"In what other land save this one
is the commonest form of greeting
not 'Good day,' nor 'How d'ye do,'
but 'Love'?
That greeting is 'Aloha' —
love, I love you, my love to you."
— Jack London

KAUAI TRAILBLAZER
Where to Hike, Snorkel, Bike, Paddle, Surf

Eighth (21st anniversary) edition, third printing
text by Jerry Sprout
photographs, graphic design production by Janine Sprout
technical consultant, Michael Sagues

ISBN: 9781793259592
Library of Congress Catalog Card Number: 99-091787

Diamond Valley Company, Publishers
89 Lower Manzanita Drive, Markleeville, CA 96120
Find us online at: www.trailblazertravelbooks.com
www.trailblazerhawaii.com (blog)

e-mail: trailblazertravelbooks@gmail.com
Published in the U.S.A. on recycled paper.

Mahalo to: Gordon and Roberta Haas; Kawika Rogers et. al. at Waipa Foundation; Mark 'Russell the Rooster' Jeffers; Chai and Chad from Wainiha; Wai–Sum at Makaleha Falls, Eric and Heidi at the Kauai Store; Moku and Koral at The Ohana Shop; Karly and Donna Hunt at Silver Falls Ranch, Chuck from Makaweli, Julie at Makauwahi Reserve, Tim, Oahu Coast Guard; Maile and Michelle at Nourish Hanalei, Robert Lockhead and family, Margaret Gill; Josh and Melissa at Ocean Paper; Leah at Warehouse 3540; Carmencita Durney at Wai'iti Botanicals; Blu Umi, Hanapepe; Thomas Daubert, Anaina Hou Community Park; John and Priscilla at Magic Dragon, Tim and Jan Gillespie; Andrew Tangel, Wall Street Journal; Uncle Onio, Lihue; Benjamin at Kamokila Village, Darla and Eliza at Kauai Coffee; Heather H. Giugni at Juniroa Productions; Michelle Ho'okana and Rosalind and Paulette, Koke'e Museum; Lynn Muramoto, Lawai Center; Eddie Taniguchi from Waimea, Surfin' Sean Moore; Jane Gray, Cleo and Uli'i at Kaua'i Museum; Kapu Kinimaka Alquiza at Kamanawa Foundation; Gwen Silva and Kevin Houk at Allerton Gardens; Susan Kanoho, Kaua'i Visitors Bureau; Hero Dave Allred; Walter (Freckles) and Kamika Smith; Lani Kawahara; Melila Purcell at Kauai Beach Resort; Jess and Sky at Kayak Kauai; Nalani Ka'auawai Brun, Office of Economic Development; Kaleo Ho'okano, Water Safety Supervisor; Mary A. Requilman, Kaua'i Historical Society; Keith Nitta, County Planning Department; Fred and Carol Tangalin; Kalani Kali; Tarey W. Low, DLNR; Frederick Wichman, Kaua'i Place Names; Beth Tokioka, Public Information Officer, Mayor's Office; Keala Senkus, Hularoom; Jodi Esaki; Bryan at JJ Ohana; Scott at Pedal 'n Paddle; Silvie Jany, et.al. at West Kaua'i Visitor Center; Edwin Hagstrom; Doug at Kaua'i Farmacy; Tebo Booth, Na Hula O Kaohikakapulani Hula Halau; Jessica and Tracy at KKCR; Lilian de Mello; Kapa'a Camera Club; Jenny Allen, Limahuli Tropical Garden; the crew at Holoholo Charters; Jo Evans, Outfitters Kauai; Denise Carswell and all at Princeville Ranch; Amy Vanderhoop; Dawn M. Traina; Joe and Lihue Kinimaka-Lopez; Aunty Rose; Margaret and Dennis Daniels; Tiane, David, and Cole Cleveland at Wailua River Kayak; Leilani Rivera Bond, Halau Hula O Leilani & Leilani Records; Titus Kinimaka; (the late) Ed and Joyce Doty at Na Aina Kai; John Cruz; Jack Johnson; Melinda Morey; Tom Ziemer and family; James the Jumper; Adventure Amy Smith; Kiko, Kapaa; Charlie Cobb-Adams; (the late) Andy and Bruce Irons; Aletha Kaohi at West Kauai Center; (the late) David Boynton; Talk Story Bookstore, Hanapepe; Mark and Tina at Hanalei Tea Company; Spark and Melissa at Coconut Coasters; Hunter Gatherer, Kilauea; Magic Dragon Toy and Art Supply, Princeville; Saa Tamba Ginlack; John Pia at Taro Patch; Prime Minister Henry Noa; Yellowfish Trading Company, Hanalei; Donald Bodine and Bob Keane, Suite Paradise. Aloha!

KAUA'I TRAILBLAZER IS DEDICATED TO THE HAWAIIAN PEOPLE,
PAST AND PRESENT, AND TO CONSERVING THE NATURAL
WONDERS, CULTURE, AND TRADITIONS OF THE GARDEN ISLE.

Waipo'o Falls

KAUAI

WHERE TO
HIKE SNORKEL BIKE PADDLE SURF

JERRY & JANINE SPROUT

A TRAILBLAZER TRAVEL BOOK

DIAMOND VALLEY COMPANY
PUBLISHERS
MARKLEEVILLE, CALIFORNIA

Table Of Contents

INTRODUCING KAUA‘I

Covering an area of 65 million square miles, the Pacific Ocean is by far the biggest single feature on Earth—as big as the other oceans combined and easily larger than the world's land masses put together. A satellite photo over the Pacific shows nothing but blue.

In the center of these waters is the Hawaiian Archipelago, some 132 islands strung in a line for about 1,600 miles, all part of the State of Hawaii. If territorial waters are considered, Hawaii is a far larger area than Alaska, but in terms of landmass, the state is the 47th smallest, larger only than Connecticut, Rhode Island and Delaware. The islands and waters from Kaua‘i north to Midway Island comprise the Northwestern Hawaiian Islands Marine National Monument.

The archipelago is the top of the Hawaiian Ridge, a mountain range standing in seawater about 5 miles deep. Snow gathers on its 13,000-foot peaks, though situated well south of the Tropic of Cancer.

NI‘IHAU KAUA‘I

OAHU

MOLOKAI

LANAI MAUI

KAHOOLAWE

HAWAI‘I

THE
HAWAIIAN ISLANDS

Considering its entirety, the Hawaiian Ridge is the tallest mountain range on Earth.

Almost all of the islands in the archipelago are sea-washed atolls, barely above a foaming surface and home to only birds and aquatic life. Ninety-nine percent of Hawai'i's 6,415 square miles is shared among its eight most southerly islands, and two-thirds of that area is allotted to just the Big Island of Hawai'i.

In terms of people, three-quarters of the state's nearly 1.5 million live on Oahu, about 100 miles southeast of Kaua'i. Maui and the Big Island each have more than twice Kaua'i's 66,000 resident and visitor population.

These are the most isolated populations in the world—about 2,500 miles from San Francisco, Los Angeles and Seattle to the northeast, and the same distance from Alaska, which is due north. (Although the archipelago extends west of the Bering Sea, the principal islands of the state do not take most-westerly honors from Alaska.) Japan is almost 4,000 miles to the northwest. To the south, southeast and southwest, 2,500 miles of open sea lie between Hawai'i and other Polynesian islands of Tahiti, Tonga and the Marquesas. The largest chunk of land southward is Antarctica.

Kaua'i (pronounced like "Hawai'i") is the northernmost of the populated Hawaiian Islands and by far the most ancient—volcanic origins date back millions of years whereas the lava has not stopped bubbling on the Big Island 400 miles to the south.

At the center of Kaua'i is 5,148-foot Mount Waialeale—Wey-ahlee-ahlee—forming the rim of an ancient volcanic caldera that, at 60 square miles, is the largest in the Pacific. Waialeale, located nearly at the center of the world's largest body of saltwater, receives the most rainfall in the world—an average of 430 inches per year. In 2018, fifty inches fell on one day in Hanalei. Over the eons, the island's caldera has evolved into Alakai Swamp—lying 4,000 feet above sea-level, the highest of any swamp environment in the world. As one Kauaian saying is translated, "At the birthplace of all waters, it rains and rains, and then it pours."

Rainfall on other parts of the island is radically less. Kaua'i's arid, leeward west shore gets 15 to 30 inches per year, its windward north shore gets 60 to 90 inches on average, and parts of eastern portions of the island get 40 to 60 inches of rain per year. The rain comes in buckets, both in storms and quick showers, followed by intense tropical sunshine that extends for days. The average temperature on Kaua'i is 75 degrees, around the clock, around the calendar. The average high varies just 8 degrees from the average low, and temperatures rarely break 90 degrees and never 100.

Although weather conditions cycle over a year—primarily winter's northerly trade winds and rains give way to summer's southerly Kona winds and drier conditions—on Kaua'i it is eternal summer. Something is always in bloom. These climatic conditions led to Kaua'i's nickname of the Garden Island. Virtually everything that can grow and doesn't require a cold snap is growing here, from redwoods to pineapples. Three of the country's five National Tropical Botanical Gardens are here.

The profusion of plant life that blankets Kaua'i in many shades of green also accents its startling topography: Rain, plus millennia of trade winds, landslides, and pounding surf have turned what was once a volcanic dome into a series of towering ridges radiating out from the center of the island to the sea, ridges above valleys and

Barking Sands Beach at Polihale State Park

canyons 3- to 4-thousand-feet deep and made of red volcanic earth held together by a tremendous root mass of tropical greenery.

These valleys yield more than a dozen rivers and large streams, the only navigable fresh water in Hawai'i. The origins of these waterways are a capillary system of streams and brooks that seep from the swamp or spring from cliff walls. Many of these contributing streams are obscured by jungle foliage, only becoming apparent after a rainstorm when dark green ridges are streaked with silvery waterfalls. Where rivers and streams meet the sea are wide slack-water lagoons extending inland from a mile to several miles before disappearing into riverbank flora or giving way to rapids and cascades. At the beach, these rivers are most often shallow, almost dammed by surf-born yellow sand. During storm conditions, the slack waters can become debris-filled torrents of destruction.

Along Kaua'i's 110-mile coast, in between the rivers and streams, are grassy, open bluffs fringed by sand and coral reef beaches. The notable exception to this landscape is Napali—The Cliffs—a 25-mile quadrant of the northwest coastline. Here ridges end in wave-battered cliffs, inaccessible by car and only partially accessible by foot. Even in Napali, however, there are little beaches with valleys that supported Hawaiian communities for centuries.

Kaua'i has the longest sand beach in the islands, as well as the longest coral reef. Many of its dozens of beaches and coves are accessible only by hikes. Generally speaking, in the winter, north side beaches near Hanalei are pounded by the trade wind's swells and the south beaches of Poipu are relatively calm. In the summer, the opposite is true, as southerly Kona winds bring bigger surf to the south and the north shore's coves become aquamarine pools. Beaches on the west and east are variable in terms of water conditions—but beach conditions everywhere can vary greatly from day to day.

Kaua'i's physical features—while perhaps beyond the scope of any engineer's or animator's imagination—are perfectly designed for recreational exploration. Roads go inland at numerous places and ancient trails rim the coast and follow ridges to dizzying heights, inviting hikers and mountain bikers. Surfing beaches are too numerous to be crowded, although on any given day the local boarders may flock to the hottest spot. Coral reefs and coves create saltwater pools—home to some 650 species of fish—made for snorkeling and swimming. River lagoons and protected bays invite kayaks and outrigger canoes. These activities combined are the only way to fully appreciate this complex island.

While ecotourism may be part of Kaua'i's future economic health, it is only a recent development. The island's powerful beauty is just a backdrop for the story of the world's least understood and perhaps most interesting human migrations. The first Polynesians, from the Marquesas, sailed here in 200 AD, followed by a second migration from Tahiti that ended in the 1400s. Polynesian life was undisturbed by any other cultural influence until Europeans and Americans arrived in the late 1700s.

Mahaulepu Heritage Trail, Hanalei Bay

GETTING TO & DRIVING AROUND KAUA'I

AIR TRAVEL
Lihue Airport, 808-246-1440.
Most flights to Kauai include a stopover and change of terminals in Honolulu. Most international airlines service Honolulu. Some airlines have non-stop flights to Kauai: Check with United. Hawaiian Airlines offers lower rates for stays of more than 30 days, and is equipped to handle surfboards and bicycles.

CAR RENTALS
All major car rental agencies are available at Lihue Airport.

PUBLIC TRANSPORTATION
A public bus with limited routes. For routes and timetables call County of Kaua'i Transportation, 808-241-6410. For access to the north shore (ten stops from Princeville to the Kalalau Trailhead), visit **Kauai North Shore Shuttle**, kauainssshuttle.com, 888-409-2702. *Stops:* Makai Golf Course in Princeville, Hanalei (at Hanalei Dolphin, Ching Young Center), Waipa, Wainiha, Hanalei Colony Resort, Limahuli Garden, and Ke'e Beach/Kalalau Trail.

DRIVE TIMES
From road's end at one end of the island to road's end at the other is about a two-hour drive—part of the island's coastline is roadless. All roads are scenic, with traffic only at junctions around Lihue and Kapa'a in the morning and evening. There are no freeways; maximum speed is 50 mph.

FROM LIHUE TO:

Nawiliwili Harbor, 2 mi., 5 mi

Kalaheo, 14 mi., 30 min.

Koloa, 11 mi., 25 min.

Poipu, 15 mi., 30 min.

Hanapepe, 19 mi., 40min.

Waimea Town, 23 mi., 50 min.

Kekaha, 27 mi., 60 min.

Barking Sands Beach, 36 mi., 70 min.

Waimea Canyon, 34 mi., 80 min.

Koke'e State Park, 38 mi., 80 min.

FROM LIHUE TO:

Wailua, 6 mi., 20 min.

Kapa'a, 9 mi., 30 min.

Anahola, 14 mi., 40 min.

Kilauea, 24 mi., 50 min.

Princeville, 27 mi., 60 min.

Hanalei, 31 mi., 70 min.

Haena, 38 mi., 85 min.

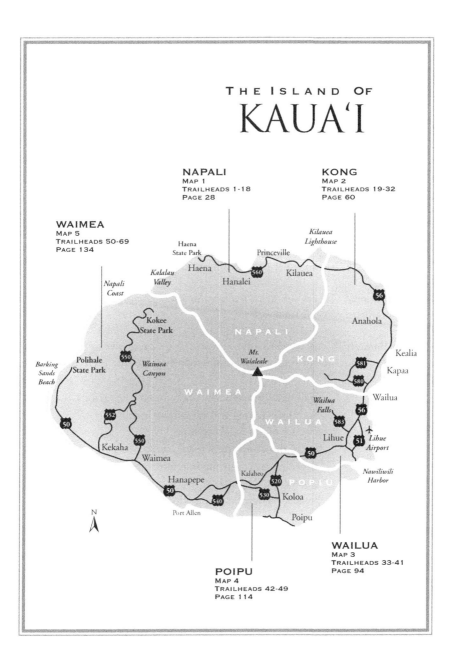

THE ISLAND OF
KAUA'I

NAPALI
Map 1
Trailheads 1-18
Page 28

KONG
Map 2
Trailheads 19-32
Page 60

WAIMEA
Map 5
Trailheads 50-69
Page 134

Kilauea
Lighthouse

Haena
State Park

Princeville

Napali
Coast

Kalalau
Valley

Haena

560

Kilauea

Hanalei

Kokee
State Park

56

Anahola

NAPALI

Mt.
Waialeale

KONG

Kealia

Barking
Sands
Beach

Polihale
State Park

550

Waimea
Canyon

581

Kapaa

WAIMEA

580

Wailua

552

Wailua
Falls

56

50

WAILUA

583

Kekaha

550

Lihue

Lihue
Airport

51

Waimea

50

Hanapepe

Kalaheo

Nawiliwili
Harbor

520

POIPU

380

540

530

Koloa

Port Allen

Poipu

N

WAILUA
Map 3
Trailheads 33-41
Page 94

POIPU
Map 4
Trailheads 42-49
Page 114

23. TRAILHEAD NAME   ACTIVITIES BANNER
     What's Best:
     Parking:
HIKE: (SAMPLE)
SNORKEL, BIKE, PADDLE, SURF

"23." Trailhead Number: These correspond to the numbers shown on the five Trailhead Maps. There are 69 'trailheads' each with one or more activities. Numbering begins on Map 1, Napali Trailheads, and numbers get bigger as you go clockwise around the island. Trailhead 69 is at the top of Waimea Canyon, on Trailhead Map 5. Trailheads that are close together numerically are also close geographically.

Trailhead name: This is the main parking for hiking, snorkeling and the other activities originating at this trailhead.

Activities Banner: This shows which of the five recreational activities are possible at this trailhead. Activities include one or more of the following, always listed in this order:

HIKE:	Trail treks, beach walks, and around-town strolls.
SNORKEL:	Both fish viewing and swimming in areas that are not in breaking surf.
BIKE:	Trails, dirt roads, rural roads, and paved paths.
PADDLE:	Kayaking and canoeing in rivers and streams, lagoons and bays.
SURF:	Surfing, boogie boarding, kite boarding and body surfing.

What's Best: Tells you, in a nutshell, what's best about this trailhead.

Parking: Gives specific directions to the trailhead and where to park. A single trailhead may include additional parking instructions to nearby activities within the same general locale.

Abbreviations used in parking directions:

Since Kaua'i is circular, with highways around its coast, compass directions change as you drive. "Toward the mountain" and "toward the ocean" are a traditional way of giving directions in the islands.

Makai = Turn toward the ocean

Mauka = Turn toward the mountains, inland

mm = Mile Marker. All island highways are marked at each mile, beginning at "0" where they originate. Marker signs show the miles from the beginning and the highway you are on. Both Hwy. 50 and Hwy. 56 originate in Lihue. Hwy. 56 goes toward Hanalei, with numbers ascending in that direction. Hwy. 50 goes toward Polihale, with numbers ascending in that direction. Driving directions are usually given heading away from Lihue, toward the higher mile marker numbers. Use your odometer to determine fractions of miles.

HIKE: The first paragraph after the **HIKE:** symbol gives the destination of each hike for this trailhead (followed by the roundtrip distance and elevation gain of 100 or more feet for that destination in parentheses).

NOTE: ALL HIKING DISTANCES IN PARENTHESES ARE ROUNDTRIP.

The second and following paragraphs after the **HIKE:** symbol give details about the hike's destination, including trail descriptions and junctions. The first mention of a **Hike Destination** is boldfaced. Hike destinations are described in the same order in which they are listed in the first hiking paragraph.

SNORKEL, BIKE, PADDLE, SURF: Following the hiking descriptions are the letter symbols for the other activities that are available at this trailhead. Descriptions and details about each activity follow its symbols. The **Location** at which the activity takes place is boldfaced. Each trailhead, for example, may have several places to surf or ride a mountain bike. Directions to each activity are either the parking directions, or otherwise noted in the text.

Activities are always listed in the same order, i.e., hiking, followed by snorkeling, mountain biking, paddling and surfing. If an activity is not available at a particular trailhead, its symbol is not listed.

More Stuff: Lists secondary activities, often less popular (and less crowded), harder to get to, or with possibly questionable access.

Be Aware: Notes hazards and gives safety tips that give an idea of hike difficulty.

TRAILHEAD DIRECTORY
A list of trailheads and their activities.

HIKE: HIKES & WALKS

PADDLE: KAYAKING & CANOEING

SNORKEL: SNORKELING & SWIMMING

SURF: SURFING & BOOGIE BOARDING

BIKE: MOUNTAIN AND ROAD BIKING

NAPALI
Map 1, Trailheads 1 through 18

KONG
Map 2, Trailheads 19 through 32

WAILUA

Map 3, Trailheads 33 through 41

POIPU

Map 4, Trailheads 42 through 49

WAIMEA

Map 5, Trailheads 50 through 69

Use caution: Venturing to the Awa'awapuhi Trail overlook is unsafe. So are the tidepools at Secret Beach

THE BEST OF KAUA'I

WHAT DO YOU WANT TO DO TODAY?

Best For Hikers—

MOUNTAIN VISTA HIKES

COASTAL BLUFFS

SHORT WALKS TO BIG VIEWS

BIRDWATCHER HIKES

FALLS AND RIVERS

GARDEN STROLLS

Smith's Tropical Paradise

Best For Hikers, cont'd—

TREES AND JUNGLE
Wai Koa Loop Trail, TH16, page 52
Sleeping Giant, TH30, page 81
Kuilau Ridge Trail, TH32, page 85
Haele'ele Ridge, TH60, page 153
Kumuwela Lookout, TH63, page 159
Halemanu-Kokee Trail, TH67, page 164
Awa'awapuhi Trail, TH68, page 167
Alakai Boardwalk, TH69, page 170

TOWN WALKABOUTS
Hanalei, TH7, page 38
Kapa'a, TH28, page 77
Hanapepe, TH51, page 137
Waimea, TH54, page 143
Koloa, DT1, page 183

LONG-AND-SCENIC BEACHES
Charos Beach, TH3, page 33
Lumahai Beach, TH5, page 35
Hanalei Bay, TH7, page 37
Secret Beach, TH16, page 52
Larsens Beach, TH20, page 62
Nukoli'i Beach, TH35, page 100
Kekaha, TH55, page 146
Polihale, TH57, page 148

PEOPLE-WATCHING BEACHES
Hanalei Bay, TH7, page 37
Kalapaki Bay, TH41, page 106
Poipu Beach, TH44, page 120

COASTAL WILDLIFE
Kilauea Refuge, TH 17, page 53
Waiakalua Beaches, TH19, page 61
Larsen's Beach, TH20, page 62
Seabird Point, TH21, page 64
Heritage Trail, TH43, page 118

HIKE-TO-ONLY BEACHES
Hideaways and Sea Lodge Beach,
  TH9, page 43
Kaweonui Beach, TH10, page 45
Wyllies Beach, TH11, page 46
Secret Beach, TH16, page 52
Waiakalua, Pila'a, TH19, page 61
Larsens Beach, TH20, page 62
Papa'a Bay, TH22, page 66
Donkey Beach, TH26, page 71
Haula Beach, TH42, page 115
Wahiawa Beach, TH50, page 135

**PORTS, PIERS,
JETTYS & MARINAS**
Hanalei Pier, TH7, page 37
Wailua Marina, TH33, page 95
Ahukini Landing, TH39, page 104
Nawiliwili, TH41, page 106
Waimea Pier, TH54, page 144

Poipu Beach

Best For Snorkelers—

BEST OVERALL
Ke'e Beach, TH1, page 32
Tunnels Beach, TH2, page 32
Kenomene and Hideaways,
    TH9, page 43
Lydgate Park, TH34, page 100
Prince Kuhio, TH45, page 122
Ni'ihau-Lehua, TH50, page 136

HIKE-TO SNORKELING SPOTS
Pila'a Beaches, TH19, page 62
Papa'a Bay, Aliomanu Beach,
    TH22, page 67
House Beach, TH26, page 73
Wahiawa Bay, TH50, page 135

A QUIET DAY AT THE BEACH
Waikoko Beach, TH6, page 36
Anini Beach, TH13, page 49
Secret Beach, TH16, TH17, page 52
Kilauea Bay, TH18, page 54
Larsens Beach, TH20, page 62
Moloa'a Bay, TH21, page 65
Papa'a Bay, TH22, page 66
Queens Pond, Barking Sands,
    TH57, page 149

LOCAL-STYLE BEACHES
Kalihiwai Bay, TH14, page 51
Anahola Beach Park, TH24, page 69
Kealia Beach, TH27, page 73
Hanamaulu Bay, TH38, page 103
Salt Pond Beach, TH52, page 139

Best For Mountain Bikers—

MOUNTAIN AND RIDGE VISTA
Powerline North, TH12, page 47
Waipahe'e Falls, TH25, page 71
Haele'ele Ridge, TH60, page 154
Polihale Ridge, TH61, page 155
Ka'aweiki Ridge, TH62, page 158

TROPICAL FOREST
Wai Koa Loop, TH16, page 52
Waialeale Basin, TH32, page 89
Halemanu Valley, TH63, page 160
Kumuwela Road, TH67, page 167
Mohihi Road, TH67, page 167

COASTAL
Kealia Beach, TH27, page 75
Kapa'a Town, TH28, page 78
Coconut Coast, TH29, page 81
Ahukini Coast, TH40, page 105

RIDEABOUT TOWN
Princeville, TH11, page 46
Kapa'a and Coconut
  Coast, TH28-29, pages 78, 80

Hanalei Beach

Best For Paddlers—

Hideaways

Best For Surfers—

Best Free Hula Shows—

Poipu Beach, TH44, page 119
St. Regis Princeville Hotel,
    DT3, page 201
Coconut Marketplace,
    DT3, page 197
Kaua'i Marriott, DT1, page 181
Kukui Grove Shopping Center,
    DT1, page 180
Poipu Village, DT1, page 185

Best For A Rainy Day—

MUSEUMS AND ATTRACTIONS

Waioli Mission, DT3, page 203
Kaua'i Museum, DT1, page 180
Kilohana Plantation, DT1, page 188
West Kauai Visitors Center,
    DT4, page 211
Kokee Natural History
    Museum, DT4, page 213

See Museums in Resource Links, page 242

**HOTELS WITH
HAWAIIANA ON DISPLAY**

Courtyard Marriott, TH29, page 80
Kaua'i Marriott, DT1, page 181
Grand Hyatt Kaua'i, DT1, page 183
Sheraton Kaua'i Resort, DT1, page 185

**WALK-AROUND
SOUVENIR SHOPPING**

Hanalei Town, DT3, page 203
Kapa'a Town, TH28, page 77
Kukuiula Village, DT1, page 184
Koloa, DT1, page 183
Hanapepe, DT4, page 209

Best Local Style Eats—
see Resource Links, page 244

Bubba's
Dani's
Duane's Ono-Char Burger
Garden Island BBQ
Hanamura Saimin Stand
Wishing Well Shave Ice
Koloa Snack Shop

Best Pacific Rim Gourmet—

Caffe Coco
Duke's Canoe Club
Gaylord's Kilohana
Grand Hyatt Ilima Terrace
Keoki's Paradise
Merriman's
Kauai ONO 560
JO2 Natural Cuisine

St. Regis Princeville

Napali

Kalalau Trail

When the Academy Award-winning movie *South Pacific* was released in 1958, Americans were left wondering where the film's magical paradise existed in real life. They discovered that this "South Pacific" was actually on the north shore of the northern-most Hawaiian island in the north Pacific—and Kaua'i became a premier destination.

With fancifully sculpted ridges, spewing waterfalls, exotic beaches and several river valleys, the north side of Kaua'i fits the image for most people's fantasy of what tropical splendor should be.

At road's end on the north shore is where Napali—or The Cliffs—begin. From here the notorious Kalalau Trail takes hikers on an arduous 11-mile trek along Napali to the Kalalau Valley, ducking into and out of other valleys along the way. Permits are required to hike beyond the first two miles. Kalalau remains a remote and mysterious place with stone terraces echoing an ancient Hawaiian village long since vanished, and inaccessible inlets, where many a bandito or recluse has successfully hidden out. The most famous desperado was Ko'olau the Leper, who, with his wife and young son, was able to evade a military assault by authorities trying to deport the afflicted man to Molokai. After three years, the disease finally overcame both Ko'olau and his son, leaving his courageous and loving wife to make the trek alone back to her village.

Near the Kalalau trailhead are Ke'e and Tunnels beaches, whose reef-protected waters are home to schools of colorful fish and a lure for snorkelers. Surfers ride the reef break at several places offshore of these beaches, near Haena Beach Park.

Just inland from Ke'e Beach is Limahuli, one of Kaua'i's three National Tropical Botanical Gardens—Eden realized. Just around the point from Ke'e, where Makana (Bali Hai) Ridge meets the ocean, is perhaps the most sacred spot in all the islands, a heiau and hula platform where cultural tradition was enacted for centuries in the form of dance and chanting. These ancient arts are still practiced there today.

Heading down the highway from Napali, several rivers and streams intersect the coast, originating in deep, steep valleys that cleave the island to its center. The Wainiha, Lumahai and Hanalei rivers are all navigable for kayakers, with a half-mile to several miles of still-water lagoons where fresh water meets the sea.

Wainiha River—the closest of the three to road's end—is noted for its rickety one-lane bridges. The river is framed by Wainiha Pali, a 4,000-foot high rippling green cliff that curls inland, serving as a high-altitude dam for the Alakai Swamp, which is on its other side. Wainiha Valley was home to the last of Kaua'i's original inhabitants, the Menehune people, 65 of whom were recorded as residents here by the U.S. Census in the late 1800s. Paddling the river here is one way to catch a view of this valley.

Lumahai, the next valley over from Wainiha, ends at Lumahai Beach, the poster shot for *South Pacific*. Lumahai is a huge sand beach with spectacular wave action.

The third river fanning out from Napali is the north shore's longest, the Hanalei. The river comes into Hanalei Bay through a National Wildlife Refuge, parts of which are open to hikers and cyclists. The river is also a major attraction for kayakers. The agricultural lands of Hanalei Valley are reminiscent of bygone days, when all Kauaian lands were divided into self-sufficient communities—each called an ahupua'a.

Hanalei Bay is a deep scoop out of the coast which today is known for several surfing beaches. The Hanalei Pier, now considered picturesque, was not all that long ago a structure vital to keeping the north shore supplied. Bowl-shaped Waioli Valley, known as the birthplace of rainbows, rises above Hanalei Town, often streaked with a half-dozen waterfalls. Joggers, hikers and cyclists will have as much fun as surfers in Hanalei, exploring not only the beach, but also the beachside neighborhood, historic church and mission, and laid-back shops.

The river-and-valley theme is less pronounced after Hanalei, as the road climbs up to the Princeville bluff. Adventure-seeking visitors may tend to overlook Princeville, with its condos and luxury hotel, but several hike-to snorkeling and surfing beaches here are among the best on the island. And inland from Princeville is Kaua'i's only trans-island trail, the Powerline, a five-star route for hikers and mountain bikers.

The bluff at Princeville gives way to Anini Beach, boasting the longest coral reef in the islands. Anini is also known for its tiny seashells, as well as its snorkeling and windsurfing. A polo field and campground, set on the lawn under spreading heliotrope trees, add to the scenery that makes this beach a favorite among many visitors.

Powerline Trail

Just around the point from Anini Beach, is Kalihiwai Bay. Kalihiwai Stream—which turns heads of drivers who pass overhead on a highway bridge—is a secret among kayakers. The beach at Kalihiwai Bay is usually a safe swimming spot and also a choice for local-boy surfers and body boarders. The offshore break at Kalihiwai Bay is a sleeper surfing spot, overshadowed by nearby Hanalei Bay.

As you leave Kalihiwai, heading toward Kilauea, the river jungle lands of Kaua'i transition into open, sloping agricultural lands, fanning out above the coast and abutting ridges in the distance inland. Hikers and cyclists can head to huge Anaina Hou Community park to see a huge mahogany forest, plus a variety of huge spreading trees. Much of Kaua'i's organic fruit and produce is grown in this region.

The highway turns inland from the coast along this segment of the island, but hikers will find a number of short trails to some huge sandy beaches, known for vistas and wave action. Secret Beach runs for two miles, ending at Kilauea Point under its historic lighthouse. On the other side of the point is Kilauea Bay, another mile-plus

arc of fine sand. Kilauea Bay also receives Kilauea Stream, a wide lagoon sweeping inland. Though access may be limited, secluded Kilauea Falls is a show-stopper.

Kilauea Lighthouse, on the massive bluff between these two beaches, is the northernmost spot in Hawai'i. The lighthouse grounds are now part of the Kilauea Point National Wildlife Refuge, and home to Laysan albatrosses, tropicbirds, boobies and a number of other exotic winged creatures. Crater Hill, above the lighthouse, is a spot not only to view birds but also a place to take in a vista of the north coast.

Hanalei

MAP 1   TRAILHEADS 1-18

NAPALI

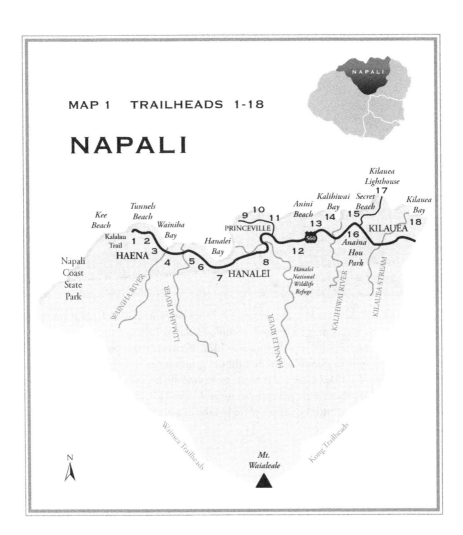

Napali Coast State Park

Kalalau Trail

Kee Beach

Tunnels Beach

Wainiha Bay

HAENA

1 2 3 4 5 6 7

Hanalei Bay

HANALEI

8

PRINCEVILLE

9 10 11

560

12

Hanalei National Wildlife Refuge

Anini Beach

13

Kalihiwai Bay

14

Secret Beach

15

Kilauea Lighthouse

17

16

Anaina Hou Park

KILAUEA

18

Kilauea Bay

WAINIHA RIVER

LUMAHAI RIVER

HANALEI RIVER

KALIHIWAI RIVER

KILAUEA STREAM

Waimea Trailheads

Kong Trailheads

Mt. Waialeale

N

NAPALI

TRAILHEADS 1-18

HIKE	HIKING
SNORKEL	SNORKELING AND SWIMMING
BIKE	MOUNTAIN OR ROAD BIKING
PADDLE	KAYAKING, CANOEING
SURF	SURFING, BOOGIE BOARDING

TH	TRAILHEAD
Makai	TOWARD OCEAN
Mauka	TOWARD THE MOUNTAIN, INLAND
mm	MILE MARKER, CORRESPONDS TO HIGHWAY SIGNS.
	USE CAR ODOMETER FOR FRACTIONS.

Note: All hiking distances are roundtrip unless otherwise noted.

1. KALALAU TRAIL-KE'E BEACH   HIKE, SNORKEL

WHAT'S BEST: Take a hike along the fabulous Napali Coast, snorkel at a picture-perfect beach, or saunter through one of the world's best botanical gardens. This is one of Kaua'i's headliners. *Note:* Reservations are required to visit this trailhead; see below.

PARKING: Take Hwy. 560 from Hanalei and continue past mm9. *For Limahuli Garden:* At mm9.6, turn left up a signed driveway. *For Kalalau Trail, Hula Heiau, and Ke'e Beach:* Continue to the parking lot at mm9.8 and park where your reservation indicates.

RESERVATIONS: Online reservations required; go to DLNR Haena State Park website, up to one month in advance. Time slots are 5 or 6 hours; successive slots may be purchased. Fees are $5 per carload, or $1 per pedestrian. Free for Hawaii residents. Visitors may also use the **North Shore Shuttle** (kauainsshuttle.com). Stops also at Limahuli Garden.

HIKE: *Kalalau Trail hikes:* Napali view (3 mi., 425 ft.), Hanakapiai Beach (4 mi., 825 ft.), Hanakapiai Falls (8 mi., 1,575 ft.); *Other hikes:* Kauluolaka Hula Heiau (.75-mi., 150 ft.); Ke'e Beach to Napali view (up to 1.25 mi.); Limahuli Botanical Garden loop (1.25 mi., 225 ft.)

The 11-mile **Kalalau Trail** along the Napali Coast begins at the trailhead kiosk on your left at road's end. *Be Aware:* Permits are required to hike beyond Hanakapiai Beach/ Falls (see page 238). The Kalalau is a tough trail. Sturdy shoes and hiking poles will help. After climbing the first rocky ramp, you'll achieve a good **view of Ke'e Beach**. After .5-mile you get a view down the Napali. The trail levels out through a cliffside garden of ti and pandanus, crosses a stream, and then widens at **the Napali view.** The iconic wave-battered cliffs line up down the coast—an awe-inspiring image. *Be Aware:* Be careful not to step off the trail; snarls of greenery hide steep cliffs.

From the Napali view to **Hanakapiai Beach**, the bumpy route dips inland again, and then drops about 400 feet through lush foliage to the beach. You need to cross

Hanakapiai Falls

the stream at beach level, which is not usually easy without getting your feet wet. *Be Aware:* Drownings occur at Hanakapiai—avoid the water except on the calmest days. Also, stream crossings are life-threatening during rains.

To **Hanakapiai Falls**, look for the trail heading inland about 30 feet after the stream crossing. The first mile is the easiest, although often mucky. You'll pass a rain shelter and a helicopter landing site, and then enter a jungle garden of bamboo, ti, ferns, huge mangos, and ancient rock agricultural terraces. About halfway to the falls you cross the stream again. The trail weaves over rocks and crosses the stream two additional times, the last one about .25-mile from the falls. (Might as well wade in your boots.) After scaling a hands-on rocky section, you reach the steep-walled amphitheater that frames Hanakapiai—a 200-foot white ribbon falling into a pool. *Be Aware:* Hanakapiai Falls is a fatiguing 8-mile hike. Be sure to note stream crossings going in to be able to find them on your return. *More Stuff:* To continue farther on the Kalalau Trail, contact the Department of Land and Natural Resources for information and a permit. See *Resource Links*, page 238.

To the sublime **Kauluolaka Hula Heiau**, begin at Ke'e Beach and pick up a stepping-stones trail that skirts the shoreline to your left as you face the beach. The trail loops around a wall, and then you walk over rocks for a short distance. At the point, where the reef opens to the open ocean, step over a sway-back palm and go hard left. Climb rugged stone steps. Stay just to the right of the greenery and go straight up toward the cliff base. You reach the top of a series of grassy terraces, about 80 feet above the sea. This spot today, as it was in antiquity, is where the ancient hula and chants are performed. *Be Aware:* Treat this place as you would a church. It is a significant cultural

Kalalau Trail

site. High waves sometimes close the trail; another route is via a road that goes to the right as you face the Kalalau Trail kiosk. Some land is private property; heed signs.

Keʻe Beach to Napali view is the shortcut to a long view of the Napali Coast. Head right along the beach. In a minute or two, look back to see the Napali Coast.

Limahuli Garden is a National Tropical Botanical Garden and it's as close to heaven as you can get on earth. The grounds are beneath the spires of Makana ("Bali Hai") Ridge and extend up lava rock terraces built by the valley's ancient dwellers. Both native Hawaiian plants and those brought by the voyaging Polynesians thrive here. The jewel of this magnificent setting is **Hale Noa** (House of Resting), an authentic thatched-roofed hut that was built at the site of an ancient foundation. The walking path skirts the hale and a stream and then winds upward, shaded by larger mango, autograph, and other trees. *Note:* Admission of about $20 is charged for self-guided tours. Hawaii residents and North Shore Shuttle riders exempt. Valid Hawaii State ID or North Shore Shuttle ticket must be provided at check-in for visitors without advanced reservations. *Advance reservations: https://ntbg.org/gardens/limahuli*

SNORKEL: Though fish are not copious, **Keʻe Beach** is an ideal saltwater pool, one of Kauaʻi's all-around best. Keep to your right as you enter a sandy shore, swimming out along the reef. The view from the water back toward the cliffs is a keeper. *Be Aware:* Water escapes this cove on the cliff side, so be mindful of the current. Avoid swimming here when surf is high, though a lifeguard station has increased swimmer safety.

Hale Noa, Limahuli Garden

2. HAENA BEACH-TUNNELS   HIKE, SNORKEL, SURF

WHAT'S BEST: Surfing, beach strolling, and superlative snorkeling with drop-dead views of Makana Ridge. Or beach hike to Keʻe Beach via Taylor Camp, a 1960s hippie enclave.
PARKING: At Haena Beach Park, mm8.75, about 7 mi. from Hanalei Bay.
Notes: Different parking spots noted for Tunnels *snorkel.* Shuttle does not stop here. Parking lot was improved in 2020; limited spaces, no reservations required.

HIKE: Keʻe Beach via Taylor Camp (2.25 mi.)

For the hike to **Keʻe Beach via Taylor Camp,** go left as you face the surf at Haena, passing **Cannons Beach**, a popular surfing spot. You'll round a point and have to negotiate rocks at the shoreline, just before reaching **Limahuli Stream**. After an easy (usually) crossing, veer inland 30 feet and go right on a wide, leaf-strewn path under a ceiling of a broadleaf trees. In 1969 this site was **Taylor Camp**, a seven-acre refuge for a hundred-plus 'hippies,' courtesy of sympathetic landowner Howard Taylor (brother of actress Elizabeth). The county condemned the place in 1973 and rousted the last residents a few years later. The path pops back to the beach at a wide, sandy stream, which is the far end of Keʻe Beach. *Be Aware:* Avoid this hike during high surf and tide, and during rains when Lumahuli Stream may be swift.

SNORKEL: The action is a 15-minute walk up the beach to Tunnels, one of Hawaii's best snorkeling venues. **Tunnels Beach parking** can be difficult. *Driving:* For the closest parking, look makai for a dirt drive at mm8.5, past Haena Street and at telephone pole #144R; it's next to a home with the address 57670. A second Tunnels Beach parking spot is .2-mile beyond the first—a dirt drive with a green chain-link fence along both sides. It's along a driveway marked by the address 57777; walk right when you hit the beach. A third, little-used (awesome!) beach access is off a private road, at mm8.25 and telephone pole #19R, just after Haena Place. The access is .2-mile in from the highway; park just before the road makes a sharp left. Access is via a short path at the end of the road. Tunnels is a 10-minute walk to your left at the beach. Tunnels has a generous swath of

Haena Beach and Makana Ridge (Bali Hai)

sand and a deep-water coral reef near shore that attracts a multitude of fish, as well as tourists. A bonus for Tunnels is the perfect view of Bali Hai—the name for Makana Ridge that originated from the movie, *South Pacific*. *Be Aware:* Haena lifeguards normally post hazard signs, but any time the surf is high you can count on rip current.

SURF: Surfers paddle the channel at **Tunnels Beach** to the reef break. **Cannons Beach** is on the other end of Haena City Beach Park. Scope the break—usually a left slide—from the unimproved turnouts (mm9) as you leave the park headed for Ke'e.

3.   **CHAROS BEACH**   HIKE, SURF

WHAT'S BEST: A beach walk with Makena Ridge views and solitude, even on busy days along this popular stretch of coast.

PARKING: Take the Hwy. 560 through Hanalei and continue past Wainiha to mm7.5. Patrons and shoppers may park in the lot for the Hanalei Colony Resort and Napali Art Gallery. Parking also just past the lot; turn makai on dirt Oneone Rd. *Alternate access for a shorter hike:* Continue to almost mm8, turn makai on Alealea Pl., and take a short path along a white fence at the YMCA camp. **North Shore Shuttle** stops here.

HIKE: Haena Point 'Rainbow Walk' (2.5 mi.)

Haena Point is a sure-thing scenic getaway for beachcombers, even on busy week-ends. Take a short access path between the resort and the restaurant—formerly called Charo's, since it was once owned by the oddball sexpot of Johnny Carson TV fame. Head to your left when you hit the sand, which is **Kaonohi Beach**. Palms mingle with ironwoods among a few low-key vacation homes inland. After about .5-mile, the homes give way to open space, part of a **YMCA camp**, and the reef encroaches on the sandy shore. *Be Aware:* Surf and reef here can be lethal. As you continue, the reef protrudes from the water, just as you reach a wide cove, noted by the half-dozen black rocks at its shore. Keen eyes will find tiny Ni'ihau-type and other shells here. A Makena (Bali Hai) Ridge view draws you along the last part of the walk. Rainbows seem to favor this beach, particularly on winter afternoons. *More Stuff:* More energetic hikers can continue to Tunnels. See parking above for access from the YMCA camp.

SURF: Too reefy for the board boys, but intrepid kite-boarders and windsurfers take to the waters between Charo's and **Haena Point**.

4.   **WAINIHA**   HIKE, BIKE, PADDLE

> **WHAT'S BEST:** A non-tourist short hike, bike ride, drive, or paddle up one of Hawai'i's most mysterious valleys—Hawaiians living here can trace their lineage back centuries.
>
> **PARKING:** Wainiha is a small outpost just beyond Lumahai Beach on Hwy. 560, after mm6. *For the beach hike*, park at bedraggled Wainiha City Beach Park: Look right for a rough turnout after Powerhouse Road. This is a **North Shore Shuttle** stop.

HIKE: Wainiha Beach (.5-mi.)

For **Wainiha Beach**, make your way from the parking area, passing rustic beach camps and entering the wide spit of sand that separates the ocean from Wainiha Stream. At the far end is the stream's mouth and a fabulous view of 4,000-foot-high ridges.

BIKE: Start in town and head toward the first of two one-lane bridges, across the **Wainiha River**. Between the bridges is a dirt road upriver that you can bike about a mile, giving you a look at tropical gardens and homestead cottages. Then backtrack and cross the second bridge and head up paved **Powerhouse Road**, on your left. It's two miles and about a 500-foot climb to the end of the road. Jungle flora and birds are at hand. Up this river valley until the late 1800s lived a 65-person colony, the descendents of the folkloric Menehune. *Be Aware:* Few tourists visit here; be respectful to locals.

PADDLE: Put in at Wainiha, in town, where the river parallels the road and a shoal separates it from the bay. The **Wainiha River** forks upstream from the bay, at the two bridges, and comes together again about a mile upstream, making a narrow island.

Kahalahala section of Lumahai Beach

5. LUMAHAI BEACH   HIKE, SNORKEL, PADDLE, SURF

WHAT'S BEST: Relax where the river meets the sea, or take a walk along the crashing surf of Kaua'i's most glamorous beach. On hot days, try a dip in the river pool.

PARKING: At Lumahai City Beach Park, around the point from Hanalei Bay, at mm5.75. Unimproved parking is before the bridge. *Alternate parking:* To access the far end of Lumahai (Kahalahala Beach), park at a paved turnout on your right (heads up!) at mm4.7, where the highway curves left. Walk a short distance up to a dirt turnout and take a trail to the left of upright poles. Walk .25-mi. down steps, through a pretty pandanus grove.

HIKE: Lumahai Beach to Kahalahala Beach (2.25 mi.)

From the parking area at **Lumahai Beach**, which is amid an ironwood grove on the bank of the Lumahai River, walk away from the river, heading onto a mass of fine sand up to a hundred yards deep (though winter surf sometimes breaches the highway). A little over halfway down the beach, the cliff draws nearer, and black rocks emerge from the sand, taking on the surf and creating bursts of spray. You may spot a coveted sunrise shell. The far end of Lumahai is called **Kahalahala Beach**. Lumahai is the cover girl among Kauaian beaches, a reputation that began during the filming of *South Pacific*. *Be Aware:* Stay well back from the shore break. Many people have been swept out.

SNORKEL: Lumahai is a dangerous swimming beach, site of many drownings and rogue waves that sweep people from the shoreline. However, during dry periods when the **Lumahai River** is slack, a large freshwater swimming area forms near the shore. Still waters are clear and green, reflecting the embankment that rises on the other shore.

PADDLE: The **Lumahai River** is a short stretch of navigable water upon which commercial outfitters are not permitted. Encroaching foliage blocks passage less than a mile up from the beach. Easy access is from the sandy shore. The Lumahai River valley, some 3,200 feet deep and 10 miles long, lies between the Hanalei and Wainiha rivers.

Waikoko Beach

SURF: Across the stream is a left-break that peels off a black-rock ledge toward the beach. This is spot for experienced surfers, who use a daring entry from the rocks.

6.   WAIPA FOUNDATION-WAIKOKO BEACH   HIKE, SNORKEL, SURF

WHAT'S BEST: A quiet beach stop across from a panoramic valley. Float in warm water and enjoy jaw-dropping views of the Hanalei ridges.

PARKING: Pass through Hanalei on Hwy. 560, cross two bridges, and park at turnout at mm4. This is a **North Shore Shuttle** stop and parking area.
Alternate (surfer beach) parking: Continue uphill to near mm4.5 and park at a paved turnout before a curving-arrow traffic sign. A steep trail leads down the embankment.

HIKE: Waikoko Beach (1 mi.)

Waikoko Beach is the continuation of Hanalei Bay beyond Waioli Stream at the edge of town. Much of the beach was eroded in the 2018 flood. You can walk back toward town from the parking area along the beach, the homestretch for joggers of Hanalei Bay, which is a mile or more. Farther along, Waipa Stream enters the bay and the sand in between is called **Waipa Beach**. *Be Aware:* The streams can be hard to cross after rains. Inland across the road is the stream-valley home to **Waipa Foundation**, a cultural-agricultural nonprofit group that hosts a weekly farmer's market and other events. Sprawling gardens make for a scenic walk-around.

SNORKEL: Waikoko Beach is a good place to take a swim with fins and mask, although fish are not usually abundant. The entrance is sandy, into deep water. The view inshore from the water is portrait quality. Waikoko is protected by a coral reef, called Pohakuopio, which juts into the bay from Makahoa Point. Use *alternate parking* above to locate the most-private beach, which has more coral and good snorkeling.

SURF: **Pohakuopio** reef creates an offshore break at the mouth of Hanalei Bay, especially during the winter. Locals check out the break from the *alternate parking*. Break is shallow upon the reef in places. This one is not for beginners.

7.   HANALEI TOWN & BAY   HIKE, SNORKEL, PADDLE, SURF

> WHAT'S BEST: Hanalei may be the best walk-around beach town in Hawaii—an old-style town fringed by skyscraper ridges that are laced with waterfalls, and bordered by taro fields, a sandy bay, and wide river.
> PARKING: Take Hwy. 56 into Hanalei Valley, where it becomes Hwy. 560. Continue to the center of town near mm2.6 and turn makai on Aku Rd. Continue on Aku to the stop sign, turn right on Weke Rd., and go about .5-mi. to parking at Black Pot City Beach Park. *Additonal Parking:* Near the Aku-Weke stop sign is the Hanalei City Pavilion. Continuing on Weke (away from Black Pot) are beach access paths at telephone pole #19 and at He'e Road, both within .4-mi. of the pavilion. Pine Trees Beach is at Ama'ama Rd., .5-mi. from the pavilion, and Weke Rd. ends not far after that at Waioli City Beach Park. *Note:* **North Shore Shuttle** stops at Hanalei Dophin, Ching Young Center.

HIKE: Hanalei Beach (2.5 mi.)

The **Hanalei Beach** walk begins at **Black Pot Beach**, the center of life for surfers, kayakers, and beach lovers. Look for the black cauldron among the ironwoods by the river. **Hanalei Pier**, a set for a number of Hollywood movies, extends from the park. Its covered dock house, rehabbed in 2013, is a cozy spot to sit on a rainy day, watch sunset, or get close to surfers. Local kids jump and fishermen try their luck. To the right of the pier, as you face the water, is where surfers park for the long paddle out to the offshore breaks and where the **Hanalei River** enters the bay—a contemplative spot.

Continuing around the bay, you'll see shore-break surfers and joggers, and pass a number of beachfront homes set among palms and gardens (one of which was depicted in *The Descendants* movie). After about .5-mile on packed sand you come to the **Hanalei City Pavilion**, the main station for the Hanalei watermen (lifeguards). From the pavilion, it's about .75-mile to **Waioli Beach Park**, which ends at Waioli Stream. You pass the picnic tables, lawn and ironwoods of **Pine Trees Beach** along the way. Across the stream is called **Waipa Beach**, which leads to the stream of the same name. Cross Waipa Stream and you're headed for Waikoko, at the far end of the bay. This walk has numerous options built in, starting at any of the access points described in the parking instructions. *Be Aware:* Hazardous during high surf; stay back. The streams can be difficult to cross after it rains.

Walkers will also enjoy tooling around **Hanalei Town**, where exposed feet outnumber lace-ups ten-to-one. Don't miss the green church and grounds of the **Waioli Mission House** on the mountain-side at the far end of town. Behind the church are rich agricultural lands of the **Waioli Valley**, "the birthplace of the rainbows." After a

rain, the 3,500-foot ridge above Hanalei reveals scores of ribbon waterfalls. Most of the inland is private property; ask permission to enter. The town features two quaint shopping areas, set off the highway on either side—plate lunches, sporting goods, coffee, surf duds, tiki-torch dining and high-end giftware. See *Driving Tours* page 203 for more on Hanalei.

SNORKEL: With its sandy bottom and shore break, **Hanalei Bay** is not known for snorkeling. But in calm conditions swimming is good around the pier at **Black Pot Beach**, where you'll see a few fish.

PADDLE: At **Black Pot Beach** is a boat ramp to put in for up-river paddles or soirees into the bay and around toward **Puʻu Poa Beach** at St. Regis Princeville Resort. To get to the ramp, go straight through the parking lot as the paved road ends. The **Hanalei River** may also be accessed at one or two openings observable along the grassy bank as you drive into Hanalei after crossing the bridge. Local outfitters also provide access. The Hanalei River runs miles into the Hanalei Valley Wildlife Refuge, below 3,500-foot ridges.

SURF: For beginners and kahunas alike, the breaks at **Black Pot Beach** combine to make it one of the best and most popular

Adventure Amy Smith of Kayak Hanalei, Hanalei Bay

spots in Hawaii. Learners and mid-level board heads like the break at the pier. Stand-up paddlers (SUPs) roam the middle of the bay. The big boys and girls go for the tiers of swells rolling in a couple hundred yards offshore, beyond the mouth of the Hanalei River—called **Bowls.** Farther out, **Queens** and **Kings**, several hundred yards farther out, only break with winter surf of 40 feet and up. Legendary surfer Titus Kinimaka in the 1990s was the first to ride Kings. The end of the pier is where to be for watching surfers. Bring your binoculars.

Pine Trees (look for the stand of ironwoods) has long tiers close to shore, a hangout for lots of locals, including pro Bruce Irons, brother of late Andy Irons, a world champion. Kauai will forever mourn Andy's death in 2010; several murals commemorate the local legend. For an onshore break, better for boogie boarding and in view of lifeguards, try **Hanalei City Pavilion** in the middle of the bay. **Waioli Beach Park** is similar to Pine Trees, a closer-in break for mid-level or better surfers. *Be Aware:* Keep a lookout for flat, frothy spots in the breaking waves, which indicate channels with rip current.

8.   HANALEI WILDLIFE REFUGE   HIKE, BIKE

> **WHAT'S BEST:** Climb for a bird's-eye view of Hanalei Valley, or stay grounded on a hike through bamboo forest to a wild spot up the river without a paddle.
> **PARKING:** Take Hwy. 56 toward Hanalei from Princeville and after crossing the river on the one-lane bridge, turn left immediately on unsigned Ohiki Rd. You enter the Hanalei National Wildlife Refuge, most of which is off-limits to humans.
> *Okolehao Trail parking:* Proceed .6-mi., passing the historic Haraguchi Rice Mill (unsigned, now refuge offices), and park on left at the improved, signed parking lot.
> *Former Hanalei River Trail:* Continue until the pavement ends, 2 mi. in. You'll see a cable across the road and a stop sign. Park as near as you can, step over the cable and walk in straight, past the house about .1-mile—not taking the drive that goes up to the right. You immediately come to the Halelea Forest Reserve checking station. *Note:* Despite the cable, this is access to the forest reserve designated by state officials. Some of the residents are not welcoming of hikers. Use your own judgment; but best to avoid these days.

HIKE: Okolehao (Moonshine) Trail to: View knoll (2.5 mi., 925 ft.) or Kaukaopua summit (4.5 mi., 1,425 feet)

The splendid, steep **Okolehao (Moonshine) Trail** rises to the best vantage point of the Hanalei coast and valley. The route was hewn during prohibition, when the Hawaiian liquor okolehao was being distilled from ti plants that grew along the trail. To begin, cross the road to the little footbridge at the trailhead and jog to your right on the mucky, red-dirt trail. Walk 40 or so yards on the road and turn left, begining a relentless climb. You leave wildlife refuge lands and enter the **Halelea Forest Reserve.** After about .75-mile and a long switchback, the road becomes a trail and footing becomes easier, at first. This key juncture is marked by a huge power pole, with a grassy view area. Cut left and head up the ridgeline. *Be Aware:* Stay back from drop-offs as you

Okolehao Trail view knoll

climb the ridge. Hiking poles will help, especially coming down if the trail is wet and slippery. Some portions of the trail are hands-on.

You'll penetrate a forest of Norfolk pine, strawberry guava, and pandanus as the trail heads inland on a series of steep ramps and benches, with roots forming a random staircse. At about 1.25 miles in, you reach a **view knoll**, a flat patch of grass with benches and a 360-degree view, a worthy destination. But more climbing remains. After one hands-on steep section and the 1.75 mile marker, you reach an "end of trail" sign. But *make sure* to take the final hairpin left and walk about 150 overgrown yards (dropping a little at first) to the **summit**, which is called **Kaukaopua**. The trail here may be washed out in sections. The summit is a flat oval adorned by ti plants that partially obscure the view of the Hanalei region. Wow. *Note:* Before taking the Okolehao Trail, you may wish to stop at the scenic turnout across from the shopping center in Princeville: Kaukaopua is the peak above the river, down from the double-tipped peak called **Hihimanu**. Named for a manta ray, this peak seems close to the end of the maintained trail—but only fit hikers with local guides should even think about it.

More Stuff: The **Hanalei River Trail bamboo forest** hike is a stomp through pig mud that is best done on a sunny day—not during rain anyway. Unfortunately, locals prohibit access, so this one may be best avoided. The trail is easy to follow, but is ingrown and dark to the point of eliciting claustrophobia. You begin in a tunnel of ferns and bamboo on a wide swath. After about .5-mile within the bamboo, the sky appears, as well as a hillock of spongy grasses too deep to trod. Then you drop down again, hearing a stream before seeing it, and finally crossing it, under overhanging branches and roots. After this thicket—all the while the trail is plainly observable—you cross a rocky streambed, veering left, and entering the bamboo again. After about .25-mile in this last, dark bamboo cave, you reach the riverbank. From the riverbank, you are able to walk through ferns to a better viewpoint of a sweeping turn of the river, a few hundred feet upstream. *Be Aware:* Make sure you know how to get back to the first river sighting, as the trail through the ferns is sketchy. Access to the trail is iffy at best.

BIKE: Ohiki Road into the wildlife refuge is a flat, 4-mile roundtrip cycle, beginning through taro fields: eye candy. Near the end of the road you will also see 4WD tracks that lead into the Waioli Valley. Some of this area is private property.

9.   PRINCEVILLE-HIDEAWAYS BEACH   HIKE, SNORKEL, SURF

WHAT'S BEST: Behind vacation homes and resort condominiums are showy sunset views and some of Kaua'i's best hike-to beaches with snorkeling and surfing.
PARKING: Take Hwy. 56 several miles past Kilauea to near mm28. Turn makai at Princeville on Ka Haku Road, passing a large fountain, and continue 2 mi. to St. Regis Princeville Resort. Public parking is on the right, just outside resort entrance station. Or, drive in to the hotel and valets will park your car for free (although a tip is appreciated).

HIKE: *Princeville Resort to:* Fort Alexander site (.25-mi.); Pu'u Poa Beach, Hanalei River and South Pacific Terraces (1.5 to 2.5 mi., 125 to 325 ft.). *Outside resort grounds:* Hideaways-Kenomene Beach (.75-mi., 250 ft.)

Fort Alexander is a stroll across the resort lawn to a pavilion on the bluff that commemorates the Russian traders' failed attempt to gain a foothold on Kaua'i in the early 1800s—an excellent spot for sunset or to check out the waves in Hanalei Bay. The fabulous **Princeville Resort** is a fave among visiting Hollywood types. From the opulent lounge area, a towering wall of glass frames a panorama of Hanalei.

To **Pu'u Poa Beach**, which is below the St. Regis, look for a beach access sign just to the left of the kiosk at the resort parking lot entrance. Access is via a concrete ramp and stairs behind the hotel. *Note:* You can also reach **Pu'u Poa Beach** by using the hotel elevators near the balcony doors: Descend to the fourth floor, walk the hallway, and then take another elevator down to the first floor. At the beach, go left under spreading heliotrope trees along the shoreline. To the **Hanalei River**, cross the small stream, head up, and go right on a trail. You'll then walk the top of a low rock wall upriver through lush flora, and see places to drop down to a black-rock bulkhead that is across from Black Pot Beach Park. For the sublime **South Pacific Terraces**, go left at the small stream and walk through a gate and up a pedestrian road. Go right immediately at the top for the best views. This is the site of the old Hanalei Plantation

Hideaways Beach, taro fields of Hanalei, Pali Ke Kua Beach

Hotel, the estate where *South Pacific* was filmed. The concrete ruins (stay off) are from a Club Med development that was wiped out by Hurricanne Iwa in 1982. The road winds up through a gardenscape for a half mile, reaching the end **Hanalei Plantation Road**; you can also drive here by turning right from the highway after the shopping center, at the police station. *Hot Tip:* Where the road ends for cars is pretty **Hanalei Organic Park**, home to Nourish Hanalei, a fantastic farm stand and cafe.. The view of the Hanalei River and Bay are superlative. Park here to walk down to **Pu'u Poa Beach**. You'll find a trailhead opening just down the road on the left, before a locked gate. The route drops through gardens and terraces (1.25 mile, 200 feet) to a postcard look at Hanalei Pier.

The funky, steep trail to **Hideaways-Kenomene (Pali Ke Kua) Beach** is on the right, just before the resort entrance kiosk. Walk a corridor between two chain-link fences parallel to the tennis courts. You then descend steeply on dirt-and-wood stairs, aided by a weathered pipe railing and then by ropes. Hideaways is a cozy swath of sand, pocketed by jungled cliffs. From the far end of the beach, a hands-on trail leads over black rock and through pandanus, a 10-minute scramble to adjacent Kenomene Beach.

Path to Hideaways-Kenomene Beach

SNORKEL: Although small, **Pu'u Poa Beach** is a decent snorkeling beach. Expect to mingle with hotel guests on this strip of reef-protected sand. Look for a sand entry and a coral section that is perpendicular to the shoreline. For the King Kong view (nine stories above), head to the balcony of the resort where you can scope out the coral. *Be Aware:* Water is shallow at low tide. A deeper sandy entry is not far left.

Hideaways Beach, a small sand cove cupped into the bluffs, has very good snorkeling—sandy entry with clear water, coral, and ample fish. And, although Hideways is on the tourist radar among Kaua'i's best beaches, the pesky hike down tends to keep crowds away. *Be Aware:* High surf offshore can cause unsafe currents, from right to left.

Kenomene (Pali Ke Kua) Beach is straight down from the guardrail at the scenic overlook about .25-mile from Princeville Resort. See *Hike* above for access. An easier access is via a concrete walkway that begins to the left of the parking lot for the **Pali Ke Kua** condominiums next to the overlook. It's near unit 106. The path zigzags steeply through a *remarkable* tropical gardenscape. Head to the far end for sandy entry points among the black rocks. Snorkeling is excellent during lower surf conditions. *Be Aware:* A sign at the start of the walkway declares that access is for residents only. Use your own judgment and proceed at your own risk. Avoid swimming here during high surf.

SURF: **Hideaways** is a locals' surfing spot, with consistent offshore rollers. Driving in to the beach, park near a scenic overlook to observe conditions—a guardrail marks the overlook. On the trail down to the beach (not an easy board carry) you'll also come to a viewing spot, about 30 feet above the water. Surfers also lug boards down the public access to **Pu'u Poa Beach**; under some conditions, it's a shorter paddle out the channel from there to catch the river mouth break off of Hanalei Bay.

10.   QUEEN EMMAS BATHS   HIKE, SNORKEL

> WHAT'S BEST: A hike-to beach and a shoreline pocketed with volcanic swimming pools, both giving a faraway feel at close-by places. But watch out for high surf.
> PARKING: Two different spots. For both, take Hwy. 56 past mm27 and turn into Princeville on Ka Haku Rd.
> *For Kaweonui (Sea Lodge) Beach,* Go .5-mi. on Ka Haku, turn right on Kamehameha toward the Sea Lodge Condominiums. Continue to midway in the compex. A signed trailhead with designated parking spots is on the left. *For Queen Emmas Baths,* continue on Ka Haku past Pepelani Loop, and turn makai on Punahele Rd., about .5-mi. before reaching the Princeville Hotel. Go down Punahele about .25-mile and look for a designated, 12-car parking area. *Be Aware:* This lot fills up early. The trail at times may close due to safety concerns. *Note:* **North Shore Shuttle** begins at Princeville Makai Golf Club, 4080 Lei O Papa Rd.

HIKE: Queen Emmas Baths (.5 mi. to 1.5 mi., 175 ft.); Kaweonui (Sea Lodge) Beach (1 mi., 185 ft.)

The path to secluded and pretty **Kaweonui (Sea Lodge) Beach** traverses down a grassy bluff, hugging the dense flora of a stream. At the bottom, avoid a stream crossing by cutting left behind a pumphouse and crossing a concrete driveway (where an alternate trail comes down from 3577 Keoniana Road). After rejoining the trail, make sure to keep left at a confusing juncture. The trail then descends on steps through a pandanus grove to the coast. Follow the trail left among ironwood trees to the mouth of the small bay. The last part of the route is cut into a rock face and requires hands, but it's not difficult. Kaweonui is a deep pocket of sand in a black-rock cove with plenty of greenery at the backshore. *Be Aware:* This trail can be slippery.

Queen Emmas Baths are black-rock tidal pools and intricate reef openings named for King Kamehameha IV's Queen Emma, who soaked here. Footing is bad on the first .25-mile walk down. At one spot near the bottom, hands may be required. You pass a small, photo-worthy waterfall and pool. Continue around to your left, walking the rocky bluffs and shoreline for about .5-mile. *Be Aware:* Exposed roots make for difficult footing. Observe wave action before venturing out on rocks. Use routes farther from the shoreline and avoid this area during high surf. People have drowned at these baths, so be extra careful. Stay back from wet rocks.

SNORKEL: On calms days the tide pools of **Queen Emmas Baths** are good places to relax and enjoy views of the vast Pacific. You can gear up with mask and fins, or just bob around in warm water. The best pool is about .25-mile from where the trail meets the coast. *Be Aware:* Observe wave action for ten minutes before entering; people have been swept away during high surf. Don't swim if surf comes over the rocks. Most winter days are unsafe for swimming in the baths.

The reef offshore of **Kaweonui (Sea Lodge) Beach** limits shore break, often making for good snorkeling among a fair number of fish, coral and maybe a turtle or two. You will usually find privacy at this little known, scenic cove. *Be Aware:* Privacy means you are on your own. Water is normally shallow. The safest area is near shore to the right as you face the water.

A swimmer barely avoids drowning on an unsafe day at Queen Emmas Bath

11. WYLLIES BEACH   HIKE, SNORKEL, BIKE

WHAT'S BEST: The 'back way' to Anini Beach will be high on the beach-hike list among independent travelers. Leisure cyclists can take a spin through the green bluffs and vacationland of Princeville.

PARKING: Take Hwy. 56 to Princeville, just beyond mm27. Enter on the main entrance on Ka Haku Rd. (To drive directly to Willies, Anini Beach on page 48.)

For the bike ride: Park on the right at a turnout just .1-mi. in, at the fountain, and just before a sign for Queen Emmas Dr.

For the hike or snorkel at Wyllies Beach: Continue for about .25-mi. and turn right on Wyllie Rd., also marked by a sign for the Pahia-Kaeo Kai condos. Go about .4-mi. and park in the public lot to the right of the entrance to the Westin Villas.

HIKE: Wyllies-Anini Beach (.5-mi. to 3 mi., 225 ft.)

To **Wyllies Beach**—which is actually at the far end of **Anini Beach**—walk the tree-lined path between the Westin resort development and the golf course. The wide trail opens to a big view of the beach and then descends into a shaded canopy of trees, alongside a stream. It's steep, but not hazardous. You pop out to the beach from an umbrella of heliotrope and ironwood trees. As you begin the beach walk, look back to memorize the spot to pop back in when the time comes. At the beach, head right and cross shallow **Anini Stream**, which is often blocked by a sand dam at the shoreline, and continue along the shore to **Anini Beach**. At one point, about .75-mile into the stroll, you need to leave the beach at a black-rock point, hopping up to the quiet road for a short distance and then back down to the beach. Anini Beach campground will be in view after the point. Windsurfers, campers, kite-boarders, and (guess what) polo players spice up the beachscape.

SNORKEL: The fresh water from the stream, in which coral cannot live, makes **Wyllies** a sandy-bottomed swimming area, protected by a reef farther out. Water clarity is only fair near the stream. Wyllies is a very good spot to take a swim, which is not that easy to find during winter surf. The best snorkeling is by a pool formed by black rocks, a couple hundred yards down the road. *Be Aware:* During higher surf, an extremely dangerous rip current develops farther out, where surf breaks and water escapes through an opening in the reef. Use caution. Stay closer to shore.

BIKE: The **Mea Hoʻona Nea** bike trail, taking off behind the gate across the road from the fountain, is a 3-mile roundtrip, rolling ride to the **Princeville Golf Club**. To continue from the golf club, turn right out to Hwy. 56, which has an adequate paved shoulder. *More Stuff:* As the Mea Hoʻona Nea bike path leaves the golf course, and just before it becomes a path on a frontage road, look for a gate on your right; the road here, at the Church of the Pacific, is directly across the highway from the road leading up past the stables to Powerline Trail north, TH12.

12. POWERLINE TRAIL NORTH

WHAT'S BEST: Hike or pedal past the peaks and streams at the heart of Kaua'i. Begin overlooking Hanalei Valley and then scale a ridge on Kaua'i's only cross-island trail.
PARKING: Take Hwy. 56 past the Princeville Airport. Turn mauka (left) about .4-mi. past mm27 on Kapaka St.—look for a yellow intersection sign and a horse-shaped sign for Princeville Ranch Stables. Go 1.8 mi. up to the end of the street, behind a water tank at a signed trailhead.

HIKE, BIKE: Powerline Trail (13 mi., 1,900 ft., one-way to Keahua Arboretum, TH33, but the interior trail is overgrown. Hikes of shorter lengths are described below. See *More Stuff* for Princeville Ranch and Princeville Botanical Gardens.

The full **Powerline Trail North** is an all-day hike best attempted by prepared hikers on dry days with long pants and machetes. But you can enjoy a botanical wonderland and river views by going in partway. The other trailhead is at the Keahua Arboretum, TH33. The route offers open vistas and lush greenery. Ruts and puddles are common. The trail attracts mountain bikers, and you'll find single-track trails looping from the main road.

Kualapa Ridge, the great divide for this route, is about 7 miles in to an elevation of almost 2,000 feet—or about half as high as the other ridges of the island's interior. You encounter a number of ups and downs along the way, and flora sometimes chokes passage. But, just into the hike, look for a falls to the right on a shoulder jutting out from the trail. Then, *less .5-mile from the trailhead,* a side trailleads to the right through ferns and trees to a good vantage point of the **Hanalei Valley**—river rapids below and possibly waterfalls across the way. This scenic side trail continues and joins the main

Powerline Trail

Princeville Ranch, Kalihiwai swimming hole

route, revealing a waterfall view not long thereafter. The middle segment of the Powerline Trail, after about 2.5 miles, is a long, open ascent through swampy ferns and a dwarf ohia forest. All the dead tree spires are remnants of Hurricane Iniki of 1992. All you see is part of the **Halelea Forest Reserve**.

More Stuff: The **Po'oku Heiau** site serves up an exquisite view of Hanalei Wildlife Refuge, but for now access is not permitted. *Driving:* Park on your right at the water tank, about .2-mile in from the highway on Kapaka. Walk a grassy two-track to your right, which contours the hillside. Two acres atop the hill are the site of the heiau, which historically was used to teach celestial naviagation and also for training in the lua, the Hawaiian martial art. *Be Aware:* A development for five-acre homes is planned. A seven-acre, nonprofit Po'oku Heiau preserve is part of the plan, but the public may be left out. Access now is trespassing.

More Stuff: The Powerline Trail borders the 2,500-acre Princeville Ranch, on which the Carswell family—stewards of this natural treasure for many generations—now operates **Princeville Ranch Adventures**. (See *Outfitters* in *Resource Links,* page 238.) You can see this stunning place on foot, swimming, by kayak, or zinging through the air on a zipline. Aficionados of sublime greenery will appreciate **Princeville Botanical Gardens**, set on nine acres in a lush stream valley. Tours move at a leisurely pace. *Driving:* Turn left at Ahonui Place, about one mile up from the highway. Call ahead for reservations. An admission is charged.

13. ANINI BEACH   HIKE, SNORKEL, PADDLE, SURF

WHAT'S BEST: Leisurely hikes along the longest coral reef in Hawai'i, and taking a dip with the fishes. Anini has the total package for a tropical vacation day trip.
PARKING: Turn makai on Kalihiwai Rd. (second), which is past mm25, about 2 mi. beyond Kilauea—on an uphill grade after crossing the highway bridge over the river.

For Hanapai Beach: Bear left downhill on Anini Dr., continue for .5-mi.to the coastline, and park at a dirt turnout on the right under trees where the road turns left.
For Anini: Continue along Anini Dr. , where there are several access paths: at address 3530, across from address 3611 (the better), and at address 3650. The main parking is 1.5 mi. in from the highway at Anini Beach Park. The road ends at Wyllie Beach (see page 46); the last .75-mile is an unmainted private easment road.

HIKE: Anini Beach (up to 2.75 mi.)

The road to **Anini Beach** reaches sea level after about .5-mile from the highway, and then runs about 2 miles along the shore before ending at Anini Stream. The beach park area covers a .75-mile segment in the middle. Use one of the beach access paths noted above for a longer beach walk or start at the beach park, where windsurfers and high-flying kite-boarders provide entertainment at Kaua'i's best spot for these sports.

The coral reef, hundreds of feet offshore, makes for a wave-free coast, and trees provide pockets of shade. You leave the park after about .5-mile and walk the road a bit, around **Honono Point**, which is marked by a telephone pole on the ocean side of the road. After the point, you enter a tropical nook and sandy cove where Anini Stream enters the sea. This trail connects with Wyllies Beach, TH11.

SNORKEL: With its fabled reef, the snorkeling at **Anini Beach** is good, but shallow water, strong current, and coarse sand keep it from getting the highest marks. Even so, many claim this as their favorite. Good snorkeling is at the camping section of the beach park, just after crossing a little bridge. For more private beachgoing, use the beach access paths noted in the parking section; better snorkeling is at address 3530. *Be Aware:* Surf surge escapes through a channel between the windsurfing area and the camping area at the beach park. A series of pipes leading from near the shore out to

Anini Beach

the reef mark the channel. You want to enter the water to the left of that. Currents can be swift in the shallow waters near the channel.

For a quick snorkeling getaway try **Hanapai Beach** when the surf is calm. A sandy entry awaits at the far end, but that's also where rip current happens. Also, at the other end of Anini, around Honono Point, is a safe swimming spot. Look for **Baby Beach**, a sandy pool near the road, protected by a small crescent of black rocks that attract fish.

PADDLE: The reef far offshore of **Anini Beach** makes for a safe and scenic lagoon for salt-water paddling—the best on Kaua'i. Put in near the campground and work your way inside the reef. *For excellent stream kayaking:* Keep right on Kalihiwai Road not far from the highway and drive down about .75-mi. to unimproved parking at road's end.

SURF: **Anini Beach** is known more for windsurfing and kite-boarding, launching from the middle of the beach park as noted by signs. Board surfers like **Hanapai Beach** for its rocky left-break called **Wires**.

14. KALIHIWAI BAY   SNORKEL, PADDLE, SURF

> WHAT'S BEST: Surfing a deep-water break (and watching surfers!), taking a paddle up a lesser-known exotic river, and playing in the waves at a locals' beach. Get out of the car and hang around for a while.
> PARKING: Take Hwy. 56 past Kilauea. At about .75-mi. past mm23, turn makai on Kalihiwai Rd. (first). It's before the highway bridge. Go 1 mi. down to the beach park.

SNORKEL: No real snorkeling here, but during dry periods, slack green waters of the **Kalihiwai River** form a pretty swimming pool near the shore, very similar to the one at Lumahai. The rest of the beach is also excellent for family wave play and a day at the beach. Kalihiwai is a winner for tourists looking for a local-style beach.

PADDLE: The .75-mile slack waters of **Kalihiwai River**, with bananas and other fruits in the small river valley, impart a faraway feel. Commercial trips are not permitted here. The navigable part extends about one-quarter mile inland from the bridge, to below thundering Kalihiwai Falls. Access is in the trees at the far end of the bay (or across the river, as noted in the previous trailhead for stream paddling).

SURF: **Kalihiwai Bay** is a consistent and popular surfing spot, favored by some of Kaua'i's best wahine wave riders, like Bethany Hamilton-Dirks. To be a spectator, stop on the way down, .75-mile from the highway, at an unimproved two-car turnout before the guardrail (or check out *Paddle* above for a panoramic view). When conditions are right, this is one of Hawaii's best viewing spots. A four-tier right-break extends from the mouth of the bay inland, usually breaking close to the cliff. Entry is to the right as you reach the beach park. Body boarders like the shore break by the river. *Be Aware:* Get friendly with locals before paddling out. They protect their surf turf.

Secret Beach

15. SECRET BEACH   HIKE, SURF

WHAT'S BEST: A hike-to, beach-lover's beach, with a long sand-and-surf walk and dramatic view of Kilauea Lighthouse on the cliffs above. Hike down and find a spot to lose your sense of time.

PARKING: Take Hwy. 56 to past Kilauea. Just before mm24 and a guardrail, turn makai on Kalihiwai Rd (first). Pass the first driveway to the school bus yard, and then turn right, just .1-mile from the highway, on a dirt road cut through a 15-foot-high embankment. Continue .3-mi. to unimproved parking by recently built homes.

HIKE: Secret Beach (.5-mi. to 2.25 mi, 175 ft., depending on beach walk.)

Secret Beach, officially Kauapea Beach, might be renamed Not-So-Secret Beach, since this access is widely known. The beach is a long and deep deposit of fine sand, running from below the lighthouse at Kilauea Point. The trailhead is between newer homesites, a dirt path in the shade of broadleaf kamani trees and bananas. You then steeply descend wood-and-dirt steps, roots, and rocks—all of which can be slippery after rains. You walk the last hundred yards or so through a flourishing pandanus grove. Secret is divided into three segments: "First" Secret Beach is the part you first access from this trail; "Second" Secret is the middle part that has black rocks poking up along its surf line; and "Third" Secret is the last beach, which is nestled up to the cliffs that lead out to the lighthouse. Keep your eyes peeled seaward for spinner dolphins. *More Stuff:* Go to the left as you get to the sand for a scenic short walk onto a low bluff with tide pools (though winter surf can fill them with sand). *Be Aware:* Be very alert for rogue waves, which can be lethal, both on the rocks and anywhere along the shore. High surf and tide sometimes closes off access to the far end of Secret Beach.

SURF: Secret Beach commonly has an onshore break that is dangerous, especially during winter months. During calmer periods of onshore break, Secret is good for body boards, and during some winter storms the locals ride the offshore swells at Third Secret, nearest the lighthouse *Be aware:* Get advice on hazards from locals.

Stone Dam, Wai Koa Loop Trail

16. ANAINA HOU COMMUNITY PARK

HIKE, HORSE

WHAT'S BEST: Hike, cycle, or just hang out at this 500-plus-acre private park. Anaina Hou may be an example of millennial ecological living, but it is rooted in the Hawaiian tradition of the *ohana*—the extended family that holds a community together. *Note:* **Stone Dam hike** may be closed through 2019 and beyond due to flood damage.

PARKING: Take Hwy. 56 toward Kilauea. *For Common Ground trailhead,* turn left just before Kilauea at mm22.8 on Kuawa Rd. and continue about .75-mi. to its end. *For Anaina Hou Park (main) trailhead,* pass the turnoff to Kilauea and turn left at mm23.7; the park visible from the highway. Sign use waiver here. *For Dog Park trailhead,* continue to mm24.4, turn left on Kahiliholo Rd., go .5-mi. and look for the park on your left.

HIKE: Wai Koa Loop Trail: Anaina Hou Park Trailhead (5 mi., 325 ft.); Common Ground to Stone Dam (1.25 mi., 150 ft.); Dog Park to Stone Dam (3 mi., 200 ft.)

Often enough, when a dot.com millionaire (the late William A. Porter, E-Trade) buys land in Hawaii, the result is a big estate with a locked gate. Not here. Porter's **Anaina Hou Community Park** ("the gathering place") has opened the door into an agricultural wonderland set below magnificent mountain ridges. On site is the **Namahana Cafe**, the place to enjoy island-fresh delectables on a large deck. Out back is **Kaua'i Mini Golf**—but forget about windmills and wide-open clown mouths. This 18-hole beauty, with a stream and footbridges, is a walk through a botanical garden that traces the history of island greenery from native plants to Polynesian species and modern exotics. The grounds host a **farmer's market**, friday-night music, and movie nights. Kids will the love the **Porter Playground**, with playsets covering an acre or more.

The **Wai Koa Loop Trail** is one of the better family exercise walks in Kauai. *Be Aware:* The trail is free and open daily from dawn til dusk, but you must drop in at the cafe to *sign a use waiver.* Beginning from the park, the route dips under an overstory of leafy trees and Cook pines, crossing a stream and then hitting a straightaway though a uniform grove of young yet stately **mahogany trees** (the largest planting in the country). Birdsong is the soundtrack. After about .75-mile, you reach the main loop junction. Go left. You then zigzag past more mahogany trees, as well as palms and ironwoods, before reaching outer gardens of the former Common Ground. Then go left at a signed spur trail to the idyllic **Stone Dam**—whose waterfall, bamboo forest, and terraced grounds are the scenic centerpiece of the trail. The loop continues passing the greenhouses of **Kauai Fresh Farms** and the still waters of **Kalihiwai Lagoon**. Next up are the **Community Gardens**, a picturesque assemblage of small farming efforts. After the gardens comes the nonprofit **North Shore Dog Park**, where you can get a doggy fix before continuing. *Note:* Stone Dam is under repair through 2019.

The old **Common Ground to Stone Dam** parking option is the shortest way to see the most scenic elements of the Wai Koa Loop Trail. For an intermediate distance walk, use the **Dog Park to Stone Dam** access, and go counterclockwise (right).

HORSE: Magnificent **Silver Falls Ranch** is home to some of Hawaii's best trail rides. *Driving:* Continue up Kahiliholo past the dog park and go left on Kamoʻokoa Road. The ranch's trails cover 80 acres of botanical gardens and are set below the jagged green ramparts of the 15,000-acre Haleleʻa Forest Reserve. The falls, a wide cascade, drop into a perfect swimming hole where lunch is served. The place is surreal, and well-worth adding to your recreational regimen. Daily tours accommodate all riders.

17. KILAUEA POINT REFUGE AND LIGHTHOUSE   HIKE

WHAT'S BEST: Take a gander at magnificent shorebirds and crashing surf at the lighthouse and national wildlife refuge on Hawaiʻi's most northerly point. Nearby is a locals' walk to a "movie star" falls—but access may be restricted.

PARKING: From Hwy. 56, turn makai toward Kilauea on Kolo Rd., near mm23. Jog right to behind the gas station and then left on Kilauea Rd. *For Kilauea Point National Wildlife Refuge:* Continue makai for 2 mi. Pass a first lighthouse parking lot and go down a steep road to the paved lot. Admission is $10. *For Crater Hill:* About .25-mile before the entrance to the lighthouse, park at Iwalani Road, the entrance to Seacliff Plantation, a development.

For Kilauea Falls (and Kahili Beach): Before the lighthouse on Kilauea Rd.(about .3-mile past Kong Lung store) turn right at a paved Kilauea Quarry Road. Drive in .3-mi. and park at pavement's end; or continue .75-mile on a smooth cinder road to park at estate driveways.

Kilauea Lighthouse

Kilauea Falls (trail probably closed)

HIKE: Kilauea Point Refuge (.5-mi.); Crater Hill (1.5 mi., 250 ft); Kilauea Falls (3.25 mi., 425 ft., *may be closed*. Hike is 1.75 mi. 200 feet if you drive the cinder road.)

Kilauea Point Wildlife Refuge and Lighthouse, draws many tourists to the most northerly part of the main Hawaiian Islands. You look down 200 feet to seas crashing on tiny **Mokuaeae Island**. North from here are the 100-plus small islands that comprise the Northwestern Hawaiian Islands Marine National Monument. Tropicbirds, Laysan albatrosses, and great frigatebirds soar about, while waddling the grasses are nene, or Hawaiian goose, the state bird. Shearwaters and red-footed boobies nest on steep hillsides. In the seas, whales and spinner dolphin vie to steal the show. Binoculars are provided for free. A visitors center offers exhibits and gifts, but the best information is available from volunteers at the **Daniel K. Inouye Lighthouse**. The lighthouse dates from 1913; it was dedicated to the late Hawaiian senator in 2013. Free tours available. *Notes:* The point's hours are 10 to 4, closed Sunday and Monday, and holidays.

Crater Hill, a former volcanco that is now grassy knob above the lighthouse, gives up views of the north coast. Starting at a pedestrian access gate, the walk is along the broad grassy margins dotted with palms of the widely spaced **Seacliff** estates. This is a local's favorite. Few cars drive the road. Bear left on Makana'ano Place, where you will get sea views of Kilauea Bay. At a cul-de-sac near the top, go through an opening for the view, including the lighthouse. You can't go to the the very top of Crater Hill.

Kilauea Falls is a beautiful baby Niagara, a fifty-foot high, 150-foot wide white curtain falling into a swimming oval nearly 200 feet across—featured in the 1998 adventure comedy, *Six Days, Seven Nights. Be Aware:* In 2004, The Kilauea Point National Wildlife Refuge Expansion Act authorized the purchase of 234 acres that include Kilauea Falls. Public access is part of the plan but not yet realized. For years, people accessed the falls via a shared easement on private property. A landowner recently closed the trail. Locals are working to re-open it. **From the parking**, descend a road through profuse flora, including a sprawling banana patch. After about 15 minutes, as you begin to get stream valley views, go right at an unsigned road that drops and traverses right (though you need to keep right and climb a little after the first descent). The route drops into a tree tunnel in a bird-rich forest from where the stream is visible. Then take a concrete drive down steeply left and then go up another ramp. The route then pierces a thicket of bamboo, ferns, and ape (*ah-pay*, elephant ear plants). You'll reach a bedrock section of the stream and ascend another 5 minutes before coming to the fabulous vista across the large pool to Kilauea Falls. *More Stuff:* Continue walking on the main road to reach **Kilauea Bay** at the stream mouth and near Quarry Beach. The panoramic hike to the bay is nearly 5 miles, round trip, with some 475 feet of elevation.

18.   KILAUEA BAY-KAHILI BEACH   HIKE, PADDLE, SURF

> **WHAT'S BEST:** Put this beach with a stream on the A-list with Kaua'i's other out-of-the-way wonders. Nearby is one of Hawaii's better botanical gardens.
> **PARKING:** Take Hwy. 56 toward Kilauea. Turn makai .6-mi. after mm21 on Wailapa Rd. *For Kilauea Bay:* Continue for .4-mi. and veer left down a steep but well-surfaced dirt road for .6-mi. to unimproved parking area at beach. Avoid this road during rains. *For Na Aina Kai Gardens:* Continue less than .5-mi. to the end of Wailapa Rd.

HIKE: Kilauea Bay to Quarry Beach (.75-mi.) or Kilauea Iki Beach (up to 1 mi.);

For **Quarry Beach**, head down the beach to your left as you face the water. You need to cross the stream and walk to your right to the viewpoint at the old quarry, bordering the wildlife refuge. Walking the other way on the bay's soft sand—called **Kahili Beach**—you quickly leave the beach and walk up flat rock ledges, gaining 50 feet, to a grassy perch just out of the salt spray. Continuing down from there is a small sweet beach—**Kilauea Iki**—which extends to the cliffs of Keilua Point.

More Stuff: **Na Aina Kai Botanical Gardens & Sculpture Park's** 240-acre grounds are decorated with more than 100 life-sized bronze statuary in garden settings, a hedge maze, and a huge pond with fountains—all the vision of Joyce and the late Ed Doty, who began the effort in 2000. The gardens give way to ocean-views from a hardwood plantation that extends to a wild beach. *Notes:* An admission is charged.

PADDLE: **Kilauea Stream** curves inland for more than a mile, wide and deep through an open valley with upland views, before losing itself in dense foliage and river rock. Go through two upright pipes on a narrow road to the riverbank.

SURF: Locals like the offshore break at the riverside mouth of the bay, called **Quarry Beach** or **Rock Crusher**. Spectators can cross the river to the quarry to view surfers looking down the barrel of the wave. *Be Aware:* Shore breaks can cause injuries.

Kong

"Kong" is the familiar name for the pointed peak on Kaua'i's northeast shore, looking much like the head of the mythical ape, forever watchful seaward. The peak's real name is Kalalea, which in Hawaiian means "prominent." But Kong's fifteen minutes of Hollywood prominence came not from *King Kong*, but as an opening shot for *Raiders of the Lost Ark*.

The gap-toothed ridge in which Kong is centered, commonly called the Anahola Mountains, is the subject of Kauaian mythology that has been altered by recent geology: The ancient "Hole in the Mountain," an opening through the ridge behind Kong, was said to have been made when a rival king from the Big Island threw his spear across the entire island, piercing the ridge and earning the kingship for his effort. In the mid-1990s, a landslide closed the hole to a tiny crescent.

Kong's ridge is a branch of the Makaleha Mountains, the east-side range that intersects the sloping forest reserve and agricultural lands that sweep around the coast from Kilauea on the north to the Royal Coconut Coast on the east. This area is known for numerous hike-to coves, beachcombing beaches and coastal bike trails. With several trails and four-wheel drive roads leading into forest reserves, the Kong region also offers an excellent inland access toward Mount Waialeale and adjoining ridges.

Heading away from Kilauea toward Kapa'a, begins a long coastline, perhaps the least-hiked of Kaua'i's accessible shore. Waiakalua beaches are among the best-kept secrets, featuring three coco palm coves. Down the coast from Waiakalua is Larsens Beach, better known and much larger—more than two miles of coral beach and ragged reef, fringed by low bluffs. Tide pools, reef currents and wave action make Larsens' shore ever-changing, and winter trade winds bring eclectic flotsam ashore.

Continuing toward Kong from Larsens, the coast becomes a series of coves and inlets large enough to be called bays—Papa'a, Moloa'a, Aliomanu and Anahola. Moloa'a Bay, though the site of several homes, is a classic getaway cove for sunbathing, swimming, and short hikes along its bluffs. Off-highway paved roads around Moloa'a, including the one to Larsens, make this a place to tour on a bike. Anahola Bay, just below Kong, and Aliomanu Bay, which lies beside Anahola, offer three snorkeling and surfing beaches, a navigable stream and a variety of beach hiking. Bordering Hawaiian Homelands, Anahola is the most-Hawaiian community on this side of the island.

Around the point, on the Kapa'a side of Kong, are miles of coastline accessible by foot and mountain bike—some of it wild, and some of it through resort paths and beachside parks—extending all the way from Anahola along the Royal Coconut Coast to the Wailua River. Surfers and boogie boarders in this neck of the woods head for Donkey Beach, Kealia Beach or Wailua Bay, while snorkelers duck in at one of several lesser known spots behind funky Kapa'a Town and the hotels of the Coconut Coast.

Makaleha Falls trail

Anahola Bay, Coconut Marketplace

This coral-reef coast is not without its paddling waters, with two streams to inland areas that practically no one paddles. Unlike other streams on the island that fit this description, Kong's are closed to kayak outfitters. Outrigger canoes and kayaks also stroke the waters off the coast, although Kaua'i newcomers should check with locals before venturing beyond the breakers in a kayak.

Some of the best inland hiking is to be had on this east portion of the Kong trailheads. Above Kealia is the Spalding Monument, pointing the way toward the upper Makaleha Mountains and Waipahe'e Falls. Above Kapa'a on Olohena Road is more access toward these mountains, as well as three trailheads to Nounou Ridge, better known as the Sleeping Giant. The landmark Sleeping Giant is a forest reserve and excellent viewpoint to get a bearing on the east side.

Heading up the Wailua River—the place where the first ali'i, or kings, chose to call home—leads to the Keahua Arboretum. From the arboretum, bikers and hikers can pick up the south end of the Powerline Trail that connects with Princeville on the north shore, or head up another ridge that twists through jungle to abut the Makaleha Mountains. Another trail from the arboretum leads to an up-close look at Mount Waialeale, below the rippling waters of its vertical face. Also from the arboretum are trails that poke out to views of Kilohana Crater above Lihue.

The rural roads around Kapaʻa and the Coconut Coast are also a scenic tour for cyclists wishing to catch a glimpse of local-style living and maybe snag a papaya at an honor-system fruit stand. Behind the Sleeping Giant is a gardenlike expanse.

After a day spent recreating, Kapaʻa Town is a good choice to grab a smoothie or a shave ice, and walk around the quaint streets and neighborhoods—a blend of the cultures that combine under the umbrella of aloha to make Kauaʻi. Buddhist temples stand near Catholic churches, and juice bars adjoin sushi bars and Hawaiian diners.

Anahola Stream, Coconut Coast in Kapaʻa

MAP 2   TRAILHEADS 19-32

KONG

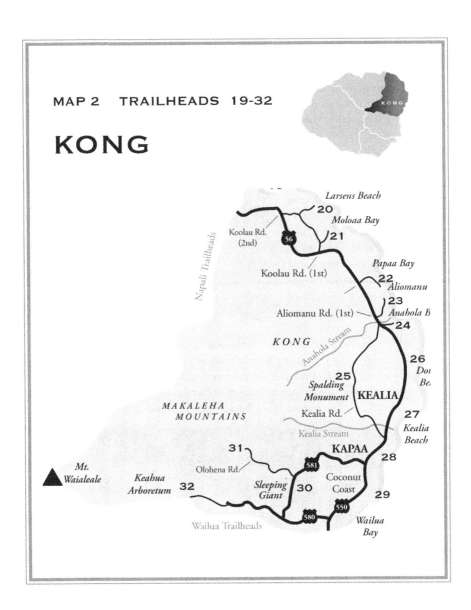

KONG

T R A I L H E A D S
19-32

HIKE	HIKING
SNORKEL	SNORKELING AND SWIMMING
BIKE	MOUNTAIN OR ROAD BIKING
PADDLE	KAYAKING, CANOEING
SURF	SURFING, BOOGIE BOARDING

TH	TRAILHEAD
Makai	TOWARD OCEAN
Mauka	TOWARD THE MOUNTAIN, INLAND
mm	MILE MARKER, CORRESPONDS TO HIGHWAY SIGNS

Note: All hiking distances are roundtrip unless otherwise noted.

19. WAIAKALUA BEACHES   HIKE, SNORKEL, SURF

WHAT'S BEST: Adventurous hikes to idyllic, hidden tropical beaches. This is why many people come to Kaua'i.
PARKING: Head beyond Anahola on Hwy. 56, past second Ko'olau Rd. Turn makai on N. Waiakalua Rd., about .8-mi. past mm2. Go .7-mi. on N. Waiakalua to end of road at cul-de-sac, and turn left at telephone pole #17 on dirt road, which is lined with ironwood trees. Go .2-mi. to unimproved parking. Leave car free of valuables.

HIKE: Waiakalua Beach to Kaluakai Beach (.75-mi., 175 ft.); Pila'a Beaches (1.75 mi., 175 ft.)

Waiakalua Beaches are jewels tucked away on a remote section of coastline, part of the Hawaiian Islands Trust and Conservation Area. Start down the steep trail, improved by log steps. At a viewpoint not far from the trailhead, look right: You'll see the more secluded **Pila'a Beaches**—palm-fringed crescents of sand on a black rock coast, under jungled cliffs. **For all beaches**, proceed down over roots and a slippery section aided by a rope, in shade all the way. One short rock section requires attention to foot place-ment, just above the soft sand beach. Go left to **Waiakalua**. Heliotropes, ironwoods, and palms grace the coarse-sand shore. You are likely to see seabirds. But watch the ground, too, since big monk seals like to haul out here. At the end of the beach is a boulder-rock point. Scramble for a few minutes and you'll come to a **Kaluakai Beach**, below Na Aina Kai Gardens, which is private property.

To reach the pretty **Pila'a Beaches**—a 'fantasy island' getaway—go to the right when you reach the bottom of the trail at the water. It's a tricky .5-mile scramble on black boulders at the edge of coastal vegetation. After the balancing act, you'll cross a small stream and reach the first beach, which is backed by a parklike lawn. Normally, you can reach the second beach, which is home to several cottages, by walking sand between boulders around the cliff. Both beaches are beautifully situated among palms and other beach trees. A tech tycoon (hint: M.Z.) owns all the acreage inland. *Be Aware:* Hiking poles and sturdy shoes will greatly aid the half-hour of boulder hopping along the coast. *More Stuff:* A short distance down from the trailhead is a mountainside fisherman's trail to the right that traverses steeply to Pila'a, but is difficult to follow; the coastal route, though not a cake walk, is easy to follow.

SNORKEL: **Waiakalua Beaches**, on pretty days, fill the bill for an ideal tropical beach, the perfect place to take a dip with the fishes. For a better swim, make the hike to **Pila'a Beaches**. Cross the stream and immerse yourself about midway along the first beach—superb! *Be Aware:* These beaches feature an exposed section of reef with strong and confusing currents. Get a good read before venturing in. A primary rip current travels directly outward from near the stream.

SURF: Surfers take a gander at **Waiakalua** from the viewpoint mentioned in the hiking section, and die-hards carry their boards down. This is a place for locals and advanced surfers to look for something exciting. Because of the reef break and remoteness, Waiakalua is a risky surfing area. During periods of epic surf, big-daddy wave riders, partnered with buddies on jet skis, ride the rolling mountains: quite a show.

20.   LARSENS BEACH   HIKE, SNORKEL

> WHAT'S BEST: Larsens is definitely not on the tour-bus circuit. Roam an open beach-scape for miles, looking for wildlife and a well-chosen place to take a dip.
> PARKING: Take Hwy. 56 past Anahola and turn makai at first Ko'olau Rd., which is about .75-mi. past mm16. Drive past Moloa'a Rd. and, at 2.25 mi. from hwy. turnoff, turn makai again, sharply right at a beach access pole. It's at telephone pole #7 and address 7200. Go .9-mi. down to a large parking area. Leave car free of valuables. *Note:* Ko'olau Rd. loops around to Hwy. 56. Coming from the north, turn left on Ko'olau just after mm20 and proceed 1.1 mi. to the Larsen's road.

HIKE: Kephui Point (3.5 mi., 425 ft.)

Larsens Beach is visible from a grassy perch a short distance down from the parking—the beach is about 200 feet below and little more than .25-mile away. **Kepuhi Point** is beyond two beach segments, lying to your left as you face the water. Take the trail down, and continue through groundcover at the backshore. (You can also take one of several spur trails to the beach and walk left on the sand.) Along Larsens Beach you will discover drifts of yellow sand beside tilting sections of broken reef, foaming with aquamarine tidal action—an ideal home for seabirds and marine life, such as monk seals and turtles. The backshore slopes fairly gently into ironwoods and broadleaf beach trees. *Be Aware:* You may see a few nude people, although nudity is unlawful on state beaches in Hawaii. They usually don't cover up for passersbys.

Telephoto shots at Larsens Beach of monk seal, baby albatross

The first part of Larsens is also called **Ka'aka'aniu Beach**. After this first .5-mile beach, leave the sand on a trail over a .25-mile stretch up and over a low point and dropping down to the next beach segment, a cutie called **Waipake Beach**. At the far end of Waipake you may see monk seals resting in the sand or on the reef (stay back). Rising at the end of the beach is a ruddy, hog-back bluff. Veer left on a gradual route before coming to the end of the beach, and follow a sketchy trail through ironwoods, staying close to water's edge. Do not disturb Laysan albatross nests on the hillsides. You will come to a lush gully. Jog left, away from ironwoods, and follow vague route across the stream in the gully, and then up through the red-dirt trail on the other side. **Kepuhi Point** is set low to the surf, with a frothing tidal pool, little sea arch, and a blunt tip that thwarts the sea to create a thunderous display of white water. You'll find various vantage points. *Be Aware:* Inland is private property; use coastal paths.

SNORKEL: **Larsens Beach** is known for lethally dangerous swimming. Before dropping down to the beach, study the reef from the viewpoint mentioned in the hiking section. You'll be able to spot the main blue channel, at the far left of the beach; current usually runs right-to-left and out this channel. Throw a stick in the water to see which way it floats, and once you enter the water, be mindful of the direction your body starts moving on its own. Still, on certain days in the right spot, Larsens is a beautiful place to get in the water with mask and fins. The second beach over, **Waipake**, is the better choice for swimmers. Check out the protected sand beach just as you drop down, a prime spot for a day at the beach. *Be Aware:* Do not swim here without making sure it is safe. Conditions are often hazardous farther out. No lifeguards here.

21. MOLOA'A BAY   HIKE, SNORKEL

> **WHAT'S BEST:** A lush tropical bay, made for an afternoon of swimming, short walks and relaxing. Though homes encircle the parking area, privacy is a short hop away, with whales offshore and seabirds as your beach buddies.
> **PARKING:** Take Hwy. 56 past Anahola, pass mm16, and turn makai on first Ko'olau Rd. Go 1.25 mi. and turn makai again on Moloa'a Rd. Continue down .75-mi. and park where the road makes a left, in assigned spots or on road without blocking driveways.

HIKE: Seabird Point (1.5 mi., 125 ft.); Moloa'a Forest Reserve (.75-mi., 150 ft.; different parking area, see hiking description.)

From the parking to **Seabird (Kalaeamana) Point**, walk the road to the left (facing the water), passing beach homes. Cross **Moloa'a Stream** and continue around the fine arc of this medium-sized bay to the far end. Under heliotrope and ironwood trees (a fine wild park) is a sign for the shearwater preserve and **Moloa'a Bay Ranch Coastal Trail**, part of the state's Na Ala Hele system. Take the path to the right along the rocks near the cliff, leaving the bay behind on a short ascent. On the upslopes before reaching the point, Layson albatrosses have been known to rest or make their awkward, "gooney bird" take-offs. If you see these birds, or the smaller shearwaters, give them room. Stay on a contour at the edge of the bluff, skirting a grassy area, until reaching a sturdy fence that marks private property. A trail continues on the ocean side of the fence—but the going gets rough in brush and then gets beyond rough.

Moloaʻa

The **Moloaʻa Forest Reserve** is not a spectacular hike, but it is a rare place to access the **Anahola Mountains** on this side; the trailhead is below a pointed peak named Amu. *Driving:* Continue past the first Koʻolau Road for 1.5 miles. You'll be going up a grade, passing a series of guardrails; as the guardrail's end—and about .1-mile after mm18—look mauka for a grassy turnout and a large silver mailbox. Park on grass shoulder on either side of road. *Be Aware:* The trailhead is hard to see on this busy road. You might end up passing it and hanging a U-turn.

Beginning at the mailbox, which reads "B-14, Hunter Checking Station-Moloaʻa," walk up the grassy embankment. Then go through the closed, not locked, metal gate to your left and follow the wide path as is curves upward toward Anahola. After a little more than .25-mile, notice a grass-cut trail veering left—the hunter's road continues toward Anahola. The left veer takes you a few hundred feet to a blue-water viewpoint of Moloaʻa Bay. Also of interest on this little-used trail: Halfway to the viewpoint spur described above, you'll see a red-dirt embankment, from which a poor trail leads. This trail gives you an option to look at Amu, a feature of the Anahola Mountains. *Be Aware:* Hunter's area; weekdays are best for hiking.

SNORKEL: The far end of **Moloaʻa Bay** is sheltered by black-rock reef, making this an interesting place to snorkel around, with good visibility on calm days and enough fish to make it interesting. Moloaʻa is an excellent place to take a plunge and go back to the beach mat. *Be Aware:* Avoid the rocky areas during periods of high surf. The better choice for snorkelers is the **Moloaʻa Baths**: Access the beach between the last two houses. Walk right about 200 yards to some palm trees, where a finger reef protects the shoreline. You'll find several "baths," or channels in the coral, just right for a swim when the tidal conditions are right. The family will enjoy poking around the tide pools.

22. PAPA'A BAY-ALIOMANU BAY

WHAT'S BEST: A one-two punch: Aliomanu contributes to Kaua'i's wealth of beach-comber's specials. Pretty Papa'a Bay is for snorkelers willing to take a short, wild walk.
PARKING: Take Hwy. 56 past Anahola and Hokualele Rd. and turn makai on second Aliomanu Rd., only .1-mi. past mm15. Go .1-mi and turn left on Kalalea View Dr., toward Aliomanu Estates. Continue 4-mi. and then turn makai (right) on a paved road normally marked by a beach-access pole. *For Papa'a Bay:* Go .25-mi. and park at a grassy turnout where the road turns right. *Note:* A lot sale may alter this access point. *For Aliomanu Bay:* Make the right and park in the lot visible just down the road. *Note:* Papa'a Rd., the next road north of second Aliomanu Rd., is also a way to get to this beach if you're coming from the north shore. Turn makai and follow beach access signage for about .5-mi.

HIKE: Papa'a Bay (1.25 mi., 125 ft.); Anahola Bay (2 mi.)

To reach the dreamy beach at aquamarine **Papa'a Bay**, go directly seaward toward an access pole and through an opening to the left of a gate. After a short distance, hang a left on a red-dirt trail in tall grass that skirts the bluff in front of homes. You'll be walking through tall grass. At the far end of the bluff, a steep trail leads down through ironwoods to sea level. From there, pick your way inland. For the last 75 yards, you'll have to walk over large black boulders (be mindful of surf). At the far end of the beach are a small stream and coral shallows, a good spot to log beach time. The two large homes behind the beach, built by a Hollywood mogul, are now owned by a tech tycoon.

Aliomanu Bay is a shallow depression in the coast between Papa'a and Anahola bays. From the parking, head down a red-dirt road, that makes easy curves to the beach, less than .25-mile away. Shell seekers love this beach. To **Anahola Bay**, head to your right at Aliomanu Beach. You'll walk the coarse sand at first and then pick your way around **Kuaehu Point**, which is below a lone house with a fading blue roof. High tide may make for a wet trip around the point, but this beach is made for wading. Once around the point is Anahola Beach, as described in the Anahola Lagoon parking in TH23.

SNORKEL: **Papa'a Bay** can be a good snorkeling spot on calmer days, as the cove offers protection from the surf. A coral reef just offshore the stream is a fish hangout, while turtles like the deeper water near the black rocks on the route in. Swimming in the bay is normally clear and calm. *Be Aware:* During higher surf, a left-to-right rip current forms near the stream mouth, but it normally dissapates in the bay. Stream runoff after rains decreases water clarity.

Aliomanu Beach has excellent scenic values, with kamani and ironwood trees interspersed along a a generous swath of coarse yellow sand along a two-mile-long coral reef. Rocks and shallow waters make for interesting wave action and tidal surges. All in all, this is a decent beach for snorkeling, although don't expect large, sparkling schools. *Be Aware:* Shallow waters, confused surf, and unpredictable northeast exposure can make for strong currents, especially in the winter.

Far end of Papa'a Bay

SURF: Locals head to **Papa'a Bay** to take advantage of a quick-breaking, offshore swell, called **Flags**. These fast-riding waves can be available at any time of the year. The usual entry point is in the rocky area where the trail first reaches sea level.

23. ANAHOLA BAY · · · · · · · · · · · HIKE, SNORKEL, PADDLE

WHAT'S BEST: Snorkel, beachcomb, or paddle. Though not normally on the list of starred attractions, charming Anahola may just become your first choice for a getaway.
PARKING: Take Hwy. 56 past Kealia and turn makai on first Aliomanu Rd., which is past the Anahola Post Office and just past mm14. Go .5-mi. down the paved road to stream mouth at beach. Park there or at one of several access points along the .75-mile long beach road. Good access is near a beach reserve sign near address 4746, and also just before the one-lane road section. *Anahola Lagoon parking:* Take Hwy. 56 past Anahola and turn right on second Aliomanu Rd., just after mm15. Pass Kalalea View Dr., continue .4-mile, and turn left on Kukana (sign may be missing). Beach access is on the right at .1-mile, at utility pole 5114C and just past a lava wall. Take care not to block driveways.

HIKE: Anahola Beach (up to 3 mi.); Anahola Lagoon (.75-mi.)

Anahola Beach, where the **Anahola Stream** flows down from nearby Kong and enters the bay, is a narrow, long strip of pale yellow sand along a broad reef. Ironwoods, coco palms and several kinds of broadleaf trees shade widely spaced beach cottages. The stream bank near the surf line is one of those perfect spots to sit awhile. Start the beach walk with the stream at your back, heading for Kuaehu Point and Aliomanu Bay. About halfway on the walk, a few beach cottages sit close to the water and you may have to walk the top of a short seawall for a bit during high tide, or stay on the road to an unsigned access near address 4934—this access may still be obscured by residents.

Portrait-quality **Anahola Lagoon** (different parking) is an easier, more scenic way to reach the far end of the beach. From the access path, go right on sloping sands to a stream. You'll receive a romantic look at Kong, rising in the background, framed by cocopalms over still waters. Grassy banks make a for a parklike setting.

SNORKEL: All in all, **Anahola Bay** is a decent snorkeling beach, with clear pools, a moderate number of fish, and a long coral reef. You'll find sandy access in selected spots, although rough coral borders much of the shore. In summery conditions, the best water play is at the sandy stream mouth. *Be Aware:* Rip currents head out channels, particularly during high-surf. Also avoid the river mouth area when the river is high.

PADDLE: The **Anahola Stream** lazes inland almost a mile before entering tangles of flora near the highway overpass. The Anahola Valley is lush with tropical fruit trees. Birdsong dominates the airwaves. This is a non-commercial paddling area, but you'll usually see a canoe or kayak parked in the ironwoods at the stream bank, where Aliomanu Road comes down. *Be Aware:* Flash floods occur after heavy rains.

24. ANAHOLA BEACH PARK   HIKE, SNORKEL, SURF

> **WHAT'S BEST:** Stop in for a swim on the locals' side of the bay, taking in views of the Anahola Mountains in afternoon sun.
> **PARKING:** Take Hwy. 56 past Kealia. Turn makai on Anahola Rd., past mm13. You'll see a right-turn lane at a guardrail and a right-arrow sign. Drive .75-mi. to white-rock sign and palms noting the beach park. Veer left, and continue to the end of road.

HIKE: Anahola Beach Park to: Anahola Stream (1.25 mi.) or Pahakuloa Point (2.5-mi., 225 ft.)

Anahola Beach Park is the home beach for the Hawaiian community of Anahola. To **Anahola Stream**, go left on the beach, with its beautiful views of the Anahola Mountains, seen through a healthy grove of coco palms. You'll pass the camping area and the rustic **Kumu Camp Retreat** before reaching the usually placid mouth of the stream—across from the main parking for TH23.

For Pahkuloa Point, take the dirt road just beyond beach parking, past picnic tables through ironwoods. On a gradual rise amid trees, the road rounds **Kahala Point** and then breaks open to grassy slopes. Avoid spur roads left and, about .5-mile from the trailhead, and you will reach rock-and-sand **Lae Lipoa Beach**. At the end of this beach,

Anahola Beach Park

follow the road as it ascends inland, passes another small rocky beach, and reaches the point. From here, you'll see across a cliffy cove to where fishermen drive in from Kealia. *Be Aware:* Though wild and remote, people can drive the coastal road from Anahola.

More Stuff: **Taro Patch** is a botanic wonder and the sometimes site of earthy cultural events and music concerts. *Driving:* Turn right on the next street after Kikoo Loop going toward Kapaʻa from Anahola. Drive across the 1921 bridge and park. A stream-side trail of about .25-mile ends at the lawn and tropical gardenscape,. *Be Aware:* Ask permission to enter; if no one is around, call John at Taro Patch-Anahola Ancient Cultural Center. The site suffered significant damage in the 2018 flood.

SNORKEL: The waters off **Anahola Beach Park** are shallow and the water clarity is normally above average. You'll have decent snorkeling and relatively safe swimming, with sandy entry points. *Be Aware:* High surf conditions can create strong current.

SURF: The reefy right-break off Kahala Point toward the beach park is sometimes called **Unreals**. The real draw here, for body boarders mainly, is **Pillars**, about halfway between the beach park and the stream. *Driving:* Coming from the highway, turn left on Poha Road and go less than .25-mile to the beach, site of the tiny tent cabins of rustic Kumu Camp. *Be Aware:* Pillars can have a nasty break onto a shallow sand bar.

25. MAKALEHA FALLS - SPALDING MONUMENT   HIKE, BIKE

WHAT'S BEST: Two hikes in mountains above Kealia: One can be either a stroll to a swimming hole, or a Tarzan-only trek through bamboo to jungly waterfalls. The other is a stroll at a decrepit monument with blue-water views of Kong and the Anahola Mountains.

PARKING: Take Hwy. 56 from Kapaʻa toward Kealia. *For Makaleha Falls:* Turn left (watch for traffic) on Malihuna Rd., just as you reach Kealia Beach. Go uphill behind the school and turn right on Kawaihau Rd. Continue for 4.5 mi. and turn left on Kahuna Rd. just after a bridge. Park after .4-mi. at a turnout just before water tanks. *For Spalding Monument:* At the far end of Kealia Beach, go left at Kealia Rd., about mm10.5. Head uphill on a paved road through bougainvillea. As you pass through fields, look for line of Norfolk pines up and to your left, which mark Spalding Monument. The defaced monument is 2.25 mi. from Hwy. 56.

HIKE: Makaleha Falls to: Swimming Hole (.5-mi, 100 ft.), or Falls (5.25 mi., 375 ft.). Spalding stroll (1.5 mi., 150 ft.—or more.)

For both **Makaleha Falls hikes**, walk past and then behind the water tanks to join a rooty, often muddy road under a high canopy of leafy trees. Ferns, moss, and birdsong accent the trail. At the top, you cross a side stream to an 'island' with a **swimming hole** to the right, and also to the left in Makaleha Stream, set below a low cliff.

To Makaleha Falls, continue up through a hau thicket up for about 200 feet, and look for the old concrete workings of a bridge in the stream. This is the crossing. (Without crossing, the trail continues up through the hau thicket to a water pipe.) *Be Aware:* This hike should be avoided when the stream is running swiftly (rather than in pools) or when it is raining—or may be raining in the mountains. Flash floods and currents can be lethal. The trail is hard to follow, requiring stream crossings, mud stomping, bouldering, and climbing over branches and trees. Count on 4 to 6 hours. Don't bother to remove shoes for crossings. Okay, time to proceed. After the crossing, you penetrate a bamboo forest, with the stream on the right. The trail climbs up left, and then returns to the streamside (take the second choice to do so). After crossing a small sidestream, you'll need to cross the major one, just below a confluence. Falls lie above the confluence on both streams. It's "easier" to boulder up to the falls to the right rather than fight the hau thicket. No two groups take the same trail, making route-finding difficult. The falls are classics—tiered white ribbons down green cliffs: a big pay-off.

With birdsong as a soundtrack, the **Spalding stroll** is is a birder's delight down a wide dirt drive fringed by tall Norfolk pines that lead away from the palm-encircled monument. The embankment and flora sometimes obscure views, but you do get looks of the Kapaʻa coast on your left and close-ups of a moist woodland valley on your right. In about .75-mile, at another ranch gate, is a big panorama inland. *Note:* The monument to honor a pineapple scion probably remains in dreary disrepair. Kauai Ranch, a walled estate, has barred other former access in this area. *More Stuff:* The washed-out road continues down **Hauaʻala Road** into a lush stream valley.

More Stuff: A hunter's road—on the left, .9-mile toward Anahola—has traditionally provided recreational access to the Anahola Mountains. A new gate with signage now makes it iffy at best. The main road continues inland toward Kaneha Reservoir, and ends near **Waipaheʻe Falls**—a former tourist attraction that has been fenced off for years.

BIKE: The **Spalding stroll** road continues down to Kealia on a slippery, rutted road, connecting with **Hauaʻala Road**, which is part of an inland ride described in TH27, Kealia Beach. To make this fairly difficult loop, you hang a left at the bottom of Spalding Road and ride out to the highway along the stream. From the highway, go left to Kealia Road, and pedal back up to Spalding. All of this is about 6.5 miles.

26.   DONKEY BEACH   HIKE, SNORKEL, SURF

WHAT'S BEST: A big beach offers room to roam on a wild-and-scenic coastline. With a high-end development planned on the upper slopes, Donkey Beach may not be the wild hideaway it once was, but it still delivers top-level scenic goods.
PARKING: Take Hwy. 56 past Kealia Beach. Pass mm11 and the Kealia Kai development. Look for signed trailhead parking, makai at the top of the hill, near mm11.5.

HIKE: Donkey Beach (1.25 mi., 225 ft.); House Beach (2 mi., 225 ft.)

Rental cars mingle with surfmobiles at the trailhead parking. **For both hikes**, take a concrete path down through a long, leafy tunnel. **Donkey Beach**, rarely called by its real name, Kumukumu Beach, is a short distance to the right on the coastal bike path. It's one of those better-known secret beaches, but its .5-mile wide crescent of

Donkey Beach

sloping sand remains pristine. Try walking down immediately on unmarked routes and trudging the sand to the right. Then walk up to treed **Paliku Point**, where a picnic pavilion is sited on grass terraces. You can then stroll the bike path. *Note:* The official beach access is off the path, toward the other end of the beach.

To **House Beach**, also known as Anapalau Beach, head away from Donkey Beach, going to your left on the bike path as you face the water. The paved path ends in about .25-mile, but the coastal trail doesn't: Take the dirt trail and then go right across a stream gully (with small falls and pools). At a tee-junction you have a choice: You can go right, passing a small cove of **Ahihi Point**, after which the trail climbs, and then drops to a rugged contour close to the water. Or, an easier route is to go left at the tee junction: You'll follow a grass-fringed path up along a rail fence, up and then down to ironwoods. After passing an old cane road gate and a sinkhole (danger), look right for a long tree-tunnel road down to the House Beach. The cove no longer has a house. You'll find ample sand between nests of black rock and shade trees.

SNORKEL: With a shore break, **Donkey Beach** is seldom a good snorkeling spot. *Be Aware:* Surf and rip currents can make this a dangerous Donkey. Snorkeling at **House Beach** is better—one of the best on the Coconut Coast during ideal conditions. On calm days, try walking out to the point (Anapalau) to the far left as you face the water, toward the lone ironwood, and swimming back in toward shore—through deep, clear water. You get a view of Donkey Beach from the point. Precautions observed, House Beach is a very good snorkeling experience. Families will love the **keiki (kid's) beach**, with a protected, sandy entry, located to the right as you face the water.

SURF: **Donkey Beach** is on the circuit for east-side surfers, but the break is better at Kealia. Avoid the chopped-up shore break by surfing inside the point to the right as you face the water, where waves peel off into the beach. Other boarders ride the tiers mid-bay. You can tell if the surf is up by looking for surfmobiles and pickups parked at the trailhead. *Be Aware:* A shore break means impact injuries.

27.   KEALIA BEACH   HIKE, SNORKEL, BIKE, PADDLE, SURF

WHAT'S BEST: Coastal biking and hiking, beachcombing, whale-watching, spacing out, and body-boarding: Kealia has it all for a beach break all day long.
PARKING: Take Hwy. 56 through Kapa'a toward Anahola. You'll see two improved parking areas. Look for a right-turn lane at mm10 or, .25-mi. beyond that, turn into larger lot near four picnic pavilions.

HIKE: Kealia Lookout (1.75 mi.); Donkey Beach (2.75 mi.)

To the **Kealia Lookout**—where you may spot a whale during winter migrations—walk to your right as you face the water. Either stomp the sand or use the wide paved path that, along with series of small pavilions and footbridges. Near the far end of the beach, about .5-mile from the parking, you cross **Kealia Stream**. If the water is high, use the bike-pedestrian bridge near the highway. At the end of the beach, continue another .25-mile to a point visible from Kealia Beach, below the scenic turnout on the highway.

To **Donkey Beach**, go to your left as you face the water, walking on a former pineapple haul road that has been paved and is now used by hikers, cyclists, and surfers. About .5-mile along on the road from Kealia, you'll round a gully and come to a pavilion just inshore of an **old pineapple pier** that hangs over crashing surf. On the way to Donkey Beach, you'll pass by a pleasing pavilion, set off the path to the right, and cross a footbridge before dropping down to the large baylike beach.

SNORKEL: To your left as you face **Kealia Beach**, a black-rock breakwater creates a sandy area for swimming, although fish are not abundant. *Be Aware:* Stay out of the water on big-surf days, and watch out for current sweeping the inside of the breakwater.

BIKE: From **Kealia** is Hawaii's best coastal path, scenic and open—part of the **Kapa'a Coastal Bike Path** or Ke Ala Hele Makalae ("the path that goes by the coast"), which opened in 2009. You have options: Ride toward **Donkey Beach**, as per hiking description. The route beyond Donkey becomes a trail, not a path. The ride has its ups and downs, but is essentially flat, curving with the coast. You can also ride the other way from Kealia, toward the **Kealia Lookout**, and continue on the coastal path for about two miles to Kapa'a. In **Kapa'a Town**, TH28, you hook up with a coastal route taking you almost to Lihue.

Kealia Beach

Another option from Kealia, is the **Haua'ala loop**, which takes you on a wild, less-traveled, 5-mile swing through the Kealia Stream valley. Take off toward Kapa'a on the path, crossing the Kealia Stream on the footbridge. Then cross the highway (heads up) and take a right, up Mailihuna Road. Pump uphill, past Kapa'a High School, joining Kawaihau Road .6-mile from the highway and into the 'burbs. Now the fun starts. Hang an immediate right down **Haua'ala Road**, which takes you down quickly to the valley, with views of the stream, shaded by banana plants and massive broadleaf trees.

Kapaa Coastal Bike Path

After about 1.5 miles, Haua'ala Road becomes dirt and crosses over **Kealia Stream**—water may be flowing over the road—surrounded by pools and under large monkeypod trees. Shortly after this serene juncture, and an uphill stretch, the road hairpins back toward the ocean, now on the other side of the stream. Just after the turn-back, you'll see the dirt road that comes down from Spalding Monument—be sure to go right here, on the lesser path at telephone pole #100. Haua'ala Road continues its loop, down now, through puddles, surging roadside grasses and overhanging, vine-encrusted limbs. After this wild, rutted stretch, you pop out at small agricultural homesteads and reach exotic views of Kealia Stream. Then the tree tunnels transition to pasture and marshlands, about a mile inland. Continue back to Kealia Beach.

PADDLE: Kayakers should park at the footbridge, very near mm10. **Kealia Stream** gathers the waters from several streams and has navigable water for about 1.5 miles inland. Birdsong is pronounced. This is a stream not used commercial outfitters.

SURF: The shore break at **Kealia Beach** invites short-board surfers and body board-ers, often several dozen at a time. Body boarding is often good off the breakwater to the left. Near the stream mouth at the other end, swells also attract surfers, although be aware of submerged rocks. Although Kealia can be good at any time of year, the onshore trade winds fight the break. Many breaks are close in, just right for spectators. Kealia is an ideal stop late in the afternoon to settle in an watch the surfing scene. *Be Aware:* Kealia is one of Kaua'i's most dangerous beaches, with rip currents, exposure to trade winds, and a shallow, onshore break. Head and neck injuries are possible.

28. KAPA'A TOWN   HIKE, SNORKEL, BIKE, SURF

> **WHAT'S BEST:** Tool around a colorful Kauaian town, on foot or by bike, and enjoy one of its several coral beaches. Try Kapa'a on a sunny weekend to see the mix of cultures that blend to create island-style living. Then take a short hike inland to a hidden waterfall.
> **PARKING:** The Kapa'a Town trailhead covers a 1.75-mi. portion of coast, beginning near mm7, just past the Kapa'a Shores condos, and extending to Kou Rd. on the other end of town, behind Otsuka's furniture store. *For parking:* Turn makai on Keaka Rd., at the gas station, drive a short block, and park at Niulani Rd. along the water. *Note:* Additional access points are imbedded in activity descriptions below. *For Ho'opi Falls:* Head toward Kealia on Hwy. 56 and turn mauka on Kawaihau Rd. (just past Otsuka's). Continue for almost 3 mi. and turn right on Kapahi Rd. Go .25-mi. and look for a gate on the left, about .1-mi. before the end of Kapahi.

HIKE: Kapa'a Town stroll (up to 4 mi.); Ho'opi Falls (.75-mi., 200 ft.)

Begin the **Kapa'a Town** stroll (say *Ka-pah-ah*) at the Keaka Road parking spot and head toward the Waikaea Canal, about .75-mile to your left at the water. Inshore is a quiet several-block-wide grid of beach cottages. The sliver of reef-protected water is

Kealia Beach

Fuji Beach, which is a draw for kite boarders and moms with toddlers. An arty footbridge leads across the canal to the large sandy beach behind the Pono Kai condos. **Pono Kai Beach** extends to **Kapaʻa County Beach Park**, with picnic pavilions and restrooms, which is behind a soccer field that borders the highway. For most of this hike, you either walk the beach, a greenscape, or the bike path. Palms and ironwoods shade the way. Keiki birthday parties, town events, and fishermen enjoying a daytime brewskie or three add to the atmosphere.

Passing the beach park—having walked .75-mile from the Waikaea Canal—you reach a footbridge at **Kapaʻa Library**. The pleasant path continues for another .25-mile, passing a community center and swimming pool, and coming to an end behind Otsuka's at Kou Road.

Pono Kai Beach

On the way back, you may wish to take a look at Kapaʻa Town: Walk the beach path back to the soccer field, and continue right on Niu Road. Then go left on the main street. Food carts will tempt tummies. The colorful cabins at **NoKa Fair** across the highway are brimming with Hawaiian fashion and art. Lots of other authentic, island-made stuff is at **The Kauaʻi Store**, just down the highway. Continue the main street to Inia Road and cut through the condos to the beach and take the path back to your car.

Tucked away in a neighborhood, **Hoʻopi Falls** won't be a vacation highlight, but it is a pleasant-enough, woodsy getaway. Head down the dirt road at the gate and within ten minutes you'll reach the stream, under a canopy of large monkeypod trees. During low water, take a lower trail across bedrock downstream; in higher water, take a trail that veers right, about 40 feet above the stream. In either case, you'll reach the falls in about 5 minutes. Two 20-foot cascades fall through a bedrock gorge, providing swimming holes and places for wannabe rock climbers to explore.

SNORKEL: **Fuji Beach** is a sandy area for toddlers and moms. From Keaka Road, walk or drive two blocks to where Makaha Road comes in. The little beach section is between Makaha and Panihi roads. You'll see a long, shallow pool near the road. This is a place to take a dip or let the kids splash around.

Pono Kai Beach, the best swimming beach in Kapaʻa, extends to your right as you face the water at Kapaʻa County Beach Park—which is behind the large grass field at Niu Road. Pono Kai Beach has ample sunny sand and shade trees. The sandy shore provides easy entry, and you'll find interesting rocks and a reef not far out, although schools of fish are uncommon. Current is generally onshore. Visibility is often only fair. *Be Aware:* Don't drift too far out, especially if swells are large; outgoing current develops under these conditions.

Coral Reef Beach—which you can access most easily by parking at the Kapaʻa Library and walking to your left across the footbridge—has shallow waters, but decent places of entry with the best fish along this part of the coast. Water clarity is good. For drying off, you can choose between a small strip of sand and a grassy area with shade among palm trees. *Be Aware:* Rip tides here can be dangerous, and sharp coral is also a factor.

BIKE: The **Kapaʻa Coastal Bike Path** (Ke Ala Hele Makalae) is the best easy going family ride in Hawaii. Read the hiking description for coastal walk, or just get on your bike and roll. *Note:* The town has numerous bike rental places, but Coconut Coasters is centrally located on the path and has a fleet of reasonably priced, spiffy beach cruisers; see *Resource Links,* page 239. Cheapo bike rental places have sprung up along the path. Starting near the Kapaʻa Shores condos on Niulani Road, make your way along path and footbridges, hugging the coast and heading toward Kealia. At the far end of town, near mm9 behind Otsuka's—across from Kawaihau Road—the route is wild-and-scenic to Kealia Beach—and beyond.

Going the other way on a bike, toward **Wailua**, is not quite as simple, but not difficult, either. To connect with the Coconut Coast, TH29, follow the path when it ends and stay on Niulani Road bike lane. You loop out to the highway at the Kapaʻa Shores condos. Don't cross the highway. Stay on the ocean side and cross the canal bridge at the Bull Shed Restaurant. You can ride the sidewalk and then turn seaward toward the Kauaʻi Courtyard by Marriott. Or, better yet, turn well before the Marriott into the apartment lot near the restaurant (have faith) and find the trails at Waipouli Beach County Park, which take you to the beach at the Marriott. See Coconut Coast mountain biking descriptions to take it from there.

SURF: **Kapaʻa Town** is not surf city. But local boarders sometimes try the reef break outside of Waikaea Canal. Head for the boat ramp on Kaloloku Road, and look seaward to the right. Due to shallow break and tricky currents, don't try this area unless the local boys are out there. The real wave action in Kapaʻa is among high-flying kite-boarders who put in at the end of **Baby Beach**, in a section called **Fuji Beach**.

Kapa'a Bike Path, Fuji Beach, Coconut Coast

29. COCONUT COAST

WHAT'S BEST: Strolling or pedaling Kaua'i's lesser-known resort coast, with its classic coco palms and quiet coral beaches. Take a mellow walk to start or finish the day.
PARKING: Take Hwy. 56 from Lihue and cross over the Wailua River. Pass mm6 and park makai at Coconut Marketplace.

HIKE: Coconut Coast stroll (up to 3 mi.)

The **Coconut Coast** is a 1.5-mile long coral beach sometimes called Papaloa, running from Wailua Bay to Waipouli, the area between the river and Kapa'a. This is Kaua'i's easy-walking, low-key coastal resort stroll. The modest hotels, spread apart, seem kitschy compared to the time-share behemoths going up elsewhere in Hawaii. From the parking, walk through **Coconut Marketplace** (check out Kauai Coffee and the upscale ABC store with take-out) and past the Islander on the Beach resort to a tree-lined water's edge. Go to your right on the paved path, passing the with-it Lava Lava Beach Club (eats, drinks) beside a strip of yellow sand. Just past the Kaua'i Sands, walk out a trail to a patch of greenery, which is contemplative **Alakukui Point**, where you'll find remains of **Kukui Heiau**, a fishing temple. From the point, skirt sandy tidepools at the shore of two small coves, behind tasteful Lae Nani condos. If you hop black rocks at the end of these tidepool coves, you will reach the outer point of Wailua Bay.

Going the other way, to your left from the Islander, you have a choice between the paved path or the beach, which is a narrow strip of coarse sand and exposed reef running along a low bank fringed by palms and ironwoods. You'll pass a large fenced resort site—alas the grass field, which had survived for decades, is no longer. You'll reach the **Kaua'i Courtyard by Marriott**. Visit the lobby to see orginal oil paintings by Herb Kane. Crossing a small ditch on the other side of the resort, you are again in an open area, with ironwoods and a coral beach—the scenic, usually quiet **Waipouli Beach Park**.

SNORKEL: On **Papaloa Beach**, just behind the Islander on the Beach as described in the parking instructions, you'll find sandy entrances in an otherwise sharp-coral beach with the reef running close to the shore. A fair number of fish swim here, and snorkeling can be good. *Be Aware:* The water is shallow and sometimes made turbulent by winds and wave action. *Cool tip:* Families and dawdlers will like the tidepool beaches at the **Lae Nani condos**, reachable via the short walk described above. A nice rock-rimmed pool is to the left as you face the water.

Waipouli Beach Park, just to the left as you face the water at the Coutyard Marriott, has the best sand in the area and several places that are shielded relatively from strong currents and wave action. Drive on Aleka Loop along a grass field to the public access path that is to the right of the resort as you face the water. *Be Aware:* Shallow waters, currents, and wave action combine to make this coast a place to take precautions.

BIKE: The **Coconut Coast** is ideal for exploring on a slow-moving mountain bike. Hug the water, being watchful for pedestrians. Between the coastal paths and the highway, roads and parking lots provide safe passage. To connect with **Kapa'a Town** (and the coastal path to Kealia) you can ride the coast most of the way, though you need to pop out to the highway past the Kaua'i Courtyard by Marriott, and cut back in again just past the Kapa'a Shores. Inexpensive bike rentals are offered at the Marriott.

Going the other way, towards Wailua Bay and **Lydgate Park**, you need to ride through the Coconut Marketplace parking lot and pick up Papaloa Road, which fronts the highway before joining it. At Wailua Bay, pedal the bike lane on the bridge over the Wailua River. After the river, drop left into Lydgate Park, TH34, where a new concrete bike path makes for easy going. (Another route is available near the highway.) At the far end of Lydgate, adventure riders can connect with Kaua'i Beach, TH35.

30. SLEEPING GIANT

HIKE

WHAT'S BEST: A tree-lover's hike to an east-side landmark, 1,200-feet high, with coastal and inland views. This forest reserve ranks high on the list of excellent half-day hikes.
PARKING: Three different trails lead to the top of Sleeping Giant.
For the Sleeping Giant West (mountain-side) Trail (best, shortest): Take Hwy. 580, Kuamo'o Rd., mauka from Wailua Bay. Continue on Hwy. 580 for 2.5 mi. and turn right on Hwy. 581, Kamalu Rd. *First access:* Go about 2 miles on Hwy. 581, past Heamoi Place, and park at telephone pole #11. *Second (shorter yet) access:* Continue .3-mi. past the above access and turn right on Lokelani Rd. Continue .3-mi. as road curves and ends at paved parking. (From Kapa'a, you can also drive up Olohena Rd., go left on Hwy. 581, and make the first left on Lokelani Rd.)

For the Sleeping Giant Kuamo'o trail (not recommended for summit): Take Hwy. 580, as noted above, only at 2.3 mi., look for a sign and trailhead parking on your right across the highway from Melia Street.

For the Sleeping Giant East (ocean-side) Trail: Head toward Kapa'a on Hwy. 56 from the Wailua River and the junction of Hwys. 56 and 580. After .25-mi. at a traffic light, turn inland on Haleilio Rd. Drive about 1 mile and look for a trailhead as Haleilio makes a big sweep around to the left—near a pump station.

Sleeping Giant

HIKE: Sleeping Giant summit via West Trail (3.25 mi., 775 ft.); Sleeping Giant via Kuamoʻo Rd. trail (to Vista Hale picnic shelter 1.5 mi., 325 ft., or summit 5.5 mi., 925 ft.); Sleeping Giant summit via East Trail (4 mi., 1,050 ft.)

All Sleeping Giant trails are part of **Nounou Mountain Forest Reserve** in the state's Na Ala Hele trail system. The Nounou Mountains, as you can observe from the coast, would be part of a ridge connecting with Kalepa Ridge, TH37, were it not long ago cleaved by the Wailua River. *Be Aware:* The trail is steep and often muddy. Hiking poles help. Drop-off hazards near the summit. Hands required in two short sections.

For the **Sleeping Giant West Trail**, which is the most direct way to the top, begin the hike by passing private homes on a gentle upslope. (The second access, from Lokelani Road, joins this grassy stretch after about .25-mile.) After .5-mile into forest, you reach the Kuamoʻo trailhead junction on your right, and then pass through stately Norfolk pines. The trail then switchbacks steeply, traversing a variety of trees planted in the 1930s by the Civilian Conservation Corps. You meet the East Trail, coming in from your left. Veer right and climb to a **picnic shelter** near the top for views of the Coconut Coast, Wailua River, and the Makaleha Mountains. **To the summit**, keep going to the right as you face seaward as the trail drops and then snakes up a ridgeline. One steep section before the top of the Giant requires your hands, but it is not dangerous. *Be Aware:* Thrill seekers will want to tiptoe to the left near the top to reach the chin of the Giant, but take your time since slips here lead to a free-fall.

The Sleeping Giant Kuamoʻo trailhead is best for the shorter walk to the **Vista Hale** picnic shelter or for a wooded, birder's car-shuttle hike to the mountainside trailhead; it is a circuitous way to the summit. You begin in a pleasant grassy easement and then cross a footbridge over **Opaekaʻa Stream**, well above the falls. The trail switchbacks through hau and guava before busting out to a view of Kalepa Ridge at the picnic shelter. The route then undulates along the west side of Nounou Mountains through richly varied forest, meeting the mountainside trail described above after about 2 miles.

The Sleeping Giant West Trail requires the most elevation. Its main upside is the blue-water views on the way up. It is also sunnier and you'll see more flowering shrubs, compared to the more forested mountain side of the ridge. Fewer hikers use this access, which joins its sister route about .25-mile from the picnic area near the top. The trailhead is a shorter drive.

31. OLOHENA HIGHLANDS   HIKE, BIKE

WHAT'S BEST: Hiking or biking an open ridge into the island's tropical interior, or riding around the rural countryside above Kapaʻa to get a take on local-style living.
PARKING: Take Hwy. 56 to the center of Kapaʻa Town and turn mauka on Hwy. 581.

Hwy. 581 is Kukui Rd., which becomes Olohena Rd. Take Olohena up for about 6 mi., making sure to bear right where Hwy. 581 turns left and becomes part of Kamalu Rd. Continue up Olohena on narrower paved section until it ends at a jct. with Waipouli Rd.

HIKE: **Moalepe Trail (3 mi. to 6 mi., 300 to 700 ft. depending on hike selection.)**

The **Moalepe Trail**, one of the lesser-used segments of the Na Ala Hele state hiking system, begins on a gradual incline, a red-dirt road flanked by pasturelands. (It is great option, due to the heavy use of the trail at its other access, from Keahua Arboretum.) White egrets often wing their way up a narrowing valley. To your back are blue-water vistas and a good look at the Anahola Mountains. After a mile the ridge narrows, with ferns, eucalyptus, and monkeypod trees at arm's length. At about 1.5 miles, the **Kamali Ridge** across the valley is dramatically close, on its way to abut the **Makaleha Mountains**, which in turn are heading toward Waialeale.

After the 1.75-mile mark, the trail becomes decidedly steeper, gaining most of its 700-foot elevation on the way to join the **Kuilau Ridge Trail**, at 2.75 miles into the hike. Gravel is often added to this section, to aid equestrians, but count on big mudholes winning out in the long run. You'll get close-ups of the Makaleha Ridge all the way. The trail junction—actually the trails just blend together, getting renamed in the middle—is at a hairpin left turn. The Kuilau Ridge Trail is described in TH32, Keahua Arboretum. *More Stuff:* The Moalepe Trail to the Kuilau Ridge Trailhead is a 4.5-mile car-shuttle, which works out well if you have a non-hiking driver in the group. *More*

Kuilau Ridge Trail

Stuff: Another easy-hiking spot nearby is the Wailua Game Management Area: When driving up Olohena, past the 581-Kamalu Road junction, turn left on Pu'uopae Road. Aftter .5-mile, turn right on Kalama and continue 1 mile to the **Rice Gate** at road's end. This is a birder's walk that eventually connects with the Moalepe Trail.

Bike: The **Moalepe Trail** is a gradual rise for nearly 2 miles, but after that, count on standing in the pedals. This trail is popular among equestrians, and horses turn the route into pudding—although gravel patches remedy this for a while. Although this trail does connect with TH32, Keahua Arboretum, it is not well-suited to mountain bikes on that end—it's muddy and wheels damage portions of the trail. Ride in on Moalepe for about 1.5 miles. Then try the countryside pedals on paved rural roads.

32.   KEAHUA ARBORETUM   Hike, Bike

What's Best: Hike, bike or picnic in the tropical highlands—to the basin of Mount Waialeale, along a jungle ridge. Or head out across the island to Hanalei Valley. Several of Hawaii's prime forested hikes are right here. So is a sacred forest.

Parking: Take Hwy. 580, which is Kuamo'o Rd., mauka at the Wailua River. Arboretum parking is about 7 mi. from Hwy. 56. Cross the one lane bridge (over the former spillway) and park at a large paved lot. Limited Kuilau Ridge parking is .1-mi. before the bridge.

Note: The **Waikoko Forest Management Road**, across the bridge, was wiped out in places by the flood of 2018. It was due to be gated closed for repairs (weekdays only) beginning late 2019 and extending for several months. Four-wheel drive vehicles are preferred, .1-mi. past the parking.

Hike: Keahua Arboretum circle (1 mi., 150 ft.); Kuilau Ridge Trail (4.5 mi., 550 ft.); Powerline Trail hikes: Kualapa Ridge (9.5 mi., 1,600 ft.), or trans-Kaua'i car-shuttle (13 mi., 1,700 ft.); Waialeale stream convergence (6 mi., 250 ft.); Waialeale (Blue Hole) basin (10 mi., 780 ft.) *Notes:* Hiking distances are from bridge parking. Different parking for Kaua'i's Hindu Monastery-Sacred Forest (.25-mi.)

The tame stroll around this trailhead's namesake **Keahua Arboretum** starts with an oh-wow weave through **rainbow eucalyptus** and continues to prime spots to have a picnic in a riverside garden setting. **For the hike**, cross the road, through the colorfully striped trees, to the top, a picnic shelter sits above a grassy basin, planted with both native and introduced tree species by the University of Hawaii. Then drop back down and head upriver, past a picnic pavilion, to a popular rope-swing **swimming hole**. Cross the river, if it's low; or doubleback and cross the bridge to the trail on the other side. On the way to the pool, are two shelters, the second of which is at the rope swing.

The **Kuilau Ridge Trail** is a hike to remember. The trailhead is about .1-mile before the bridge parking area—on your right driving down. The beautiful forest walk begins up an often-wet dirt road, with tree-filtered views of Waialeale basin in the distance

Kuilau Ridge Trail

and two stream drainages in the foreground—bursting with shrubs, vines, and trees. You can also see the Powerline Trail making its way to the Kualapa Ridge. At about 1.25 miles, the trail levels, reaching a large grassy area with **picnic shelter**. From the picnic shelter are views seaward of Sleeping Giant and Hoary Head and, straight ahead, of anvil-shaped Makaleha Ridge. Butterfly seekers and birdwatchers join hikers at this sublime spot.

Press on for the best stuff. The trail jogs right from the picnic area, and, for the next .5-mile, you're on a narrow, twisting ridge, amid lush tropical greenery with a Japanese-garden feel. A variety of birds will be seen and heard. This squiggly ridge is one of the most striking and scenic walks on Kaua'i. *Be Aware:* The profuse greenery at the edge of the trail hides steep drop-offs on either side. Stay on the trail.

Crossing the ridge, the trail makes a switchback, climbing to your right and then descending over a stream on a footbridge. *Note:* A sign at the footbridge says this is the end of the Kuilau Trail; disregard the sign and continue. For the next .5-mile you ascend a straight, wide path, through a tree tunnel formed primarily by peeling paperbark trees (from which paper is not made). At the top of the tree tunnel is a small grassy opening, where the trail hairpins to your right. This is where Kuilau Ridge joins **Moalepe**, the end-point for this hike. To get other views of the **Makaleha Mountains**, as well as the Kapa'a coastline, head down the Moalepe Trail for about .5-mile. Continuing all the way to the Moalepe trailhead, makes for a 4.5-mile car-shuttle hike.

Despite its dreary name, the **Powerline Trail** is an excellent trek through a wonderful snarl of tropical greenery—tree ferns, ti, bananas, and a who's-who among leafy trees. The best bet is to walk in a distance that suits your mood and turn around, rather than attempting the marathon trek to Princeville. The trail begins about .1-mile from the arboretum parking, on your right after the first uphill across the bridge. You'll see an uninviting rocky ramp going up. The **Kualapa Ridge**, the high-point of the journey, is nearly 5 miles in on the Powerline Trail, a rollercoaster ascent. The route's initial climb gives way after five minutes to a grassy road under monkeypod trees. You'll swerve and undulate through a ferny forest, chugging upwards, with views toward the Kuilau Ridge and waterfalls, about 2.5 miles in. Birds are profuse, and greenery narrows the route. The trail takes a 300-foot dive into a stream valley before the final ascent to the ridge. *Be Aware:* Grass and ferns crowd the trail in places, but the footing is reliably flat. You will up close and personal with plantlife and will also have to step around downed branches.

From the Kualapa Ridge you can see down the more gradual north slopes of the trail to the Hanalei Valley, and, looking the other way, the upslopes of the Kilohana Crater area and the Sleeping Giant. These views are in addition to close-ups of the wrinkled ridges beside the Powerline Trail. The **trans-Kauai hike** (to Powerline Trail North, TH12) is an all-day trek to be attempted by fit hikers on a sunny day. The middle third of the trail is overgrown, through a boggy forest that is still recovering from Hurricane Iniki in 1992. *Be Aware:* Bring plenty of water, food, rain gear, and hiking poles.

To the **Waialeale stream convergence**—where three streams join—and to **Waialeale basin**, a point 4,000 feet directly below the fabled peak, stay on the Waikoko Forest Management Road. On the 4WD road, you circle up and behind the forest gardens, drop down and cross a second spillway and walk (or drive) up a grade, under a canopy of subtropical trees. After the second spillway, you come to where power towers cross the road. From the power towers, the road undulates heading fairly straight for a mile, and then it makes a right, beginning a west-heading approach to the Waialeale basin. Continue for .5-mile. Then, for the **Waialeale stream convergence**, take a right-bearing fork. You'll see a sign announcing Hunting Unit C and telling people not to pick up lost dogs. This right fork follows a water ditch for a mile and ends under a tree canopy alongside the swift-flowing North Fork of the **Wailua River**, at a gauging station. If you carefully cross the river on rocks, you'll discover a point at which two major streams join the Wailua River, which is coming down from the Waialeale and headed for Wailua Bay.

For the **Waialeale (Blue Hole) basin**, take the left fork at the Unit C-dog sign. From this fork you are 2.5 miles from the basin. Continue up a grade through eucalyptus, avoiding spur roads and trails. After .5-mile from the fork, you pass a spur road on the left to a picnic area, and enter an open forest of monkeypods and African tulip trees. After the picnic road you'll pass a yellow metal gate, and then come to a gate, with tall concrete poles that frame a view of Waialeale (known as 'Jurassic Park Gate'). Beyond the gate, the relief becomes pronounced, and the scenery really darned pretty. Be careful of getting too close to overgrown viewpoints that disguise drop-offs. The rutted road ends at a gauging station, a rough-poured concrete dam, creating a face-on spot

to sit and enjoy the fast-flowing North Fork of the Wailua River. Across from the dam is a profusion of jungle greenery, leaves as big as elephant ears lost within great vine tangles—and a view of the concave face of **Mount Waialeale**, with a half-dozen gouges in its vertical face that become waterfalls.

More Stuff: Across the river at the dam, a sketchy trail leads through the jungle and along rocks to the **Blue Hole** at the foot of Waialeale. Plan on 8 hours, roundtrip from here. A swimming hole is a worthy halfway destination. Though marked by ribbons, the trail is difficult and should be attempted only by fit hikers traveling in pairs on nice days. Dense flora, slippery rocks, and flash floods are among the potential dangers. You need to drive all the way to the spillway to have a hope of reaching the Blue Hole.

Toward Waialeale Blue Hole

Powerline South Trail, Arboretum swimming hole

For roadside contemplation, try two stops at the 51-acre grounds of **Kaua'i's Hindu Monastery**: The tiny **Sacred Forest** is on the main road on left as you head mauka near mm5, at 7345 Kuamo'o Road. This spot will calm everyone down, whether they like it or not. The **monastery** itself is down the road about .5-mile; turn on Kaholalele Road, near mm4.5. The church, garden, and visitors center is at 107 Kaholalele. The groomed banyan on the path to the church is a world unto itself. *Note:* Visitors are asked to use one of the sarongs supplied at the teahouse to cover up shorts while on the monastery grounds. Normal hours are 9 to noon.

BIKE: The **Kuilau Ridge Trail** is used by some advanced riders, who don't mind trails that are steep, muddy and rutted. You also can begin this cycle at another access point: Moalepe Ridge Trail, TH32, above Kapa'a. The best intermediate-level mountain biking option for Keahua Arboretum—one of the best rides anywhere—is the **Waialeale basin** trail, as described in the hiking section. Although mud may fly, the elevation is reasonable over the 5 miles, and the roads are very rideable, cobblestones notwithstanding. The toughest climbing for this ride is during the first mile as you negotiate steep hills on either side of the spillways. From the spillways, the ride is gradually up. On a bike, you can afford to explore the spur roads—although make sure to keep your bearings. *More Stuff:* An adventurous option off this trail is to cut left where the power towers cross the road, as described in the beginning of the basin hikes. A network of roads lead to the **Wailua River** watershed, above the falls. Some of this area may be private property, however. You make the call.

Powerline mud, waterfalls on Mount Waialeale

Wailua

Wailua Falls

When the ancient Polynesians completed a 2,500-mile voyage from the South Pacific, thus making their mythical homelands a reality, their first steps were on the banks of the Wailua River. In the years to come, they built seven heiaus—temples—along the course of the river, the last near its source at Mount Waialeale. The heiaus line a sacred path from the bay to the birthplace of all waters.

For centuries, Wailua was the homeland of the aliʻi, or kings, and all royals in the Hawaiian Islands could trace their lineage to this river valley on Kauaʻi. Wailua in Hawaiian means, "waters of the spirits," a name reflecting the Hawaiians' reverence for their ancestors and kinship with nature.

Short walks from Wailua Bay and Lydgate Park lead to three heiaus, including one nearly intact. Intact heiaus are rare on Kauaʻi, since, when Christianity was embraced by the royals, the heiaus were sometimes used as livestock pens or rocks were removed for roadwork. Also at the mouth of the river are the remnants of a 'city of refuge,' a place where vanquished warriors or criminals could escape to do penance.

Wailua Bay is the best surfing spot along the coast between the river and Nawili-wili. But most people get on the water here in canoes and kayaks, heading up the widest, deepest, longest river in Hawaii. A simulated Hawaiian village and the Fern Grotto, both tourist attractions, may be seen from the river. Naturalists can observe native subtropical vegetation, such as hala and hau trees, along with the rare pili grass, used to make grass houses, that still grows on the banks.

Beginning at Lydgate and extending toward Hanamaulu Bay are several miles of secluded beaches. This coast runs along the Wailua Golf Course as well as behind a resort hotel. At Nukoliʻi (Kauaʻi) Beach, strollers will find interesting bits of coral and shells, and often will be able to see net fishermen casting from shore. Mountain bikers can find a trail most of the way—pushing the wheels as needed in one spot—completing a continuous run of coastal pedaling that goes from Hanamaulu Bay to Anahola Bay.

Hanamaulu is a locals' beach, where families gather on the weekends. Its sheltered cove makes for safe swimming as well as boogie boarding, and the bay's waters are safe for kayakers who can paddle out to Ahukini Landing at its mouth. An annual outrigger canoe race begins at Hanamaulu, heads into open water, and finishes by rounding Ninini Point and entering Nawiliwili Harbor.

The coast between Ahukini Landing and Ninini Point, despite being behind

Fern Grotto

Paddling by the Sleeping Giant on the Wailua River

the airport, is a scenic ride or hike, and Ninini, with its lighthouse, is an eye-popping spot to watch cruise ships enter the harbor under Hoary Head Ridge.

Nawiliwili Harbor, Kaua'i's largest port, displays both the muscle and romance of a tropical island. Walking around Nawiliwili, or riding a bike, can easily take up a day. Included in that day might be swimming or surfing at Kalapaki Bay, the beach below the Kaua'i Marriott Resort that features Duke's Canoe Club. Walks along two breakwaters and a small harbor for cruising sailboats add charm to the lively harbor. Cruise ships offload tons of tourists.

Almost unnoticed in the harbor, but one of its more remarkable features, is Huleia Stream. The stream's calm waters lead into the Huleia National Wildlife Refuge and past the Menehune Fish Pond. Some of the movie *Jurassic Park* was filmed here, and, although private property restrictions prohibit exploring the shore, much can be seen from the water.

The most-visited spot in the Wailua area is Wailua Falls, a few miles inland. A very steep (possibly closed) trail takes hikers to the base of the falls. In ancient times, warriors dove from these falls to prove their courage to prospective wives. In more recent times, the falls were depicted in television's *Fantasy Island*.

The entire Wailua area can be viewed from Kalepa Ridge, which runs just inland, parallel to the coast between Wailua Bay and Hanamaulu Bay—a vantage point of historical significance. From the sandalwood trees that grew on this ridge, Kauaian warriors kept watch for a dozen years, beginning in 1795, for the invasion of Kamehameha the Great—an attack that never came. Once, a fierce storm on the Kaua'i Channel thwarted Kamehameha's ships, and a second invasion fizzled when warriors were stricken by disease after they again had set sail for Kaua'i.

The sandalwood trees on Kalepa Ridge were clear-cut in the early 1880s and the fragrant wood became Hawai'i's first export. A hundred years later, from a bunker on the ridge, American soldiers kept watch during World War II for another invasion that never came. The ridge affords a mid-distance view of the coast and a panorama inland of the Kilohana Crater and Mount Waialeale.

Kaua'i Marriott Resort on Kalapaki Bay

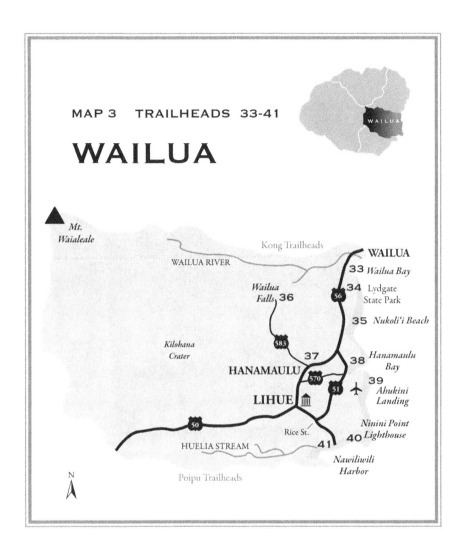

MAP 3   TRAILHEADS 33-41

WAILUA

WAILUA

Mt. Waialeale

Kong Trailheads

WAILUA RIVER

WAILUA

33 *Wailua Bay*

Wailua Falls 36

34 Lydgate State Park

56

35 *Nukoli'i Beach*

Kilohana Crater

583

37

38 *Hanamaulu Bay*

HANAMAULU

570

39 *Ahukini Landing*

51

LIHUE

Ninini Point Lighthouse

50

Rice St.

40

HUELIA STREAM

41

Nawiliwili Harbor

N

Poipu Trailheads

TRAILHEADS

33-41

HIKE	HIKING
SNORKEL	SNORKELING AND SWIMMING
BIKE	MOUNTAIN OR ROAD BIKING
PADDLE	KAYAKING, CANOEING
SURF	SURFING, BOOGIE BOARDING

TH	TRAILHEAD	*Note: All hiking*
Makai	TOWARD OCEAN	*distances are roundtrip*
Mauka	TOWARD THE MOUNTAIN, INLAND	*unless otherwise noted.*
mm	MILE MARKER, CORRESPONDS TO HIGHWAY SIGNS	

33. WAILUA BAY
HIKE, PADDLE, SURF

WHAT'S BEST: A vacation variety pack: Walk the shore or paddle up the river of kings, the most sacred place in the Hawaiian Islands. Or take excellent family strolls to Kaua'i's largest heiau and its most underrated botanical garden.

PARKING: The jct. of Hwys. 56 and 580 chops this trailhead up into four parts, although everything is located close together. Read hiking descriptions for places to park.

HIKE: **Wailua Beach (1.25 mi.); Malae Heiau (up to .5-mi.); Wailua Marina and Smiths Tropical Paradise (up to 1.5 mi.); Birthstone Heiau and Royal Coco Palm Grove (.5-mi.)**

In spite of its on-road location, **Wailua Beach** is a scenic stroll, especially when the river is running high after rains, colliding with choppy incoming surf. *Driving:* Access is easiest if you're heading from Lihue toward Kapa'a; cross the river in the right-hand lane and use the parking lot on your right immediately after crossing the river; if you miss this one, park at a second turnout at the far end of the bay. When the river is low, you can wade the sand bridge at the river mouth and connect with **Lydgate Park** (you can also get there via a pedestrian lane on the highway bridge). Beauty seekers will want to curl right and walk under the bridge and inland for a view up the wide river; this is where local canoe clubs put in. Or, heading left as you face the water, you can make your way around Alakukui Point and connect with the **Coconut Coast**.

The **Wailua Marina and Smiths Tropical Paradise** is where paddle wheel boats depart for **Fern Grotto**. *Driving:* Head across the bridge going toward Lihue and turn right immediately. The grotto is a large dripping cavern creating acoustics for the old-timey serenade provided by your guides. The river boat tours, operated by the Smith family for generations, are a kitschy classic and well worth the price of tickets. The marina docks, surrounded by several grassy acres, yield a superlative view across the wide Wailua toward the Sleeping Giant. The cultural and botanical gardens inside **Smiths Tropical Paradise** are also well worth the modest admission price. Footbridges span lagoons amid flowering tropicals and forests of native and fruit trees. Kaua'i's Japanese, Polynesian, and Filipino heritages are represented. Shrieking peacocks waft down from towering banyans. You'll likely give the place two thumbs, especially if kids are along. *More Stuff:* For easy-access river kayaking, try **Kayak Kaua'i**, located inside.

Though plant growth often hides **Malae Heiau**, it is the most intact of seven heiaus the ancients constructed, beginning at Wailua Bay and extending to Waialeale. *Driving:* Heading toward Lihue, cross the bridge, pass the entrance to Smith's, and look for a dirt turnout. You'll see a gate for a cane haul road. Head through that gate and look right for a grassy path that leads a short distance up to, and around, the 300- by 400-foot edifice. Its walls are about six feet high and more than twelve feet wide, vertical in the center and sloping down around the perimeter. *Notes:* The heiau is periodically cleared of brush, but it grows back quickly. Take care not to disturb the walls of this sacred place—officially a state historic site since 1928.

At the **Birthstone Heiau**, a stairway with pipe railing leads up from behind this historic site to a small Japanese cemetery and a tree-filtered view of the Wailua River. *Driving:* Go less than .5-mile up Hwy. 580 and park on the left at the **Wailua River State Park Poliahu Area**. Across the street from the Birthstone Heiau is small arboretum, a State Soil and Water Conservation Park. Next to the park is the **Royal Coconut Grove**. The royal grove lies behind the old **Coco Palms Resort**, closed due to Hurricane Iniki. Elvis stayed here when filming *Blue Hawaii*. (Plans to rebuild are *slowly* in the works.) The lagoon inside predates the hotel, built for enjoyment by Queen Emma. Entrance to the grove is prohibited, but you can get a good look at it by walking along the road.

PADDLE: Kayakers may access the **Wailua River** by turning on Hwy. 580, Kuamo'o Road, and making an immediate left, just past Smith's ticket area, into a Wailua State Park boat launching area. The Wailua Marina also has a boat launch area. This is Kaua'i's most popular river, and kayak rentals and tours are limited to prevent overcrowding. Even so, it can get cozy. **Kayak Wailua**, is an excellent choice for independent travelers who want the enrichment provided by competent guides. They are family owned and run small daily tours. As mentioned, **Kayak Kaua'i**, is located at the Smith's Marina. See *Resource Links* page 239 for these and other outfitters.

The Wailua is very wide, with several miles of slack waters. Two miles upriver is a confluence: The left fork is the South Fork of the Wailua River, which comes from Wailua Falls; the right fork is the North Fork of the Wailua River, which comes from Waialeale basin. The Wailua was the landing spot for the ancient Polynesian mariners, where the first Hawaiian settlements were established. **Fern Grotto**, part of Wailua

Lydgate Park, Fern Grotto tourboat, Malae Heiau

Uluwehi (Secret) Falls

River State Park, is a little more than 2 miles upriver, just up the left fork. The right fork leads past the privately owned **Kamokila**, a recreated Hawiian village where much of the movie *Outbreak* was filmed. Many tours go past the village and take out a little farther up, where the river narrows at rapids and shallow water. A trail leads from the left side of the river for about a mile to **Uluwehi (Secret) Falls**, a popular destination.

SURF: With its eastern exposure and river-mouth location, the surf at **Wailua Bay** varies more than most placcs. Surfers take advantage of an offshore break, from about the middle of the bay extending over to **Alakukui Point**. Body boarders try the shore break, though shallow water makes this hazardous to your health. The sails of kite-boarders will also be seen above the bay's waters. *Be Aware:* Swimming can be dangerous due to rip currents near the river and the other side of the bay.

34. LYDGATE PARK
HIKE, SNORKEL, BIKE, SURF

WHAT'S BEST: A short walk of historical significance or a longer beach walk. Kids will love a fantastical play area and the island's safest snorkeling. Lydgate is one of Hawaii's best family beach parks.

PARKING: *From Lihue:* Take Hwy. 56 toward Kapaʻa and turn makai at mm5, on Leho Dr. Follow Leho, turn right on Nalu Rd., and continue to large improved parking lot. *From Kapaʻa:* Take Hwy. 56 toward Lihue and turn makai after crossing the river, at left-turn lane for the Aloha Resort; this is also Leho Dr. as it loops back out to Hwy. 56. Then turn left on Nalu Rd. *For Lydgate Play Bridge:* Drive to the south end of Leho Dr.(Lihue end) and take Nehe Rd. a short distance to a parking area.

HIKE: Hikinaʻakala Heiau (.25-mi.); Lydgate Beach (up to 3 mi.)

At the **Hikinaʻakala Heiau**—located at the river mouth just above the beach and below the Garden Inn by Hilton—are interpretive signs, describing heiaus in general, and this heiau in particular. Not much remains, but this was the first of seven heiaus leading inland from the bay toward Waialeale. Adjacent to the heiau are the remains of the **Hauola City of Refuge**, a place for Kauaian miscreants to go during periods of banishment from proper society. *Be Aware:* Don't enter the interior of the heiau.

Lydgate Beach, a state park with showers and restrooms, is the first stretch of beach that starts at the mouth of the Wailua River and extends about four miles, almost to Hanamaulu Bay. Interpretive signs add interest to a walking path. Large **Kamalani Playground** and picnic area is just inland of the park's man-made snorkeling pools. Heading away from the river on the beach, you pass a midway picnic area, and then the **Play Bridge**. The developed area of the park is about .5-mile long, after which ironwoods encroach on a fairly narrow strip of yellow sand. A wide concrete bike path runs parallel to the coast, through a camping area. The park's surprise on this end is a five-level, mazelike Play Bridge that could accommodate several classrooms of scurrying little people. Continuing on the beach, you'll pass the Wailua Golf Course, beyond which are the sands of **Nukoliʻi Beach**, TH35—this is an appealing car-shuttle stroll.

SNORKEL: **Lydgate Park** features an oval, man-made swimming area, which breaks the surf near the river mouth. This large pool provides snorkeling free of concerns

Lydgate Park

about riptides. Fish at times may be outnumbered by snorkelers in the shallow water, which can sometimes be turbid due to wave action outside the enclosure. Lydgate is ideal for children. It's a sure thing for a swim and gets high overall marks.

BIKE: **Lydgate Park** is a pleasant segment of bikeable shoreline, connecting on one side with TH35, **Nukoli'i Beach**, and on the other with TH29, **Coconut Coast**. Heading toward Kapa'a and the Coconut Coast, ride up to the highway and take the new bridge bike lane, closest to the ocean. Biking the other direction, toward Lihue, roll along the concrete path, hugging the coast, until a dirt path ends past the Play Bridge. Eventually you spill out onto the sandy road along the beach. You can also push through sand or ride along the out-of-bounds perimeter of the golf course.

SURF: **Black Rock**, at the mouth of the Wailua River off of Lydgate Park, offers a fairly deep reef break. It's a long paddle, to a right-break. Best for intermediate-level surfers.

35. NUKOLI'I (KAUA'I) BEACH   HIKE, SNORKEL

> WHAT'S BEST: Comb the east side's longest beach, looking for coral and shells, and watching Hawaiian net fishermen. You get far away in an instant.
> PARKING: *First (easiest) Nukoli'i access:* From Lihue or the airport, head toward Kapa'a on Hwy. 56—from the jct. of Hwys. 56 and 51. Turn makai on Kauai Beach Dr., .25-mi. past mm3, toward the Kaua'i Beach Resort. Turn right just before resort lot, and follow the road .4-mi. around to developed lot, which is Nukoli'i Beach Park. *Second (undeveloped) Nukoli'i access:* Continue .5-mi past Kauai Beach Dr., nearly to mm4, and turn makai on a dirt (Nukoli'i Beach) road along the edge of the golf course. Follow the road, past a racetrack and around to parking area among ironwoods at beach.

HIKE: **Nukoli'i Beach (up to 4.5 mi.)**

Starting at the beach park, which is maintained by the resort, at the **first Nukoli'i access**, take off down the beach to your left as you face the water. Nukoli'i is also called **Kaua'i Beach** and Kawailoa. This beach sees few visitors, especially beyond the immediate grounds of the resort. At any time of the day you may see net fishermen, plying their ancient trade. About .5-mile from the beach park, you pass the resort, where you cross a ditch. A sandy road, closed to vehicles, parallels the beach. Nukoli'i extends more than two miles, joining the beach behind the golf course—where the second access area described above brings you in—and continues seamlessly to Lydgate Park.

SNORKEL: Wave action, shallow reef, and rip current team up to make Nukoli'i Beach an iffy choice for swimmers. One exception is **Kaua'i Keiki Beach**, a small reef-protected pool that is straight out and a little to the right of the beach park facilities; even so, the tide has to be right to make this work. Another possibility for adult dipping is the beach section that is up the beach, past the resort and just beyond the drainage ditch. Stay close to the shore during high surf.

Nukoli'i Beach

36. WAILUA FALLS

WHAT'S BEST: Viewing the falls, from above or below, a scene many will remember from TV's *Fantasy Island.*
PARKING: Turn mauka on Hwy 583 which is off Hwy. 56, between Hanamaulu and Lihue. *For top of falls viewing:* Take Hwy. 583, also called Ma'alo Rd., 4 mi. to the end at the falls parking area. *For bottom of falls hike:* After passing under a cane-haul bridge near mm3.6, look for a paved turnout on the right with a guardrail; park at a dirt turnout at the beginning of the guardrail. *Note:* Signs may indicate that this trail is closed.

HIKE: Wailua Falls (1.75 mi., 275 ft.)

Be Aware: This trail may be 'closed,' though hikers are a common sight. In any event, drive to the falls viewing area before beginning this hike. If the river level is high at the top of the falls (normally it is comprised of twin cascades), or if it is raining, do not take this hike. Also *do not* take a lethal trail that is to the right at the falls overlook.

For the **Wailua Falls trail,** walk the paved road to near the middle of the guardrail, where the trail is clearly visible, and begin a steep and often slippery descent. Roots and branches make for steps and handholds, but the trail is not dangerous. After reaching the bottom, head upriver a short distance through ferns and a shade canopy, courtesy of huge mango trees. The trail becomes sketchy, and reaches a ledge. Cross the river here; don't start up the ledge. On the other side, a hard-to-follow trail leads upriver to the vast pool beneath the falls. Follow your ears and watch your footing. *Be Aware:* Falling rock is a danger under the falls. Don't cross swift waters.

More Stuff: From the end of the parking area at the falls, you can hop across a grassy ditch to a road in former cane fields that leads to a river crossing, .5-mile away.

37. KALEPA RIDGE   HIKE

> **WHAT'S BEST:** Walk the path of Kauaian warriors, a sweeping mid-elevation vista of the Wailua coast, Kilohana Crater and interior mountains. A Kaua'i classic.
> **PARKING:** Take Hwy. 56 toward Lihue from its jct. with Hwy. 51. At .4-mi. past the jct., turn mauka on narrow Hulei Rd., behind the red-roofed senior center. Go .25-mi. and park at a chain-link fence, with a pedestrian opening to the right. *Note:* Property owners (Grove Farm) are not liable for your safety.

HIKE: Kalepa Ridge (3 mi. to 8 mi., 425 ft. to 1,600 ft.)

Kalepa Ridge, an underrated hike, is where Kauaian sentinels once kept a watchful eye seaward for Kamehameha's invading ships from Oahu—which twice were thwarted, first by a storm, and then by disease. Walk through the chain-link gate and up the concrete ramp. You'll gain 400 feet in elevation and pass a water tank. Continue to where the concrete ramp turns sharply left, and go right. Take the left-forking trail at this point—the right-forking trail crests the first Kalepa view knob, but is very steep on the downside. *Be Aware:* Tour helicopters fly over the first portion of the ridge. A few dirt motorcycles use these trails, particularly on weekends; give them right-of-way. Same goes for wild pigs. The route is muddy after rains, and hiking poles will help with footing.

The Kalepa Trail, like life, has its ups and downs. After the viewpoint at the beginning, the next major knob on this ridge is **Kokomo**, nearly 1,000 feet up from the trailhead. At its base is the junction of two trails, F1 and F2, both of which contour around; F2, inland to the left, is half as long as F1 and avoids 200 feet of elevation loss and gain. (You can also make a loop out of these two trails.) A gradual ascent follows after F1 and F2 join. You will then come to another fork, where F3 contours left, while another route heads up the next knob, **Nailiakauea**. Beyond Nailiakauea is another protuberance, called **Mauna Kapu**. Just below this feature, as you face inland, is the Wailua River and **Fern Grotto**. Mauna Kapu is about 2 miles from Kokomo. The ridge, comprising the Kalepa State Forest Reserve, is an ideal place to gain a perspective on the entire east side of Kauai. Flora is profuse. You'll encounter tree tunnels of ironwoods, Cook pines, and shrubs, including strawberry guava. Views are both seaward and inland, to the green expanse of agricultural lands that were once part of the Kilohana Crater.

38. HANAMAULU BAY   HIKE, PADDLE, SURF

> **WHAT'S BEST:** Picnic or swim at a locals' beach with a Hollywood history.
> **PARKING:** Turn makai off Hwy. 56 on Hanamaulu Rd., at a traffic light. Hanamaulu is .5-mi. toward Lihue from the jct. of Hwys. 56 and 51. On Hanamaulu Rd., go .2-mi. and veer right on Hehi Rd. Continue 1 mi. down to the beach park.

Kalepa Ridge

HIKE: Hanamaulu Beach Park (up to 1 mi.)

No hiking trails lead from **Hanamaulu Beach Park**, but short walks inland through boggy banana fields and around the park and beach of this cozy bay, will give you a look at the east-side's most Kauaian beach and community—on the weekends, expect a family party in one of the picnic pavilions.

Hanamaulu Bay is the only indent in a seven-mile coast running from Wailua Bay to Nawiliwili Harbor. Looking out to sea, on the right mouth of the bay, is Ahukini Landing, TH39. Hanamaulu Bay was the scene for several of the earlier movies shot in Kaua'i, including *Pagan Love Song*, in 1950, and John Wayne's 1963 classic, *Donovan's Reef*. Check out the ironwood grove at the stream's mouth.

PADDLE: **Hanamaulu Bay** is the launching spot for canoe races that go around Ninini Point and into Nawiliwili Harbor. Although novice kayakers might want to avoid that voyage, except on the calmest of days, Hanamaulu is perhaps the best place to safely venture into the saltwater, with intimate views of the bay, shrouded with coco palms and ironwoods. You can even get a few strokes inland on the stream, .25-mile or more, amid bananas and lush fields.

SURF: A gentle onshore break invites safe boogie boarding and body surfing, though the local boys don't often clamor to catch these combers.

39. AHUKINI LANDING   HIKE, SNORKEL, BIKE

WHAT'S BEST: Say a scenic aloha before leaving Kaua'i, or on any day, with a walk around a historic pineapple pier. Or try the surprisingly good snorkeling waters.
PARKING: Take Hwy. 570, which is Ahukini Rd., toward Lihue Airport and veer left, staying on Ahukini. Go 1.5 mi. to road's end.

Ninini Point Lighthouse

HIKE: Ahukini stroll (.5-mi.)

That **Ahukini Landing** can be so close to the airport is testament to Kaua'i's scenic beauty. Once a principal shipping dock for the flourishing pineapple trade, Ahukini today is a state-run fishing pier. The pier area is an interesting stroll, with a view of Hanamaulu Bay and a downward look at fish and the occasional manta ray or turtle in clear water. Ahukini's black rock breakwater is another walk option, as is the 'glass beach' to the right as you approach the parking area. The most common activity here is the "park 'n' stare," a tradition among Hawaiian drivers taking a break from the world. *Be Aware:* Observe waves before going onto the breakwater.

SNORKEL: With no beach and a dreary curbside appeal, **Ahukini Landing** will not impart love at first sight. But the water is deep and clear, sheltered by the breakwater, and fish are plentiful among scattered coral knobs. Entry is easy, over rocks. All in all, Ahukini gets high marks. *Be Aware:* Stay behind the breakwater to avoid wave action. Also, stay clear of the fishing pier and other areas closed to swimming.

BIKE: A fine dirt road fronts the shoreline from **Ahukini Landing** all the way to **Ninini Point**, TH40. The shoreline road is marked by a pipe gate, just before Ahukini Road makes its 90-degree turn on the way to the landing.

40. NININI POINT   HIKE, BIKE

What's Best: From the lighthouse is an exotic look at ships entering Nawiliwili Harbor. Sit a spell, and then take a long, level jog or bike ride along the coast and a resort lagoon.

Parking: Take Hwy. 51 from the Lihue Airport toward Nawilwili. At .6-mi. past Hwy. 570 (the airport road) turn left at beach access, which is Ninini Point Rd.; you'll see an entrance station for the Kaua'i Lagoons. Follow Ninini Point Rd., curving left and then right. *For Ninini Point:* At 1.75 mi. from highway—with the Kaua'i Lagoons Marina on the right—go left on what looks like a cart road. Pass hole #4 and continue along a fence for .4-mi. *For Running Waters:* Keep going straight at the Kaua'i Lagoons Marina for a short distance and park in designated spaces behind the (probably) closed center.

HIKE: **Ninini Point (less than .5-mi.); Running Waters Beach (1 mi., 150 ft.)**

Kukui Point in Nawilwili Harbor

Ninini Point is just down the dirt road from parking area. You'll see **Ninini Lighthouse**, which sits close to the sea at the mouth of Kalapaki Bay, also the entrance to **Nawiliwili Harbor**. Across the bay is Hoary Head Ridge, a backdrop for the white cruise ships that slide past the point. Try to time your visit when a cruise ship is departing, often around 5 p.m. Litter detracts from the scenic beauty. *Note:* You can also reach the lighthouse by continuing up from the Mariott. Follow signs for public access.

Rugged **Running Waters Beach** is pocketed between the Ninini and Kukui points. A concrete path begins below the former Whaler's Restaurant. The route descends on a shared portion of a golf path before reaching a steep, rutted trail to the sand. Black rock shelves add interest to a coastal exploration. *Be Aware:* Be wary of waves and currents. Running Waters is almost always dangerous for swimmers.

BIKE: To bike the **Ahukini coast**, take a grassy, two-track road to your left as you face the water, going behind the fenced installation. You'll roll along ironwoods and a low-set bank on a rugged coastline. In about .5-mile you reach **Kamilo Point**. Finally, at 2.5 miles, the road joins with Ahukini Road. *Note:* Another option for cyclists is to park at the entrance station and tour the area in a 10-mile loop. Start by riding out to Ninini Point and then down the coast to Ahukini Landing and back. Then pedal over to to the Kaua'i Marriott on the path that encircles the resort's huge lagoon.

41.   KALAPAKI-NAWILIWILI   HIKE, SNORKEL, BIKE, PADDLE, SURF

WHAT'S BEST: Get a look at the guts and the glitz of tropical Pacific seafaring life and enjoy Kalapaki Bay, which lured Kaua'i's first major resort. Or paddle up a river into a wildlife refuge. It's easy to spend the day poking around Nawiliwili Harbor.

PARKING: Take Hwy. 50 to Lihue, turn makai on Rice St. and continue about 2 mi. down. Or take Hwy. 51 toward the harbor from airport, turn left on Rice St. When almost down to the harbor, turn left toward the Kaua'i Marriott, on Ho'olaulea Way.

Nawiliwili Harbor

Pass the resort's main entrance and turn right on Kalapaki Circle. Then turn right toward beach access and continue down to a 150-space parking lot. *Alternate or overflow access:* Pass the resort entrance, continue on Rice-Hwy. 51, and park at beach access on the left just before crossing a small concrete bridge. *For Kukui Point and Running Waters Beach:* After turning on right Kalapaki Circle, pass the beach access noted above. Instead, keep left to Shoreline Public Access and parking for Chapel by the Sea.

HIKE: Kalapaki Beach walk and Nawiliwili Jetty (up to 2.25 mi.); Kukiʻi Point (.5-mi, 100 ft.); Nawiliwili Small Boat Harbor (1 mi.)

For Kalapaki Beach walk and Nawiliwili Jetty, skip out to the beach from the parking area and go right, either on sand or the paved path through the the resort's poolside gardenscape. You'll probably want to duck into the grounds of the **Kauaʻi Marriott**. Go up stairs to an elevated promenade with balconies over a glamorous pool. In the lobby, check out the *Princess*, the huge koa canoe, circa 1860, that belonged to the great Prince Jonah Kuhio. In the front of the resort is a **lagoon** with koi ponds, waterfalls, and colorful birds. Built in 1962, as the Kauaʻi Surf, this resort prompted a zoning law requiring that future island buildings be "no higher than a coco palm."

Continuing around the .25-mile curve of sand of **Kalapaki Beach**, you will pass **Duke's Canoe Club**, named for Olympic champion Duke Kahanamoku. Inside are lots of historic photos, and Duke's trusty surfboard, *Papa Nui*. Outside again, walk over a footbridge to **Nawiliwili Beach Park**, a canoeists' enclave and locals' hangout, behind the Anchor Cove shopping center. **Nawiliwili Jetty** extends seaward from the beach park, about .5-mile into the harbor. You can drive out the entire distance, but a path closer to the water gives you a look at surfers. In the boatyards across the road, you may see the *Hokulea* drydocked, for this is where the replica sailing vessel is sometimes outfitted. To your right from the end of the jetty is Huleia Stream and the small boat harbor. Hoary Head Ridge rises seaward.

Kuki'i Point is the mini-lighthouse across from Nawiliwili jetty light at the entrance to the harbor. The short walk delivers a large scenic payoff. From the parking by Chapel by the Sea, walk to the end of the road. Go right on a golf course path, which curves down, around and then below a green. Then follow a rocky trail to Kuki'i Point.

More Stuff: From the same parking lot, a path the skirts the new resorts and golf course .75-miles to **Running Waters Beach**. The last part of the walk is over a smooth-lava shelf favored by fishermen. Running Waters was more of a scenic getaway before the institution-like Kalanipu'u Resort was built in 2010. You can shorten the hike by driving to the defunct shopping center at the road; see TH 40 for the walk from there.

To **Nawiliwili Small Boat Harbor** is a gateway for sailboats to the open Pacific, and for kayakers to the wildlife refuge and Huleia Stream. *Driving:* It's about a mile from the Marriott. Pass Anchor Cove Center going away from Kalapaki. Turn left on Wilcox Road and pass Matson shipping and the anchorage for the massive cruise ships. Continue and then turn left on Halemalu Road toward the boat harbor, and **Niumalu Beach Park**. Several kayak outfitters, as well as sailing and fishing guides, are based in this low-key area. The sailboats will strike a romantic chord for anyone who has fantasized sailing the South Seas. For the full effect, walk the **jetty** that shields the harbor along the fresh waters of **Huleia Stream**—an underrated jaunt.

Running Waters Beach

SNORKEL: **Kalapaki Bay** is not known for fish-peeping, but relatively sheltered waters do provide a scenic and reliable place to don the mask and fins. Waters are fairly murky. People lap swim just offshore of the beach. Kalapaki is a roomy bay, but if you drift too far off shore you might run into trouble with surfers and boating lanes.

Running Waters is better for sight-seeing and relaxing than anything else. Large waves from varying directions wash the rocky shore, making this a turbulent area for swimming on most days. But, during calm periods, Running Waters is known as a good area for experienced snorkelers who don't mind the new imposing resort development.

PADDLE: Kayakers will enjoy stroking into well-protected **Kalapaki Bay**, but keep an eye out for surfers and boat traffic. For access to the **Huleia Stream**, go to the Nawiliwili Small Boat Harbor, as described above. Outfitters there rent kayaks and offer guided tours up the wide stream, which goes into the **Huleia Wildlife Refuge**. The refuge was a setting for the movies *Jurassic Park* and *Raiders of the Lost Ark*. It is not readily accessible on foot. As wide as any river except for the Wailua, the stream curves

Duke Kahanamoku

inland for about 2 miles. About 1 mile in, you pass the **Menehune Fish Pond,** a streamside reservoir constructed by Kaua'i's legendary settlers around 200 to 400 AD. A mile past the fish pond, waters ripple over a cascade, the end of navigable waters. No hiking is permitted inland, except with a licensed outfitter. *Be Aware:* Brace yourself for a headwind on the homeward paddle.

SURF: **Kalapaki Beach** is the site of Duke's Canoe Club, named for surfing legend Duke Kahanamoku. His hardwood longboard is displayed inside. Duke's beach has several good surfing spots, although often too tame for the local boys. The onshore break is suitable for bodyboards. Farther out, near Kuki'i Point, is an area called **Lighthouse**, a left-slide next to a rock wall suitable for good surfers only. Near the breakwater across from lighthouse is an area sometimes called **Hang Ten**, near the right side of the bay; Hang Ten also has rock hazards. Both these Kalapaki spots often suffer from low surf. On the other hand, good breaks for beginning and intermediate surfers may be found on any given day. **Kalapaki Bay** is also an excellent choice for stand-up paddlers.

KAUAI MARRIOTT
WEATHER STATION

IF THE COCONUT IS WET...	It's Raining
IF THE COCONUT IS SWAYING...	It's Windy
IF THE COCONUT IS HOT...	It's Sunny
IF THE COCONUT IS COOL...	It's Overcast
IF THE COCONUT IS BLUE...	It's Cold
IF THE COCONUT IS SHAKING...	Earthquake
IF THE COCONUT IS GONE...	Hurricane

Up to the Minute
Weather Report prepared as a Courtesy
by the Kauai Marriott   Aloha!

Jetty walk, Nawiliwili Small Boat Harbor, Marriott weather station, Kalapaki beach boys

Poipu

Along the Mahaulepu Heritage Trail

The last volcanic eruptions on Kaua'i took place 40,000 years ago from craters that are now obscured by cacti and brush, a long tee shot from the golf links and resort hotels of Poipu Beach. Kaua'i's first eruptions were 10 million years ago, under the sea.

More recently, but long ago in the 1300s, the Poipu shores at Mahaulepu were the scene of a great battle, when a powerful king from the Big Island, having conquered all the other islands, landed here with a flotilla of war canoes. The Kauaian king, Kukona, outfoxed the powerful enemy, coaxing the invading forces inland, where they were defeated. Rather than kill the captured king, Kukona is said to have taken him on a tour of the island. The next unified invasion of Kaua'i was not attempted for almost 500 years, by Kamehameha the Great, and his forces did not succeed either.

Beginning in Mahaulepu, which is on the ocean side of Hoary Head Ridge, and extending to Lawai Bay, the south coast is a varied coastline of reef-protected coves, wave-bashed bluffs, and sandy beaches. These features make Poipu ideal for hiking, cycling, and all water sports. Horseback riding is also popular here.

On the arid bluffs between Shipwreck Beach and Mahaulepu is the Heritage Trail, known for shorebirds, whale viewing, and historic sites—one of the best coastal walks in the Islands. The Grand Hyatt Poipu at Shipwreck Beach is rated among the world's top tropical resorts, a recommended walk-through.

The whole coast from Spouting Horn to Mahaulepu is well-suited for exploring on a mountain bike, some of it by zigzagging through resort areas and other parts by riding on four-wheel tracks and disused cane roads. One dirt road, just up from the Poipu-Spouting Horn junction, leads inland to parts of the island not reachable by any other means.

Windsurfers are drawn to the waters with the surfers off Shipwreck Beach. Ocean kayaking and canoeing are popular within the protected waters of Poipu Beach, but paddlers should get the advice of a local before stroking out to sea.

Poipu Beach is flanked by resorts and condominiums, basking in the south shore's desertlike climate. In the winter, Poipu will have sun when the rest of the island may not. The beach is a two-mile run of small sandy coves separated by short peninsulas, creating pools suited for snorkeling and swimming. Surfers come here year around to Brennecke's Beach, but the real surfing action along this coast is during the summer when Kona winds bring larger swells.

Koloa Landing, at Whalers Cove, today is often bypassed by tourists heading for Spouting Horn or Poipu. But in the 1800s Koloa Landing was the third busiest anchorage in Hawaii among whaling and trading ships, surpassed only by Honolulu and Lahaina on Maui. Although the shore is rocky, snorkeling is good at Whalers Cove, but not quite as good as a little farther up the coast at Prince Kuhio Park. Named in honor of Prince Jonah Kuhio Kalanianaole, delegate to the U.S. Congress in the early 1900s, today the place is just "PK's." An audience gathers at PK's to watch the surfers during the summer, and in the winter the little beach is packed with snorkelers.

The road ends at Lawai Bay, not far from Prince Kuhio Park. Two of Kaua'i's three National Tropical Botanical Gardens are located up the Lawai Valley—Allerton and McBryde gardens. The gardens, part of a botanical research center working to preserve and study tropical plants, were once the retreat of a Hawaiian queen. Many movie companies, including those shooting *Honeymoon in Vegas*, *Jurassic Park*, and *Donovan's Reef*, have selected the gardens for locations. Visitors wishing to see the gardens must take a tour, starting from the visitors center across from Spouting Horn.

Spouting Horn is where pressurized sea water erupts like a geyser through a lava tube, created from sea swells trapped below. A second, larger geyser was nearby, but it was dynamited in 1910 by plantation owners who wanted to keep salt spray from cane crops. A whale-watcher's trail connects Spouting Horn to the Allerton gate.

Agricultural lands and rural neighborhoods comprise the lands sloping up from Poipu toward Kahili Peak. The hikes to Kahili Ridge provide exhilarating views of the

Grand Hyatt lagoon, Poipu Beach

south shore, as well as a close-up of the ridge's complex flora and topography. Kahili rises above Koloa Gap—the passageway between Lihue and Poipu. The view from this jungled spine was once utilized by outlaws who could swoop down on horseback and surprise their victims.

An easier walk, and perhaps the best place on Kaua'i to view the south and west shores, is Kukuiolono Park on a hillock above Kalaheo. The park will interest history buffs and botanists, as well as provide a 260-degree blue-water vista.

Shipwreck Beach, Spouting Horn, Poipu Beach

MAP 4   TRAILHEADS 42-49

POIPU

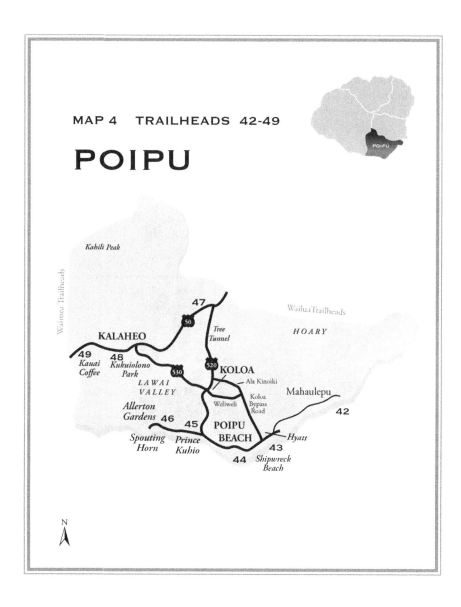

Kahili Peak

Waimea Trailheads

Wailua Trailheads

47

50

Tree
Tunnel

HOARY

KALAHEO

49   48
Kauai   Kukuiolono
Coffee   Park

530   520   KOLOA

Ala Kinoiki

LAWAI
VALLEY

Koloa   Mahaulepu
Bypass
Road

Weliweli

Allerton
Gardens   46   45

POIPU
BEACH

42

Spouting   Prince
Horn   Kuhio

Hyatt

43

44   Shipwreck
Beach

N

T R A I L H E A D S
42-49

HIKE	HIKING
SNORKEL	SNORKELING AND SWIMMING
BIKE	MOUNTAIN OR ROAD BIKING
PADDLE	KAYAKING, CANOEING
SURF	SURFING, BOOGIE BOARDING

TH	TRAILHEAD	*Note: All hiking*
Makai	TOWARD OCEAN	*distances are roundtrip*
Mauka	TOWARD THE MOUNTAIN, INLAND	*unless otherwise noted.*
mm	MILE MARKER, CORRESPONDS TO HIGHWAY SIGNS	

42. MAHAULEPU   HIKE, SNORKEL, BIKE, PADDLE

WHAT'S BEST: This wild-and-scenic coast is close to the resorts of Poipu Beach, but potholes on a dirt road can make it seem far away. Take a swim where the monk seals sun themselves, or walk along wild coast. Hawaii's largest limestone cave is a must-see.

PARKING: Take Hwy. 50 from Lihue and turn makai on Hwy. 520, which is Manuhia Rd., the Poipu tree tunnel. Go 3 mi. and turn left, before Koloa, on Ala Kinoiki. Continue about 3 mi. to a stop sign at Poipu Rd. Turn left. Conintue past the the Grand Hyatt Poipu as then road becomes unpaved. *For Makauwahi Cave Reserve*, turn right at sign for CJM Stables after about 1 mi., then turn left before the stables after .25-mi. and continue for .1-mile to parking on a dirt road. (You can also drive to the reserve; follow directions below, but turn right at a shack befor Gillin's parking.) *For Mahaulepu and Gillin's beaches*, continue past the stables road. Turn right, about 1.5 mi. from Hyatt. At 2 miles, enter gate for Kawailoa Bay; open normally from 7 to 6. Continue .4-mi to Gillin's Beach (Gillin's) parking. Turn left, continue .25-mi Mahaulepu Beach at Kawailoa Bay. *Be Aware:* Beyond the Hyatt, the road is normally unpaved and potholed.

HIKE: Makauwahi Cave Reserve (up to 1.25 mi., 100 ft.); Haula Beach (2 mi., 150 ft.); Mahaulepu Beach (1 mi.)

The **Makauwahi Cave Reserve**—Hawaii' largest limestone cave and fossil depost—has quietly become one of the state's top natural attractions. From the parking, take a dirt road to the left (the right-fork goes down the bluff to Gillin's Beach, but the cave trail also reaches the beach). The beginning reveals excellent sea views. The trail forks at post #6, but the quickest, scenic way is to stay right. You'll reach an overlook of the sinkhole, a 150-foot oval more than 30 feet deep, with an oasis on its floor that includes the native loulu palms. Circle down and pass a footbridge. On your left at post #15 is the 3-foot crawl hole entry that opens up to the sinkhole floor. The largest cave, and an interpretive table, is a the far end. After leaving the cave, don't forget to turn

left to walk the limestone walls along the stream. Then double back to the footbridge and cross to see the native-species plantings (several thousand have be re-introcuced) and also a Hawaiian 'canoe garden,' comprised of the species needed for survival brought by the voyaging Polynesians. Don't miss the large enclosures for tortoises, **Lida's Field of Dreams**; steps go over fencing. These guys (Squirt, Maurice, Pacer, et. al.) have it made in the shade. From the gardens, you can pop right out to the beach, at the far end of Gillin's. *Notes:* Cave hours are M-F, 10 to 2, weekends 10 to 4. Tours available. Please donate.

Haula Bech, Makauwahi Cave Reserve

The bright seascape from Kawailoa Bay to **Haula Beach** may inspire you to paint with watercolors. Start to your left as you face the bay—an inland road also goes in that direction. The coastal trail curls through the ironwoods along low tawny bluffs. It then drops into a cove, with a rugged little beach. Continue along the shoreline. After this first cove, you can pass unobstructed at the shoreline—a dicey little move around a post over a 15-foot drop; or cut up and inland through low ironwoods to the sandy horse trail; you'll find a gate in the fence about 50 feet down from the corner. From the fence, stroll up the slope and curve around to the right, reaching a view of the Haula Beach from an ironwood forest. Traverse inland and pick your way down *steeply* to the beach (a sand trail loops around, and takes much longer). Haula Beach is surrounded by the **Haupu State Forest Reserve**. It is a generous curve of sand, in the shadow of steep-rising Kawelikoa Point. *More Stuff:* A rugged hunter's trail leads from the upslope of the beach and switchbacks roughly up to a view spot of Kipu Kai Beach. *Be Aware:* Heed private property signs. Landowners are not liable for your saftey. A sign beyond the fence prohibits tresspassing after 6 p.m.

Mahaulepu Coast

Going the other way from Kawailoa Bay, toward **Mahaulepu Beach**, is easy going around a sandy point and then a long straightaway, bordered by the ironwoods, where you will find other trails. Monk seals commonly sun themselves at this beach—stay back from this endangered species. The far end of Mahaulepu Beach is known **Gillin's Beach**, the name of the guest cottage at the backshore. Scamper up the bluff and you'll be on the **Mahaulepu Heritage Trail** headed for Shipwreck Beach.

SNORKEL: Small **Kawailoa Bay** is enticing for snorkelers and swimming can be good, though choppy at times. Watch for sleeper waves along the shoreline. For the most sea life, swim out and left toward the low reef. Above this reef—walk to the left at the bayshore—is an excellent **keiki (kids) beach**. Locals jump from the nearby bluff.

Mahaulepu Beach, is also fairly good, best accessed from the first beach parking area. Look for cars; a short trail to the beach is hidden in a hedge of ironwoods. The best swimming is to your left, a couple hundred yards down the beach. A rock barrier, about 30 yards out and running along the shore, creates a huge oval pool for beginners and younger children. Safer spots are nearest the sandy point. For some tide pool soaking action, or nonaction, head to the beach's headland, at **Gillin's Beach**. *Be Aware:* High surf at Mahaulepu indicates dangerous current conditions.

43. SHIPWRECK BEACH-GRAND HYATT HIKE, SURF

WHAT'S BEST: The Grand Hyatt Poipu is a fitting start for a majestic nature-history walk along bluffs above the deep blue Pacific.
PARKING: Take Hwy. 50 from Lihue and turn makai on Hwy. 520, the tree tunnel road. Before Koloa, turn left on Ala Kinoiki, a bypass road. Continue several miles. At stop sign, turn left on Poipu Rd., and, just past the Grand Hyatt Kaua'i, turn makai on Ainako St., a beach access after the Hyatt. (You can also use Hyatt's large lot.)

HIKE: Grand-Hyatt and Mahaulepu Heritage Trail (4.25 mi., 275 ft.)

The **Grand Hyatt Kaua'i** is one of the world's top beach resorts. Go right at the beach parking lot and weave your way around the saltwater lagoon, up beside the pool with its waterfalls and slides, and through the resort's gardens. Inside, Asian-inspired architecture manages to be both grand and intimate. Decor includes museum quality artwork. *More Stuff:* A paved path extends from the Hyatt through the greenbelt of Poipu Kai condos, reaching **Poipu Beach Park** at Panc Road, which is off Ho'one. It starts from the side of the resort opposite beach access parking.

For the superlative **Mahaulepu Heritage Trail**, start toward your left as you face Shipwreck Beach in front of the Hyatt and walk down the beach toward **Makawehi Bluff**. The landmark bluff greets the pounding surf at that end of Keoneloa Bay—which is the proper name for the Shipwreck. (The most recent wreck of 1970 was taken away

Shipwreck Beach

by Hurricane Iniki.) Several footpaths lead to the top, where intrepid divers sometimes wow beachgoers. Shorebirds nest in rock pockets. Make your way down the coast, at first through a network of sandy paths and hardened dunes, woven amid dwarf ironwoods. The trail drops to sea level, jogs inland, and ascends along a tall wall that borders a golf course. At the top, you'll find the large, lava-rock platform and other remains of **Ho'ouluia Heiau**, a large fishing shrine. The path continues along the ledge of the golf course—watch for drop-offs, but also keep a seaward eye peeled for whales and spinner dolphins. Just before dropping into Mahaulepu Beach, the route snakes across Kamala Point. Near the water is the **Makauwahi Cave Reserve**, Hawaii's largest limestone cave; see page 115. The trail then drops to Gillin's Beach.

More Stuff: **Pu'u Wanawana Crater**, hiding in plain view, is the site of Kaua'i's most-recent eruption—recent in geological terms. *Driving:* Head mauka on Ala Kinoiki Road, up just .1-mile from the stop sign at Poipu Road. Park at a dirt turnout, walk around a yellow gate, and stay left on a two-track road that rises up to a road that goes around the crater. Go to your right about 75 feet and look for a trail leading into a thicket of upright shrubs with cacti tentacles carpeting the ground. The path twists a hundred yards and reaches a vantage point at the Stonehenge-like volcanic teeth that mark the perimeter of the crater. *Be Aware:* Access may overgrown and may be through private propery. *More Stuff:* For an 1.5 mile exercise walk, try the paved path to **Makahuena Point**. Head to your right as you face the water at the Hyatt's beachside path. The path skirts the green margins of neighborhood condos and a newer gigantic timeshare resort. *More Stuff:* History buffs can take a short walk down the dirt road from the top of the beach access lot to find state certified **archeological sites**. Centuries old rock walls are mostly covered by greenery.

SURF: **Shipwreck Beach** is a popular spot for bodysurfing and body boards, as well as short board surfers. Its popularity and location in front of a major resort hide the dangers of the waters here. Shipwreck is known for a shore break with rock hazards, swells in the winter and high surf in the summer. Make observations before entering the water, and avoid on rougher days. The coast off Shipwreck Beach is also popular among windsurfers, but only experts should venture into these seas.

44. POIPU BEACH   HIKE, SNORKEL, PADDLE, SURF

WHAT'S BEST: Surfers, strollers, snorkelers, and people-watchers all can end their quest somewhere along sunny Poipu Beach. The arid surroundings and condos are a disappointment to some, but not to those seeking blue sky when it's raining elsewhere on the island.
PARKING: Take Hwy. 50 from Lihue and turn makai on Hwy. 520, which is Manuhia Rd., the tree tunnel road. At Koloa, turn right at stop sign and then turn left at the gas station on Poipu Rd. Continue to the roundabout and go left on Poipu Rd.
First (Sheraton) parking: Turn makai on Kapili Rd toward the Sheraton, about .5-mi. after veering left. Kapili Rd. ends at Ho'onani Rd., where you turn left and park immediately on right at public access lot. This is the quieter end, farthest from the beach park.

Second (midway) limited parking: Continue on Ho'onani Rd. for about .25-mi. and park near the Kiahuna Plantation Resort. Puts you in the middle of the Poipu Beaches. *Third (Poipu Beach Park) parking:* Continue on Poipu Rd. past Kapili Rd., about .75-mi. and turn makai on Ho'owili Rd. to Poipu County Beach Park.

HIKE: Poipu Beach stroll (2.5 mi.); Moir Gardens (.25-mi.)

Poipu Beach is about a mile long, consisting of four small sandy coves separated by natural black-rock breakwaters extending not far seaward. This is not a nature walk, as beach chairs, boogie boarders, and sunbathers abound. Starting at the first parking, take a groomed path through a pleasant palm grove, around the back of the Sheraton, coming upon its sloping sandy beach. Continue, either along the beach on a path that runs parallel to where two luau show take place weekly. Lava's restaurant serves up beachside libation. Leaving the Sheraton, with its double-scoop beach, walk the greenspace of **Kilohana Plantation Resort**, a premier location for Poipu lovers.

After passing the rocky area (a former heiau site), you come to the newly refurbished, low-key luxury of the Ko'a Kea Hotel & Resort at **Waiohai Beach**. This beach soon blends into **Poipu Beach Park**. The park has a sandy peninsula, with a rocky tip, that creates a beach area to either side of the spit. Monk seals like it. The park extends inland from the beach to Poipu Road. Continuing along the park, the next, rougher beach you come to is Brennecke's, across from the restaurant of the same name. *More Stuff:* A paved path leads from Pane Street at the end of the park through resort homes to the Grand Hyatt, about 1.5 miles distant. *More Stuff:* Head up from Brennecke's on Ho'owili Street to the corner of Poipu Road to see the restoration of the ancient

Monk seal behind barrier, Poipu Beach

Poipu Beach

village site of **Kahua o Kaneiolouma**. You'll see a lava wall at the corner, framing carved statues (called kiʻi), with a pond, and ruins in the background. Only recently uncovered, Kaneiolouma is one of the most signifcant sites on the islands.

Moir Gardens, a.k.a Pau a Laka, include native plants, succulents, and a display of cacti rated among the ten best in the world. *Driving:* Go to the Outrigger Kiahuna Plantation, which is across Hoʻonani Road from the second beach access parking. Look for a Plantation Gardens sign. Begun in the 1930s, the gardens surround a lagoon and the plantation restaurant, near which is also a fabulous orchid garden.

SNORKEL: Poipu Beach commonly offers some of the safest and sunniest swimming on Kauaʻi, especially during the winter. At **Sheraton Beach** and **Waiohai Beach**, a reef offshore breaks up the swell and waves, creating a large and fairly deep swimming area. Little shore-breakers might test your balance. Fish are not copious.

At **Poipu Beach Park,** towels may carpet the sand on weekends, but the place is spacious. There are pavilions on the lawn at the backshore, but don't overlook the shaded tables to the far left as you face the water. The park inland across the street is the site of art fairs and events. Families and waders like the baby beaches to either side of the sand spit, but snorkelers can power out farther, beginning from the right side of the spit. *Be Aware:* Farther out, surfers, sailors, and reef action pose hazards. Another snorkeling spot, often overlooked because it's in the seam between the roads that fork to Poipu and to Spouting Horn, is **Whalers Cove**. *Driving:* Take Hoʻonani Road away from the Sheraton about .5-mile. Look for a turnout on the left. Whalers Cove has good snorkeling with clear water and plenty of fish, but getting past boulders at water's edge requires some balance. The cove looks better from the water than the shore.

PADDLE: **Whalers Cove**, going away from the Sheraton on Ho'onani Road, has a canoe landing. Go past the turnout described in the snorkeling section and look for a sharp left as the road heads away from the cove up Waikomo Stream. This is access for ocean exploration, recommended for calmer days.

SURF: With occasional trade swells in the winter and Kona wind in the summer, Poipu is year-around surf city. During the summer, beginners surf **Poipu Beach Park**, off the spit in front of the pavilion. The beach features both right and left breaks. In the cove next door, rougher **Brennecke's** also breaks both ways. During the summer, try the reef off **Waiohai Beach**, to the right of the sand peninsula. This is for average surfers, but a shallow reef covered with sea urchins creates a hazard. **Horseshoe** is in front of the Sheraton. This is mostly a summer beach, with a long paddle from shore. Horseshoe (a.k.a. Cow's Head and First Break) is recommended for top surfers.

45. PRINCE KUHIO PARK   HIKE, SNORKEL, PADDLE, SURF

WHAT'S BEST: This coast may lack curbside appeal, but it has some of the island's best snorkeling and summer surfing. You'll also find beaches tucked away.
PARKING: Take Hwy. 50 from Lihue and turn makai on Hwy. 520 toward Poipu. At Koloa, turn right at stop sign, then left immediately on Poipu Rd. At bottom of grade, veer right from the roundabout toward Spouting Horn, on Lawai Rd. Go 1 mi. on Lawai Rd. and park off road at Prince Kuhio Park—near Beach House Restaurant.

HIKE: Koloa Landing (1.25 mi.)

The coast along **Prince Kuhio Park** is generally rocky, developed, and close to well-known Poipu Beach. For these reasons, this good snorkeling and surfing area may be overlooked. For the off-beat neighborhood stroll to **Koloa Landing**, walk to your left as you face the water to small Prince Kuhio Park, which features a monument to Kaua'i's longtime congressional representative. You'll find grassy terraces, picnic areas, and a pond. From the park, cross Lawai Road and veer off to the water side on Ho'ona Road.

Look for a beach access pole near 5152 Ho'ona Road. Head out onto the shore, known as **Waterhouse Beach**, and make your way along the sand and then around black-rock tide pools, accented by dry areas filled with bits of white coral. Around the point is Whalers Cove Resort. Continue along the shore toward the **Waikomo Stream** inlet. You will see a wooden stairway, which is the public access to **Koloa Landing**. Go up the stairs, through the resort parking lot, and back out to Ho'ona Road.

More Stuff: **Kukuiula Bay**, a sportfishing harbor, is another good spot for a scenic break. *Driving:* Continue on Lawai Road for a mile and veer left on Amio Road. The breakwater can be walked for a whale's eye view of the bay. Also nearby are the **Shops at Kukuiula Village**, some 45 restaurants and specialty shops that feels like an old-timey two-level plantation-style sugar town. *Driving:* From the roundabout, take Ala Kalanikaumaka Road. Mature tropical trees and flowering gardens with water features make the shops a pleasant stroll, especially on Wednesdays at 3:30 when the village is jumping with the **Kukuiula Culinary Market**—organic produce, music, and artisan foods.

SNORKEL: **Longhouse Beach** is on the other side of the Beach House Restaurant from Prince Kuhio Park. Despite its unappealing roadside setting, Longhouse—also called Beach House, Keiki Cove, or PK's—offers excellent snorkeling, with enough sand, easy entrance and a nice population of fish swimming close to shore in deep, clear water. You might see a turtle swimming through coral heads. The shore of **Kukuiula Bay** features a sandy-entry, underrated swimming spot—with few people.

Waterhouse Beach, described in hiking section, has an excellent **baby beach**, a protected, shallow spot for dunking and wading—the best beach on this coast to log some relaxing beach-towel time. This may become your favorite Poipu-area beach. Snorkelers will have better luck at **Whalers Cove** at Koloa landing, which is also noted in the snorkeling section of TH44, Poipu Beach. Stream runoff muddies the water, but the cove can be a very good snorkeling venue.

Kukuiula Bay

SURF: The offshore break at **Longhouse Beach** draws good surfers, mostly during the summer. Longhouse breaks in four places, which locals call—starting from left to right as you face the water— **PK's** (for Prince Kuhio), **Centers**, **Acid Drop**, and **Heroins**. Sometimes PK's is just called Longhouse. Just don't call it late for surfin'. From April through October, people line the shore at the Beach House Restaurant to watch the show. PK's and Centers draw good surfers—none of these beaches are for beginners. The kahunas test their skills at Acid Drop and Heroins. All Longhouse breaks are well offshore, two-way breaks—and vary greatly due to wind conditions.

PADDLE: Outrigger races from Nawiliwili Harbor end at **Kukuiula Bay**, located a mile away from Kuhio Park. Another popular paddle from Kukuiula Bay is toward Spouting Horn and Lawai Bay, which is not accessible to the public via land, except for garden tours. The bay is sheltered, although you need to be mindful of boat traffic.

46. ALLERTON GARDEN-SPOUTING HORN   HIKE, SNORKEL

> WHAT'S BEST: Two of the nation's five National Tropical Botanical Gardens are right here. Across the street is Kaua'i's sea geyser, a long-standing roadside attraction.
> PARKING: Take Hwy. 50 from Lihue and turn makai on Hwy. 520 toward Poipu. Turn right at stop sign in Koloa, and then left on Poipu Rd. At bottom of grade, veer right on the roundabout toward Spouting Horn on Lawai Rd. Go about 2 mi. on Lawai Rd., turn makai and park at Allerton Garden visitors lot or the lot at Spouting Horn.

HIKE: Garden Visitors Center and Spouting Horn (1 mi.); Spouting Horn to Kaiwa Point (1 mi.); Allerton Garden (.75 mi.); McBryde Garden (up to 1.5 mi.)

Spouting Horn is Kaua'i's saltwater version of Old Faithful. Here, plumes of sea-foam erupt through an opening in a reef, powered by pressure of waves trapped below. You should watch from a safe distance behind a fence, just off a parking lot that is fringed by low-priced trinket booths. The easy-going path from **Spouting Horn to Kaiwa Point** follows the road from the parking lot to the upper gate at Allerton Garden, along one of the island's best whale watching spots. The view was enchanced in 2011, when invasive trees were cleared and replaced with natives species, Polynesian imports, and exotics.

The garden's **South Shore Visitors Center** was originally built using a grant from Bill and Jean Lane, former publishers of Sunset Magazine. It's a restored 1920s sugar plantation home, set here on the coast after Hurricane Iniki destroyed the other center farther inland in 1992. A path leads through the grounds, featuring a number of native plants, tropical fruits, and interpretive areas—a beautiful, free, and informative introduction to the island's greenery. A gift store offers books and artwork, and a 'grab-and-go' Garden Cafe that will cure the munchies with muffins, wraps, and salads. Various tour combinations are available. **All garden walks** are ticketed tours, leaving on buses from the center. Advance reservations are recommended; an admission

is charged. Admission fees go *directly* to pay for maintentance, research, and plant propagation.

The folks literally save species from extinction every day. The National Tropical Botanical Garden is a nonprofit, privately funded organization, under Congressional charter. Three of the five sites are on Kaua'i.

The **Allerton Garden** was once a retreat for Queen Emma and is known for its landscape design, fountains, statuary and flowering plants. The gardens were the brainchild of Robert Allerton, who in 1937 at age 64 bought the property and labored for many years with his lifetime companion, John Gregg Allerton. With a private beach and lush stream valley, Allerton Garden has been the set for a number of movies, including

Biodiversity trail, McBryde Garden, Allerton Garden

Honeymoon in Vegas, Thorn Birds, Jurassic Park, and TV's *Fantasy Island.* Separate botanical 'rooms' are decorated with fountains and statues. *Be Aware:* The Allerton tour does not include the beach and estate. To see these attractions, ask about the **Sunset Tour**, usually held daily. This more-expensive-but-worth-it tour also includes libation.

You're left to wander and marvel at your own pace through the 200 acres of **McBryde Garden**, a dreamland of native plants and trees, as well as spices and exotics. A free map and good signage make the garden easy to navigate. **Lawai Stream** runs down the center, punctuated by cascades, pools, huge trees, and a forest of palms. The misted tunnel of the **Biodiversity Trail** is way cool; this trail tells the story of plants on earth beginning 4.5 million years ago. The **Spice of Life** trail displays the plants we use to add zest to our daily lives. Rock-and-dirt steps weave through what seems like a jungle of fronds and flowers, until you look closer to note the cultivation that has taken place.

On the upslope of McBryde is the **Canoe Garden**, planted with the 30 or so different species the Polynesians brought with them on their 2,500-mile sailing voyage about 1,500 years ago. Providing spaces to take a break here are an authentic canoe hale (*hah-lay*), a wedding pavilion (you can book it), and (try this one) streamside benches shaded by sail-like awnings. This whole place would be thrashed by wild pigs were it not for the perimeter fencing. Independent travelers, plant peepers, and solitude-seekers will appreciate the McBryde. It's on the short list of best botanical gardens in the state—and Hawaii has many good ones.

SNORKEL: The rocky shore near **Kaiwa Point**, with no stream intrusion, is excellent for snorkeling, but *only* when surf is flat. You have to scramble down a steep bank, and entry is not the easiest. *Driving:* Park past Spouting Horn before the garden gate.

47.   KAHILI RIDGE   HIKE

> **WHAT'S WORST:** Landowners have closed the trails; hopefully one day they will reopen.
> **PARKING:** Take Hwy. 50 from Lihue. Turn mauka .5-mi past Hwy. 520, which is the turnoff to Poipu. Look for Kahili Mountain Park sign, .25-mi. past mm7. Go .75-mi. left toward the school. Continue up the grass field, between cabins and the school. Keep right past cabin number 30, and park off road when you see a water tank on your right.

Note: Access to the property and trails is now closed. Heed signs. The trails are described here in the event that landowners will one day make the ridge open to the public.

HIKE: Kahili Pine Grove (.75-mi., 200 ft.); Kahili Ridge (2.75 mi., 1,700 ft.)

For the stroll to **Kahili Pine Grove**, walk .1-mile down the road from parking, making sure to look inland to view your destination, a stand of several hundred Norfolk and Cook pines. Across from a Dead End sign, is the trailhead, which is signed. About 50

Kahili Ridge

feet in on the walk, keep right, just after the trail makes its first small step up. The trail loops around to the right, through fern hedges and then through a stand of ironwoods before leading into the grove. These are mostly Norfolk pines; their cousin, the Cook pine, has bushy branches.

The **Kahili Ridge Trail** is a challenging, hairy climb up a narrow feeder ridge that abuts Kahili Ridge. Begin at a road behind the water tower. After only .1-mile, you veer left off the road, following a a tunnel of a trail through pink-flowering shrubbery. Less than .5-mile in, and 200 feet up, you pop out to views of the 197-acre park, with Hoary Head Ridge and the Poipu shores as a backdrop. The ridge trail gets steeper, never making switchbacks, before reaching another plateau. You get a seaward view here, but now the mauka view draws attention, with four or five **waterfalls** often streaking down **Kahili Ridge**. By this juncture the trail has narrowed to a foot or two wide, falling very steeply on both sides. But any acrophobia is assuaged in most places by the thick foliage, through which you couldn't roll a bowling ball. Still, exercise caution, for what appears as an embankment to the trail may be just tufts of flora.

The trail continues flat along this ridge for just a short distance, before launching skyward again, through trees whose roots provide steps to go with branch handholds. This rise gives way to another plateau, now that much closer to the face of Kahili. You make another significant upping, your final, before reaching the windswept heights. The trail ends at a radio antenna, down the ridge from **Kahili Peak**, which is not readily accessed. *Be Aware:* Narrow sections of the trail skirt drop-offs that are dangerous, especially with wind to throw off your balance and after rains create a slick surface. Hiking poles will help greatly, especially on the descent.

48. KUKUIOLONO PARK HIKE, BIKE

WHAT'S BEST: A short walk with long views, a scent of flowers and a sense of history. This park is a peaceful retreat for road-weary visitors.
PARKING: Take Hwy. 50 to Kalaheo, which is about 5 mi. past Hwy. 520, the turnoff to Poipu. In Kalaheo, at mm11.2, turn makai at the traffic signal, on Papalina Rd. Continue, passing first Pu'u Rd., for 1 mi. Turn right on the second Pu'u Rd., and right again immediately, at the stone archway that is entrance to the park.

HIKE: Kukuiolono Park and Pavilion (.75-mi, 100 ft.)

Kukuiolono Park is a golf course and wild-chicken habitat with grounds that feature an exotic Japanese garden and a Hawaiiana exhibit of rocks with archeological significance. The gardens and artifacts are located in trees just up the hill from the parking area. Bamboo, ti, palms, and sprays of ginger surround the big rocks, whose stories are told on plaques. From the gardens a paved golf path leads seaward past a decrepit fountain from the old McBryde estate and exotic fruit trees to the picnic pavilion. Resting high above the gentle slopes of the Lawai Valley with big blue water vistas, the pavilion is a five-star picnic stop. Coco palms, ironwoods, plumeria, and Norfolk pines buffer the scene. Walter McBryde, 19th century sugar magnate, is buried in the park.

BIKE: Pu'u Road is a five-mile, clockwise loop on a one-lane country road that encircles Kukuiolono Park. Stay on Pu'u Road until Papalina Street, where you turn right. For another rural-residential ride, go down **Papalina Road**, just outside the park gate, for a mile to the administrative offices of the National Tropical Botanical Gardens. You can view upper McBryde garden from the back patio.

49. KAUAI COFFEE COMPANY HIKE

WHAT'S BEST: The perfect place for pick-me-up on the way to or from Waimea—bottomless samples. Tour the huge orchard on foot or in an open-air safari truck.
PARKING: Take Hwy. 50 past Poipu turnoff, through Kalaheo, and veer left on Hwy. 540 at its junction with Hwy. 50. Continue a few miles Kauai Company, on your left. Hwy. 540 rejoins Hwy. 50 at Ele'ele-Port Allen.

HIKE: Kaua'i Coffee coffee tour (up to .5-mi.)

Sugar plantation tours used to be a must-do, but since the last one on Kaua'i closed for keeps in 2009, the 3,100-acre **Kaua'i Coffee Company** is the only place to see Hawaiian-style agriculture in action—and to cop a free caffeine buzz while you're at it. Though an Italian company (Massimo Zanetti) now owns the company, you'll still get a family vibe at the visitors center, owning its history as the McBryde Sugar Company, and then Alexander & Baldwin, operating from the 1800s. Coffee was first planted in 1987. This place will be a repeat stop for many visitors.

An arty gift shop in the cottage is a sure thing to find island souvenirs, or to have your favorite roast shipped home. A large **outdoor tasting deck**, shaded by lattice, offers a bottomless cup of a dozen or more varieties of freshly brewed bean juice, while a television looped-video details coffee production from the field to the mug. Specialty coffee drinks, as well as baked goods and sandwiches, are available at the counter. Kaua'i now outproduces Kona. *Note:* Hours are daily, 9 to 5 (5:30 in the summer).

Sufficiently energized by Kaua'i java, vistors are free to roam a short distance from the tasting deck for a **self-guided tour** of part of the orchard. A path weaves among trees (technically bushes, related to the gardenia) with interpretive signs along the way that explain the art of creating the brew—from blossoming, to harvesting, and finally roasting. Six different varieties are grown, each with several roasting options. As was the case in the old days with sugar cane, the production process is ultra-efficient, conserving of energy and water, which is dispensed via some 2,500 miles of drip tubing. **Free guided tours** take place every two hours, from 10 to 4.

As of 2019, visitors are able to commune with many of the orchard's 4 million coffee trees by taking a two-hour tour in an open-air safari truck that ranges over several miles, from near the sea to the 1,000-foot level at **Alexander Reservoir**. The route skirts jungled **Wahiawa Valley**, featured in *Jurassic Park*, sitting below the jagged green **Kahili Ridge**. Visitors get to plant their own tree, which one day can yield a pound of coffee. At the upper reaches of the valley (the tour doesn't go this far) is **Kanaele Swamp**, which lies at the foot of the tallest peak on the island, **Kawaikini**, standing at 5,243 feet. *Note:* A fee is charged to take the tour.

Kilohana Overlook

In 1778, Hawai'i became the last major landmass to take its place on the modern globe. In that year British Captain James Cook and his ships, the *Discovery* and the *Resolution* dropped anchor in Waimea Bay, thus ending the Hawaiians' fifteen centuries without contact from the rest of the world's cultures.

Cook and his men, having sailed the South Pacific for a dozen years, recognized at once that these new people were of Polynesian descent, but prior to making landfall not even this great navigator knew that Hawai'i existed. Four hundred years had elapsed since the last Tahitian migrations, and islanders in those southern waters, like Cook, had known nothing of their descendants far to the north.

Cook's Kauaian visit lasted only three weeks, long enough to trade coveted iron nails with locals for equally coveted fruits and livestock, and for Cook and his officers to share a few peppery awa cocktails with the Kauaian aliʻi. Cook's most significant legacy, however, was not a welcome gift: Although he had prohibited fraternization with the local women, his men managed to infect them with venereal disease.

Upon surveying Kauaʻi, these first Europeans chose the gently sloping coast of the drier west side for safe anchorage. But they barely caught a glimpse of what awaits today's visitors. Not many hikers in the tropics expect to find cacti growing on cliffs of red-walled river canyons. Waimea Canyon is appropriately called the "Grand Canyon of the Pacific."

About ten miles long and almost 4,000 feet deep, Waimea Canyon takes its place alongside canyons of America's Southwest as a scenic wonder. Trails lead into the canyon, as well as along its cliffs and throughout the diverse forests that border its upper rim at Kokeʻe State Park—a wonderland for birds and myriad varieties of trees. Forests include both native varieties and others planted by the Conservation Corps in the 1930s. Within the park is Kokeʻe Museum, one of Hawaii's best, and an interpretive nature path, as well as miles of trails through forests chock-full with a fantastical array of flora. Kokeʻe Lodge, next to the museum, draws a crowd for lunch. Both the Cliff and Waipo Falls trails pop out to big views of Waimea Canyon.

The west side of Kokeʻe State Park forests gives way to Napali—The Cliffs. All along the northwest quadrant of the island, ridges and valleys fan out like spokes on a wheel, starting at road's end on the north shore and continuing around to road's end on the west shore at Polihale State Park and Barking Sands Beach. Each ridge ends at a cliff along a coast with no roads. This is a wild forest reserve area that hikers and cyclists can spend weeks exploring.

At least eight of the Napali ridges can be hiked or ridden by mountain bike. The hikes begin through tropical greenery and end at bluffs, some 1,500 feet above the surf, with canyon walls of neighboring ridges to the left and right. Viewpoints at trail's end look down at remote valleys, once inhabited, and all steeped in Hawaiian mythology.

Heading up from Kokeʻe park headquarters, the road ends at a lookout of the Kalalau Valley. Road's end is the beginning of the Pihea Trail. From Puʻuokila Lookout, the Pihea Trail starts along the precipitous rim of the Kalalau Valley and then turns inland, going across the Alakai Swamp on a boardwalk. Alakai Swamp is a 60-square mile bog of dwarf vegetation that was once the caldera of Hawaiʻi's first volcano. The boardwalk ends abruptly at a platform looking 4,000 feet down into the rippling green Wainiha River Valley and, beyond the valley, to Hanalei Bay on the north shore. Even the most avid among red-dirt adventurers may take several trips to Kauaʻi before comprehending its geographic jigsaw puzzle.

Down from Waimea Canyon is a shoreline than includes the longest strip of sand in Hawaiʻi—some 17 miles—beginning where the road ends at Barking Sands Beach in Polihale State Park. Beach hiking and surfing are superlative at Barking Sands, as well as at Majors Bay and Kekaha, two other beaches that continue around the west side from Polihale (though a military base poses some restrictions).

This trailhead section also includes two of Kaua'i's quaintest places to walk around, each distinctly Hawaiian—Waimea and Hanapepe. Waimea Town, once the island's capital, is where the Royal Hawaiians make their monthly trips by ferry from Ni'ihau. Waimea, meaning "red waters," has a river for kayakers and a bay for surfers. An ancient trail also leads up Waimea Canyon from Waimea Town, along the ancient remnants of Menehune Ditch, a water-conveyance system.

Between Waimea Town and Hanapepe is Pakala Beach, one of the better surfing beaches. Pakala is dubbed "Infinities," because the rides can go on forever. Right near Hanapepe is Salt Pond Beach Park, the best swimming spot on the west side, as well as the site of the ancient—and still functioning—salt ponds. In the 1800s, sailing vessels coveted the salt, not only for its taste, but also as a vital preservative for meats and fish.

Hanapepe is another uniquely Hawaiian town, funky around the edges with Kauaiana shops along its small main street. Browsers will enjoy the town's suspension footbridge over a river, and trails into a canyon that would be a main event were it not for nearby Waimea Canyon. Private property limits access as far as Hanapepe Falls—of *Jurassic Park* fame—but three rural roads and

Swinging Bridge, Hanapepe Falls

trails give hikers and cyclists a taste of the canyon floor. Paddlers can get the farthest into the green-and-red gorge.

Port Allen, Kaua'i's working harbor, with a power plant and commercial dock, is a taking-off point for snorkeling adventures and the "Forbidden Island" of Ni'ihau. Kayakers can try the bay before heading up Hanapepe River. From Port Allen, hikers can also walk a coast trail to Wahiawa Bay, a destination for snorkeling tours not easily reached directly, since the bay borders the private property of a coffee plantation.

The Waimea area doesn't have hotels—with one notable exception in Waimea Town, and other ventures on the drawing board—so many visitors zip through on the way to Waimea Canyon or Barking Sands. But the west side could be an island unto itself and still be a world-class destination for muscle-powered sports nuts.

Waimea Rodeo, Alakai Swamp

MAP 5 TRAILHEADS 50-69

WAIMEA

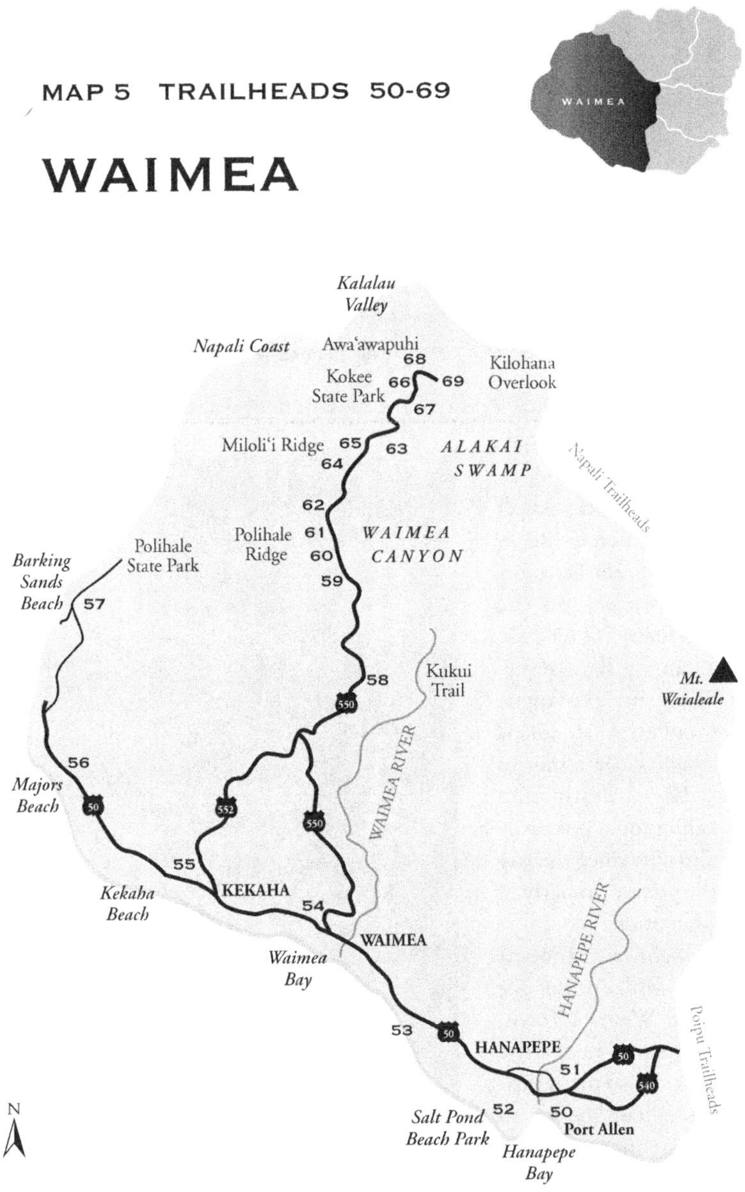

WAIMEA

Kalalau
Valley

Napali Coast   Awa'awapuhi
68
Kokee   66   69   Kilohana
State Park   Overlook
67

Miloli'i Ridge 65   63   ALAKAI
64   SWAMP

Napali Trailheads

62

Polihale   Polihale 61   WAIMEA
State Park   Ridge   60   CANYON
Barking   59
Sands
Beach   57

58   Kukui
550   Trail

Mt.
Waialeale

56
Majors
Beach   50

552
550

WAIMEA RIVER

55
Kekaha   KEKAHA
Beach   54

WAIMEA

Waimea
Bay

HANAPEPE RIVER

Poipu Trailheads

53   50   HANAPEPE
51   50
540

N   Salt Pond   52   50
Beach Park   Port Allen
Hanapepe
Bay

T R A I L H E A D S
50-69

HIKE	HIKING
SNORKEL	SNORKELING AND SWIMMING
BIKE	MOUNTAIN OR ROAD BIKING
PADDLE	KAYAKING, CANOEING
SURF	SURFING, BOOGIE BOARDING

TH	TRAILHEAD	*Notes: All hiking distances*
Makai	TOWARD OCEAN	*are roundtrip.*
Mauka	TOWARD THE MOUNTAIN, INLAND	*Visitor parking fee of $5 for*
mm	MILE MARKER, CORRESPONDS TO HIGHWAY SIGNS	*Koke'e and Waimea Canyon parks, begining pg. 151*

50. PORT ALLEN-NI'IHAU   HIKE, SNORKEL, SURF

WHAT'S BEST: Take a look at Kaua'i's sightseeing and whale-watching port, or hike to an out-of-the-way snorkeling bay. Or, spend the day cruising to the island of Ni'ihau, where you can place your face in some excellent snorkeling waters.

PARKING: Take Hwy. 50 past Kalaheo, and turn makai on Hwy. 541, Waialo Rd., at mm16. Go .75-mi. on Waialo and park at large lot near dock and outlet shops. Additional parking areas described below.

HIKE: Glass Beach (way less than .25 mi.); Wahiawa Bay (2.5 mi., 225 ft.)

Port Allen is not a place to spend an entire vacation; fuel tanks, utility pipes, and power poles are not postcard fodder. Yet the port gives you a look at what makes Kaua'i tick and offers shopping and eating opportunites. Red-dirt T-shirts are on hand, as are most of the sightseeing ships' offices. The dock at Port Allen is popular for sportfishing, whale-watching, snorkeling, and Napali Coast touring.

To **Wahiawa Bay** and **Glass Beach**, turn left on Akaula Road, which is uphill from the dock area and runs between metal warehouses and fuel storage tanks. The beach is where the road drops to the water. Colorful smooth glass pieces *used to* outnumber the sand particles, but bucket loads have been removed by collectors, and now it's an example of Yelp-gone-awry. The road continues a short distance and ends at a **Japanese** and **McBryde cemetery**. A nice-walking fishermen's path leads down the coast to the bay, winding its way alongside the edge of the shore with tide pools, a small sea arch, and a lava bridge. The trail takes a hop up from the reef and becomes a red-dirt straighaway through dry grasses to the mouth of **Wahiawa Bay.** It then curves inland toward the bay, passing access points along the way. *Be Aware:* Inland is private property, so heed signs.

SNORKEL: The ultimate Kaua'i snorkeling trip awaits 20 miles offshore at the 'Forbidden Island' of **Ni'ihau** and the tiny island of **Lehua** that lies next door—a bird sanctuary. Several tours depart Port Allen, but the most experienced and popular are HoloHolo Charters and Captain Andy's. They'll both zip you there in a diesel catamaran, and swing by the Napali coast on the way. Ni'ihau is privately owned, off-limits to all but native Hawaiians. Lehua is a cinder cone off its eastern shore. Snorkeling locations will depend on weather and sea conditions, but count on crystal clear water.

Offshore Ni'ihau and Lehua

Wahiawa Bay boasts a comfy sandy beach, ideal for sun bathers, but with shade as well. The base of its cliffs is lined with submerged rocks, and the bay is well-protected, especially during the winter when the trades blow from the northeast. Tour boats used to anchor in the bay, and the snorkeling can be very good. Just below the cemetery, is an excellent channel with a sandy nook, **Little Eternity Beach**—provided surf is very low.

SURF: **Hanapepe River mouth** (between the small boat harbor at Port Allen and the river) is a spot for beginners and boogie boarders. Small waves and rock-free waters make for safe conditions.

51. HANAPEPE   HIKE, BIKE, PADDLE

> **WHAT'S BEST:** Exploring old-style Hanapepe Town and its river canyon—on foot, by bike, or paddling a kayak. Nose around and you'll be rewarded.
> **PARKING:** Take Hwy. 50 through Kalaheo. Veer mauka toward Hanapepe on Hanapepe Rd., which is about .25-mi. past mm16. Continue a short distance beyond left turn and park near Pa Lane at parking for Swinging Bridge.

HIKE: Hanapepe Town stroll (up to 1.5 mi.); Bougainvillea path (.25-mi., 150 ft.); Swinging Bridge-Hanapepe River (up to 3.5 mi.)

Artists and craftspeople moved into quaint **Hanapepe Town** after Hurricane Iniki smacked its already dilapidated sugar shacks, and 25 years later, the result is one of Hawaii's more interesting walk-around villages. Saunter down Hanapepe Road past the 1911 Bridge and back again. You'll find historical markers affixed to some two-dozen buildings, and many quirky storefronts. To check out the pulse of the place, stop in at the nonprofit **Storybook Theater of Hawaii**, run by Mark "Russell the Rooster" Jeffers, whose television shows entertain Kaua'i's kids. The **Peace Garden** is out back. *Notes:* To see Hanapepe pop, catch an art night, normally every Friday, beginning at 6. Avoid Sundays, when the place shuts down. For more on Hanapepe's offerings, see *Driving Tours*, page 209.

For the **bougainvillea path**, walk back the way you drove in, past Ko Road, and take a paved path with a pipe railing leading up to the left. Flowering plants blanket the cliff. This short walk, which is the kids' route to Ele'ele School, gives you a perspective on the town.

A highlight is the **Hanapepe River** walk across the **Swinging Bridge** that spans the wide river—the bridge is a destination itself. A levee trail on the other side goes both to the left

Little Eternity Beach, Hanapepe swinging bridge

Hanapepe River

and right. To the left, or downriver, you walk about .5-mile, to the 1911 Bridge, about .5-mile up from where the river enters Hanapepe Bay. Going to the right across the Swinging Bridge (most scenic) takes you about .5-mile upriver, to a broad, agricultural area, with a variety of fruit trees, including bananas. Side trails lead down to two parklike spots to take a zen-break. You'll have exotic river views, looking through large broadleaf trees at the red walls of the gorge—while, on your left, as a contrast, you'll pass rusting vehicles and chicken coops. Roosters and barking poi dogs are a likely audio. The path loops away from the river, ending at a farmhouse, where Awawa Road comes in, as per mountain bike description.

BIKE: Two decent rides await mountain bikers in Hanapepe, both up the valley on different routes. **Ko Road**, which is your first right on the way into town, snakes in 1.5 miles before coming to a locked gate. Beyond the gate is a hunter's road. Ko Road is bordered in places by the 200-foot high canyon, with views of the river and a patchwork of agricultural lands. Mountain bikers can ride the other side of the river by pedaling down Hanapepe Road from the Swinging Bridge parking area, crossing the river on the 1911 Bridge, and turning right on **Awawa Road**. Awawa Road takes you 1.5 miles through a tree tunnel and past country homesteads.

PADDLE: The **Hanapepe River** makes lazy, very scenic curves inland from the bay for 1.5 miles. You see cacti as well as bananas. *Driving:* Kayakers can put in at the river mouth, off Puolo Road—backtrack from the Swinging Bridge to the highway and turn right. Cross the river and turn left immediately on Puolo Road. Continue, passing a ball field on the right, and park after .25-mile, where the road makes a sharp right. This puts you at the mouth of the Hanapepe River across from the swimming beach at Port Allen. The put-in involves a short carry. You'll also have the option of stroking around Hanapepe Bay. You need to be mindful of boat traffic in the bay.

52. SALT POND BEACH PARK   HIKE, SNORKEL, SURF

> **WHAT'S BEST:** Salt Pond is a superlative place to take a snorkeling beach break while touring the west side. Follow your swim with a seacoast hike along ancient salt ponds.
> **PARKING:** Take Hwy. 50 to .75-mi past Hanapepe River and turn makai on Hwy. 543, Lolokai Rd. toward Salt Pond Beach Park. Keep right at Lele Rd. The beach park is 1 mile from Hwy. 50. *Best access to see the salt ponds:* Keep left at Lele Rd. and then go right along the airstrip on Kuiloko Rd. This takes you to a less-used, unpaved lot.

HIKE: Salt Ponds and Pa'akahi Point (3 mi.)

Salt Pond Beach Park is an unflattering name for this idyllic beach park. From the parking, walk across the lawn of the picnic and camping area and then arc left around the beach. Don't forget to admire the offshore view of **Ni'ihau**. Almost unnoticed inland as you first leave the beach (at the alternate parking spot) are the **salt ponds** from which the ancients—and present-day Hawaiians—have extracted life-preserving salt from seawater. You need to veer inland toward black plastic: It doesn't look appealing, but make the effort. (Kaua'i's sea salt is coveted for its mix of some 82 minerals and

Salt Pond Beach Park

Ancient salt ponds

reddish color, derived from island clay.) Then backtrack from the ponds and hug the coast on a red-dirt road. The hike takes you around the chunky peninsula that forms the west side of Hanapepe Bay, across from Port Allen. As you walk you encircle Port Allen Airport, an asphalt strip that is the occasional launching pad for ultra-lights and tour helicopters. Locals have fought a plan to increase helicopter facilities here, which would disrupt the pond's historic uses. In the middle of the peninsula, Puolo Point is the loca-tion of **Hanapepe Light** which identi-fies the bay for sailors. From Puolo to **Pa'akahi Point**, the last .5-mile of the outward segment, black rocks supply the resistance for some explosive wave action. Near **Puolo Point**, dolphins and whales often swim close to shore.

SNORKEL: Nature has made a salt-water swimming hole at **Salt Pond Beach Park**, complete with a crescent of sand and swaying palms. A reef protects the shoreline, but don't drift beyond the reef, as currents get tricky not far out. Due to silt and wave action, visibility is most often just fair, and fishes are not profuse. To the right and left of the big beach are a **keiki ponds**, made for splashing. Though not huge in area, these keiki ponds have clear water and the best snorkeling, when the tide is high enough.

Camping at Salt Pond

SURF: Windsurfers and boarders alike take advantage of an offshore break at **Salt Pond Park**. It's a long paddle out, and known only as a summer spot for surfers. Some locals also try the harbr break, at the mouth of the harbor just off the airport runway— **Paʻakahi Point**. Access is difficult, down a rocky embankment, and the right-breaking swells are recommended for good surfers only.

53. PAKALA BEACHES   HIKE, SNORKEL, SURF

WHAT'S BEST: Surfers rave about Pakala's long-breaking waves, but hikers will find a long, palmy beach walk, or a shorter one, to view a quiet sugar-shack community right out of the 19ᵗʰ century. Stream runoff can spoil the aesthetics.

PARKING: Take Hwy. 50 from Hanapepe. Pass the makai turnoff to Makaweli and cross a highway bridge, at mm21, near an emergency phone. Park on highway shoulder, just on other side of the bridge. Watch out for high-speed traffic.

HIKE: Pakala Beaches (up to 2 mi.); Makaweli (1.5 mi.)

Access to **Pakala Beaches** starts just below the highway bridge. From the turnout, cross the highway and walk inside a guardrail to the bridge. A path runs beside **Aʻakukui Stream** for about .25-mile under the boughs of large monkeypod trees to the beach. Turning right at Pakala Beach—which is also called Aʻakukui Beach or Infinities, because that's how long the waves roll—leads you about 1 mile to rocky **Poʻo Point**. The point forms the mouth of Hoahuana Bay.

Going to your left at the beach, you cross the stream (if it's not too high or turbid) and follow the coco palm-lined shores and big grass field that border **Makaweli.** Makaweli is a collection of several dozen weather-worn, red-dust-stained sugar shacks, festooned with nets, glass balls, and hanging laundry, choked by tropical greenery and set in a grid of narrow, potholed dirt streets that make perfectly good sleeping spots for the occasional poi dog. Palm trees overhang a narrow strip of sand. Where the cottages end is a grass field that borders sweet **Makaweli Beach**. *Be Aware:* This is not a tourist town. Although the people here are friendly, visitors should tread lightly at this quiet community.

Pakala Beach

Beach at Makaweli

SNORKEL: The stream at Pakala has a reputation of being unhealthy due to upstream agricultural use. Better to cross the stream toward **Makaweli** and try the first beach you come to. Or better yet, head for **Makaweli Beach** at the far end of the village, one of the best places to snorkel on this coast. You can drive there from the highway; turn at the post office. *Be Aware:* Surf can make shores turbulent all year around, with rip currents in shallow waters. Be mindful of private propery; ask permission (if you see anyone).

SURF: **Pakala Beaches**, or **Infinities**, draw surfers all year, but during the summer the swells are particularly inspiring. If the surf is good, cars will be parked at the highway. To the east side of the beach, or left as you face the water, is Pakala Point, where

Plantation house, Makaweli

left-hand slides take boards up the coast to infinity. To access this break, you need to walk to your right up the beach about .25-mile and paddle out through deeper water for about 100 yards. Locals sometimes ride these fast tubes for two or three hundred yards. In the winter, the offshore break toward Makaweli can be better. *Be Aware:* Infinities has a dangerous, shallow reef. Even the big boys and girls prefer high tide.

54.   WAIMEA TOWN   HIKE, PADDLE, SURF

> **WHAT'S BEST:** This most Hawaiian of towns offers a mix: a long beach walk, a navigable river, and exotic hiking into the "heart of darkness." Waimea is the West, cowboys and all.
> **PARKING:**   Take Hwy. 50 past mm22. Cross bridge over the Waimea River. *For the beach and town walk:* Turn makai (left) at the first opportunity, on Alawai Rd. Go a short distance and park at river mouth at Lucy Wright Beach Park. *For Menhune Ditch and canyon trail:* Turn mauka (right) on Alawai Rd. After .5-mi., Alawai merges with Menehune Rd. Directions continue in the hike description below.

HIKE: Waimea Beach and Town walk (up to 2.5 mi.); Menehune Ditch or Waimea Canyon Trail (.5-mi. to 16 mi.)

You won't find many tiki torches in **Waimea Town**, but you will find some of Old Hawai'i. Outrigger canoes rest along the beach, fishermen hang out on the pier, families picnic and talk story, and cowboys herd cattle. Waimea has the most native Hawaiians among its population, including Royal Hawaiians who take the ferry from Ni'ihau.

For the **beach and town walk**, start at **Lucy Wright Beach Park**, which was the landing for the first Europeans to set foot on Hawaii, in 1778, arriving in vessels led by Captain James Cook. Not all locals remember the occasion with fondness. About

.25-mile down the beach is **Waimea State Recreational Pier**, where you can walk over the water. Cut in from the beach at the pier and go left on an alley, passing the authentic plantation cottages of the Kikialoa Land Company. (The defunct sugar mill facilities are the center for the Waimea Town Celebration, held in February.) At the end of the alley are the parklike grounds of **Waimea Plantation Cottages,** a low-key, upscale vacation spot with a striking arboretum of banyans and other giants. You can continue across the rodeo grounds (or drive the highway) to **Kikiaola State Boat Harbor**, a mile from Waimea. With a palm grove and a small bay that launches adventure cruises to Napali, the harbor is an good choice for a picnic break. Turning back from the Plantation Cottages, you can jog inland through sleepy Waimea Town's mom-and-pop commercial district. The cemetery at **Waimea Church** has most of the grave markers, Japanese and American, of key figures from the sugar cane days. The **West Kaua'i Technology & Visitors Center**, across from the old sugar mill, has been downsized, but they still have exhibits and offer historical walking tours of the town.

For both the mellow **Menehune Ditch** stroll and the (potentially) more challenging trek up the **Waimea Canyon**, continue on Menehune Road. About 1.3 miles from the highway, you'll see a **suspension footbridge**; park at a grassy turnout on the left before the bridge, or at another cliffside turnout .1-mile after the bridge. Embedded in the rock is a plaque commemorating the archeological site of the Menehunes' water-conveyance ditch, including the short tunnel section that remains. You'll also want to walk the bridge, but the roads on the other bank of the river are signed 'no tresspassing.'

For the oh-wow **Waimea Canyon Trail** along the river, continue slowly on the narrowing road for .9-mile past the bridge—the last .2-mile of which—past the junk cars at a river crossing—is unpaved. Park at the turnaround just before a house. Walk the road through a botanical wonderland of ti, bananas, heliconia, and big-leafed ape (*ah-pay*). Mowed grass makes it a park. You'll pass a stable and other buildings, some part of the Mid-Pacific Research Station. Then keep right at a lawn with bamboo railings; this is the end of strolling and the beginning of the trail proper.

You'll see a brown-and-yellow sign for hunters who are entering the **Pu'u Ka Pele State Forest Reserve**. A short distance later, make sure to follow bamboo railings up to the left, not the spur trail to the river. The going gets rougher here. Swithbacks climb about 150 feet and reach a ditch. You follow the ditch. You may need to push plants away in places and step over rocks. In about .5-mile, you'll see an Indiana Jones-type **suspension bridge** crossing 20 feet above the river. Cross this plank-and-cable bridge—the safety of which cannot be assured—and meet up with the four-wheel drive trail coming upriver. Stay on this road, as it swerves up the canyon, crossing the river.

About 2 miles in from the trailhead, the trail climbs again, about 500 feet, and follows a ditch above the river for about 1.75 miles before dropping down again to the river. By this time you may feel like you've stepped into a Joseph Conrad novel. Signs of

Around Waimea Town

civilization are to be found in the form of a water conveyance system, built in the early 1900s by sugar plantation owners. From where the trail drops to the river to where it meets the Kukui Trail, TH58, is another 3.5 miles. To see this area, you're better off taking the Kukui Trail down from the canyon. *Be Aware:* Don't attempt this hike when river is high or when thick clouds indicate mountain rains inland. Prepare for a full-fledged trek. Although Kauaian hunters are a friendly lot, this trail is best for weekdays when hunters are not present.

More Stuff: To see the humble remains of Fort Elizabeth, turn makai at mm22.3, before crossing the bridge into Waimea. In the early 1800s, the Russians established the edifice, but abandoned their efforts with the emergence of British and Americans.

PADDLE: Waimea River is navigable for maybe 2 miles inland, although after about a mile in you want to watch for rocks and debris. Not many people paddle these red-silt waters. Waimea also invites a bay-and-river combination, as waters along the beach are normally fairly calm. You're more apt to be joined by an outrigger canoc than a kayak.

SURF: The river mouth at **Lucy Wright Beach** is usually a place for novice surfers and boogie boarders. But Wright's is not always okay for keikis: Summer swells break far offshore, and build in four tiers to a shore break that can be dangerous.

55. KEKAHA   HIKE, SURF

WHAT'S BEST: Pull off the road and catch a sunset view of Ni'ihau on a miles-long sand beach hike. When rains darken the rest of the island, sun seekers head for Kekaha. **PARKING:** Take Hwy. 50 past Waimea. Pass Kikiaola Small Boat Harbor. Kekaha Beach Park access is at mm25. *Primary parking:* At MacArthur Park lifeguard station and picnic pavilions, mm27.25. *Targets Beach parking (locals, shortens hike by .75-mi.):* Turn on a dirt road, mm27.6, just after at a small bridge over a canal (across from 'Pioneer."). Drive in .1-mi. and park near ironwood trees.

HIKE: Kekaha Beach (up to 3.75 mi.)

Kekaha, not long ago a thriving sugar town, is now known for its long, fine-sand beach and as a gateway to Waimea Canyon. And when clouds hang over other parts of Kaua'i, sun often shines on Kekaha. Open sand and normally big surf stretch for miles, part of the longest sand beach in Hawaii. Offshore is a view of Ni'ihau. Dunes shift around near shore and create long sandy-walled pools. When the surf's up, you're safer on the higher flat sand. Just past the lifeguard station is **MacArthur Park**, melting in the sun, with its lawn and several covered picnic tables. *Be Aware:* With strong legs and a sense of purpose you could hoof it 10-plus miles along Majors Bay and the Pacific Missile Range Facility to Polihale State Park. Alas, since 9-11 the government boys have closed the beach about 2 miles from the lifeguard station.

Kekaha Beach

SURF: **Kekaha** gets pounded with south swells in the summer, and has predictable winter surf. But this beach is too far away from Kaua'i's other surfing beaches to be well-known or become crowded. Good-to-average surfers try their luck at a half-dozen spots. Among the most popular is the reef near mm25 at **O'omano Point**, sometimes called **Davidsons**. The reef, which provides the break, also presents a hazard. There are four other breaks along **Kekaha Beach**, from the community park to the lifeguard station. A locals' favorite is **Targets**: Use secondary parking. Walk to the right at the beach; it's offshore from the the landfill. *Be Aware:* Watch high surf before paddling out. Drownings and impact injuries do happen; don't bodysurf.

56. MAJORS

HIKE, SNORKEL, SURF

WHAT'S BEST: A beach-lover's beach, with sand two-hundred yards deep and miles long, made for surfing and bagging some R&R. The catch these days is you need to apply for permit or enlist in the military to enter the base.

PARKING: Access is at the Pacific Missile Range Facility, which is past Kekaha on Hwy. 50, at mm30. *Note:* Due to heightened security, permits are required to visit the beach. Call 808-335-7936 or Google: 'PMRF MWR guest card application.' A two-page application and background check takes up to a month to process and costs $25 per person. They may mail an application, which you can snail mail back to them at MWR, Box 128, Kekaha, HI 96752. But normal procedures call for personal pick-up and delivery. The permit is good for a year. You'd think they could make it easier.

HIKE: Majors Bay (3 or 4 mi.)

Majors Bay, another name for Waiokapua Bay, is the middle segment of the long beach—the longest in Hawai'i—that runs from the foot of the Napali coast at Polihale

State Park around to Kekaha. Majors is next to what's left of Mana, the settlement of old Kaua'i. Your permit allows access to several recreational areas, depending on what operations may be taking place on the base. One area is in the middle of the bay, and another is toward the north end, where monk seals have been known to loll about. If you need shade with your beach, however, bring it with you, since Majors is nothing but sand, air and water.

Starting at either area on Majors Bay, walk toward your left as you face the water. You'll be heading toward Kokole Point, visible from Kekaha. Majors Bay is the kind of place to get lost right out in the open, a deep expanse of soft sand that gives way to a mesmerizing view of Ni'ihau. The **Kawaiele Bird Sanctuary**, is located on the highway between the two entrance gates; easily reached but of low scenic value. Feathered friends fly into the view, among them albatrosses.

Going to your right from the parking areas at Majors you can get to the coral reef that signals the beginning of Mana Point. At certain times, you can access **Barking Sands Beach** from the base, by taking a road to the right as you enter the main gate; called Recreation Area One. The road leads to the reef at the far end of Barking Sands, and then becomes a four-wheel drive sand road. The sand road continues for about .75-mile, ending near Queens Pond at Barking Sands, as described in TH57.

SNORKEL: On occasion, swimming is possible at **Majors Bay**, but more often, all year, the surf is unsafe for snorkeling. A rip current from right to left, or north to south, is also a hazard. The best snorkeling area—the reef near the airstrip—is sometimes off-limits. Receding tide sometimes creates keiki ponds.

Majors Beach

Polihale State Park

SURF: **Majors** draws surfers, featuring some of the west side's biggest breakers during the winter. During the summer, swells can be outrageous. Some surfers head toward the north end of the base, toward Barking Sands.

57. POLIHALE STATE PARK   HIKE, SNORKEL, SURF

> **WHAT'S BEST:** Walk the Napali coast over the sands of time—where longest beach in the Hawaiian Islands ends and the Napali coast begins. Big, big mana.
>
> **PARKING:** Take Hwy. 50 through Kekaha to end of highway beyond mm32. At mm33, turn left where a sign says "Polihale State Beach." *Be Aware:* Floodwaters sometimes cause this road to close or be limited to 4WD. If puddles close out the entire road near the beginning, turn around. If not, continue for 3.25 mi. on an unpaved road, dodging its ruts and mud-holes. *For main Polihale parking:* Turn right after 3.25 mi. at a T-intersection with a large monkeypod tree and a state park sign. At 1 mi. from this junction is access to the dune camping road; park here if sand is deep on road just ahead. At 1.5 mi. is additonalparking. For main parking continue across a spillway, and park near a pavilion—1.75 mi. from the T-intersecton. *For Queens Pond:* Turn left at the monkeypod T-intersection. Drive .25-mi. and park after road turns sharply right uphill and comes to an end in deep sand—except for surfers in 4x4s who drive onto the beach.

HIKE: Polihale and Barking Sands beaches (up to 4.5 mi.)

Polihale State Park, which includes portions of **Barking Sands Beach**, is at road's end on this side of island. Here, a massive sand abuts *Napali*—The Cliffs. Inland from the tree-and-shrub-covered dune, is a wedge of agricultural lands, **Mana**. The entire beach runs for about 17 miles, but you can't walk the whole way due to restrictions at the missile-launch facility. Polihale Park has rest rooms, picnic shelters, and car-camping sites scattered in kiawe trees atop the dune, providing the most remote and the best beach camping on the island. *Be Aware:* For all hikes bring water, sun protection, and footwear to guard against hot sand.

From the parking walk onto the sloping, fine sands. Going to your right, the beach gives way to black rocks in less than .5-mile, at the base of the **Polihale Ridge**. This may be the prize spot in the park, set below towering cliffs at a beach that goes on forever. You can walk the rocks another .25-mile to Polihale Springs, or **Sacred Springs**, which flows from Polihale Heiau, where the spirits of the dead are said to have departed the island. This walk requires extensive rock-hopping.

The hike to the left along the coast in soft sand will test the legs beach walkers. About a mile from the last picnic grounds at Polihale Beach, as you begin to see coral reef offshore, the beach inland is **Barking Sands**. The beach gets its name from a "woofing" sound these 60-foot high dunes make when settling, or when someone walks down them. Kauaian mythology says the "woofing" is the otherworldly echo of an ancient fisherman's dogs—the first man to love dogs as companions rather than as a culinary delicacy. As you proceed, the reef and shoals become more pronounced—a vast, eternal seascape. *Note:* Due to military security, the beach may be closed to walkers about 1.75-mile south the beach pavilion parking, which is about .75-mile beyond **Queens Pond**. You definitely don't want to put on a ski mask and skulk inland. *Be Aware:* Don't turn your back when walking the surf line and watch out for rogue waves.

More Stuff: The **Kapaula Heiau** and other ruins are across the sandy road from the day use restrooms. Black rock walls and foundation segments are located among kiawe saplings about 50 feet from the road and stretch for a couple acres up the slope. The sites can be difficult to get to if the grasses are tall, but this is just the sort of place made for real-deal history sleuths.

SNORKEL: **Queens Pond** is often a safe swimming area on an otherwise dangerous swimming beach. Head up the sandy road and through the dunes to the beach. Queens Pond is a few hundred feet to the right as you face the water. It is formed by a crescent-shaped reef that touches the shore at the near end, making a large oval swimming area. When conditions are right, surf is spilling over the outside of the reef. Under extended calm conditions, Queens Pond can dry out and be a sand box. *Be Aware:* During storm surf rip current can be extreme at the far (right) end of the pond.

SURF: **Polihale State Park** is known for a multi-tiered shore break with lots of wave action and fairly short rides. The waves normally pound all year, with winter surf and currents posing a significant hazard. You want to consult the locals before trying Polihale; this is a big beach, and its quirks are not commonly known, since hazards shift with the sand. No lifeguards are on duty.

Polihale State Park

Another spot, but one for experienced surfers only, is **Queens Pond**. Follow directions in the snorkeling description above. The break here is right, as waves peel off where the reef touches the shore. Get advice from locals; if it's a good day to surf, they will be here. *Be Aware:* Barking Sands and Polihale State Beach are among the island's most dangerous. Swimmers should stay clear of the water in all but calm conditions.

58. KUKUI TRAILS   HIKE

> **WHAT'S BEST:** A hike to the bottom of a rainbow-hued canyon that rivals those in Arizona or Utah. This trail into the canyon is one of Kaua'i's scenic superstars. You don't need to go down all the way to have a great hike.
>
> **PARKING:** Take Hwy. 50 to Waimea and turn mauka on Hwy. 550 just past mm23, which is Waimea Canyon Dr. (*Note:* Hwy. 550 is several miles shorter and also more scenic than taking Hwy. 552, the route suggested by highway signs.) Continue on Hwy. 550 past its junction with Kokee Rd., Hwy. 552. Go .75-mi. past mm8 and look for trailhead signs on the right and park off road, or drive ahead a short distance, make a U-turn at a turnout, and drive back to paved turnout parking on the opposite side of the highway. There is also a two-car turnout on the right side of the highway at the trailhead.

HIKE: Kukui Trails: Iliau Nature Loop (.25-mi.); Wiliwili Camp, to bottom of canyon (5 mi., 2,075 ft.)

Kukui Trail

The **Iliau Loop** is a promenade around a flat area below the parking area, on which the native vegetation of the canyon rim is identified. The loop takes in a **railed viewing area**, to your left, and its inspiring vistas of the variegated red-and-green canyon walls, often streaked with a waterfall or two. You can see up **Waimea Canyon** and also **Waialae Canyon**, which wyes off to the right. *Note:* Prime picnic tables await a couple hundred yards to the right on this loop trail.

Wiliwili Camp is at the bottom of the canyon and alongside the Waimea River. **Kukui Trail** is the only way for bi-peds to walk the bottom of the canyon from the Koke'e area. Once down, you can go upriver another 3.5 miles to **Lonomea Camp**, or downriver, connecting up with the **Waimea Canyon Trail**, TH54; but most day hikers will have done enough after making it back up. The Wiliwili Camp trail begins to the right off of the nature loop trail. You start out switchbacking, and then walk out onto an **eroded promontory** that makes a destination for those not wishing to go all the way down. From the promontory, having descended the majority of the way, you hike left, traversing an eroded hillside, and then right, switchbacking down to the bottom through a leafy forest. The canyon floor, at Wiliwili Camp, is still about 600 feet above sea level and will give you a faraway, exotic feel, with towering century plants and cacti. Go left on the trail and you get to it's first hairy portion, where it is cut into a cliffside, a high-dive above the river as it courses through contorted geology.

Be Aware: Be mindful of flash floods, since river crossings, required farther upstream, can be treacherous. Prepare for a full-on day hike, with rain gear, food, and water.

59. PU'U KA PELE   HIKE, BIKE

> **WHAT'S BEST:** A short hike with quirky access to an astounding viewpoint of mythological significance. Mountain bikers can take a different flight.
> **PARKING:**   Take Hwy. 50 through Waimea. Turn mauka on Hwy. 550. *For Waimea Canyon Lookout,* turn right at signs at mm10.3. *For Pu'u Ka Pele, Lapa Picnic area,* park on the left, off road just past mm11 on shoulder at the access sign for Papa'alai Rd.

HIKE: Waimea Canyon Lookout (.25-mi.); Pu'u Ka Pele (.75-mi, 150 ft.); Lapa Picnic Area (4.5 mi., 575 ft.)

The **Waimea Canyon Lookout** gets hammered with tour buses, particularly mid-morning when the cruise ships are in Nawiliwili, but don't let that dissuade you. Railed viewing terraces on several levels provide plenty of room to behold the panorama.

Pu'u Ka Pele, or Pele's Hill, is an extinct sulfur vent located to the right of the highway, on the edge of Waimea Canyon across the highway from Papa'alai Road. The hill is said to be where Pele, the volcano goddess, left Kaua'i to create more fiery mischief farther south in the archipelago. At a pit at the top is Pele's footprint, made when she leapt

Waipo'o Falls, Waimea River at Wiliwili Camp

from the island. From the road, walk across the highway and go up a concrete driveway to a phone company building, visible from the highway. Concrete stairs and a series of log-and-dirt steps with a cable handrail aid a steep and rutted route. A fenced phone installation at the top takes up space but doesn't detract from the view. *Be Aware:* Don't venture out onto unsafe rocks. Also, although this is a historic trail within a state park and used frequently by hunters and hikers, it is along an improved easement utilized by the phone company. Use your own judgment, enter at your own risk, and stay away from buildings and lines.

Lapa Picnic Area is a bird-watcher's hike along Contour Road, which runs along the forested contour on the left side of the highway. This hike, though generally a contour, takes you through some undulation. Start down **Papa'alai**

Road. After about .5-mile the trail makes an "S" turn and crosses Koke'e Ditch. You then head seaward for another .5-mile, passing a road on your left that is the continuation of Papa'alai Road going toward two ridge roads. Pass this road and bear right, now on **Contour Road**. It loops inland through subtropical forest, turns toward the ocean for .5-mile, and finally hairpins right, back to the Lapa Picnic Area.

BIKE: A good way to get to know these Napali ridge roads is to tour **Contour Road**. Six different four-wheel drive roads head seaward from Contour Road, all going out its own ridge, each with valleys steeply falling to either side. To ride Contour Road, follow the hiking description for the picnic area, but continue past the Haele'ele Ridge Road. After another twisting-and-turning mile you reach Polihale Ridge Road and, 1.5-miles later, come to Ka'aweiki Ridge Road—hang a right here and pedal about one curving mile back up to the highway. *Be Aware:* On Contour Road, expect mud, puddles and fallen branches. It's best to use these roads on weekdays, when hunters are not present (and when the gate is usually locked).

60.   HAELE'ELE RIDGE   HIKE, BIKE

WHAT'S BEST: A tree-lover's ridge hike or bike for a bird's eye view of Barking Sands and a blue-water look at Ni'ihau.
PARKING: Take Hwy. 50 through Waimea and turn mauka on Hwy. 550 toward Waimea Canyon. At mm12, park on left, off-highway on the shoulder near a sign for Haele'ele Ridge.

HIKE: Haele'ele Ridge (13 mi., 1,900 ft.); Kepapa Spring (11.5 mi., 1,575 ft.)

Haele'ele Ridge drops to a bluff that is due east, as the albatross flies, and 1,400 feet above road's end at Polihale State Park. The red-dirt surface gets snotty with rain, so watch your footing. Haele'ele trail is a broad swath through a forest of eucalyptus, Norfolk Pines, and other trees. Beginning in **Waimea Canyon State Park**, the trail takes you into the **Pu'u Ka Pele Forest Reserve**. From the trailhead you hook left around the **Lua Reservoir**, and then cross Contour Road, about 1.5 miles in. From here you gradually come out of forest along a 3-mile descent. After about 2 miles on this descent—and that distance from Contour Road—is a side road to **Kepapa Springs**, which feeds Sacred Spring at Polihale Beach. Kepapa Springs Road is to the south, or left, becoming a trail after .75-mile. *More Stuff:* A rougher trail crosses the springs' drainage and traverses up a spur ridge, lenghthening this hike considerably. *Be Aware:* Stay well back from cliff edges.

Continuing on Haele'ele Ridge Road, you drop down the remaining 500 feet over the last 2 miles to trail's end. During the last .5-mile, through a rocky section, the trail stops being a sort-of road and becomes a true trail. *Be Aware:* Hunters use this area on weekends.

BIKE: **Haeleʻele Ridge** is ideal for fit, experienced cyclists. If caution is used, that is. Stay aware of slick surfaces, ruts, branches and roots—the route is not difficult to navigate. The difficulty comes in having the wind and strength to ride back up. Coasting down, after leaving the junction with Contour Road, saves a lot of steps.

61. POLIHALE RIDGE   HIKE, BIKE

> **WHAT'S BEST:** Exploring where the Napali begins on this side of Kauaʻi, and where the spirits of the dead left the island from a sacred heiau below.
> **PARKING:** Take Hwy. 50 through Waimea and turn mauka toward Waimea Canyon on Hwy. 550. Pass mm12, continue .8-mi., and park at picnic area on your left. Look for trailhead sign for Polihale Ridge Road. *Note:* From the guardrail at the highway is a knock-out view across the canyon to Waipoʻo Falls.

HIKE: **Polihale Ridge (10.5 mi., 1,875 ft.)**

Polihale Ridge descends steadily through a forest of pine, eucalyptus and other trees, as well as flowering shrubbery. Conditioned hikers can step out on this four-wheel drive surface. You begin at the A-plus **Puʻu Ka Pele picnic grounds**, with a newer pavilion and several covered tables. Head down and take the road to the right that follows the utility line, not the one to the right. The route jogs a the beginning and then is is due west. For the first mile or more, you drop through moist forest, reaching Contour Road. The trail from Contour Road falls steadily, through large koa trees, mixed with ironwoods and Norfolk pines. About a mile from Contour Road, and 1,000 feet farther down from the trailhead, Polihale Ridge narrows, not to a spine, but you'll see pronounced relief of the valleys on either side. *Be Aware:* Hunters drive this road on weekends and holidays.

Polihale Ridge

Puu Hinahina view

The road forks near the end, just past a small water tank, each fork a short spur leading to an exciting view from a 1,400-foot escarpment. The left fork ends at a turnaround among ironwood trees. Walk through the trees to an eroded, red-dirt area for a big view of road's end at Polihale State Park. On calm days, you will be able to hear surf pounding, and using a hang glider, you could be there in a few minutes.

To the left is canyonlike **Haeleʻele Valley**, and three ridges are visible: Haeleʻele, Kolo, and Mana. The right fork ends after .25-mile at an eroded area, looking down 1,000-feet into the **Hikimoe Valley**. The next ridge over, Kaʻaweiki Ridge, is close enough for those with keen eyes to spot a wild goat or two. You can see surf at a wild cove. Polihale Ridge, according to Hawaiian religion, was where the spirits of the deceased left the island for the other world. Aloha. A breeze normally sweeps up the cliff.

BIKE: Polihale Ridge is made for mountain bikes. It's a tough down-and-up pedal, but the down part isn't so tough. Ruts, cones, and roots, along with a slick surface, present the usual hazards, but this ride takes more endurance than skill. Save enough energy and daylight to get back up.

62. PUʻU HINAHINA   HIKE, BIKE

WHAT'S BEST: Take a short walk to a dramatic canyon lookout. Or go for a long adventure hike or bike down your choice of two west Napali ridges.
PARKING: Take Hwy. 50 through Waimea and turn mauka on Hwy. 550 toward Waimea Canyon.

For Ka'aweiki and Kauhao ridges: Go only .1-mi. past mm13 and turn left. Drive in, avoiding spur roads to the left and right, and continue straight for almost .4-mi. Park where the road forks. The right fork is Kauhao Ridge; the left fork is Ka'aweiki Ridge. *Note:* Under most conditions, you can drive another .5-mile either way at this fork, and park where each ridge road intersects Contour Road. Access is made somewhat confusing by a series of community and church camps situated between the highway and Contour Road. *For Pu'u Hinahina:* Continue to mm13.6 and go right into an improved parking lot.

HIKE: Pu'u Hinahina (up to .5-mi.); Kauhao Ridge (8.5 mi., 2,150 ft.); Ka'aweiki Ridge (10.5 mi., 1,950 ft.)

Pu'u Hinahina Lookout is sometimes overlooked, since other viewpoints precede it, but it affords a spectacular view down Waimea Canyon. Glancing left from the lookout, you can review the terrain of the **Halemanu Valley** hikes, TH63. To the right, as you face the lookout stairs, is a short path to a **lookout of Ni'ihau** and **Lehua** islands. *More Stuff:* A trailhead for the Canyon Trail is at the lookout parking lot, but you are better off using the access described in TH63, Halemanu Valley Trails.

For Kauhao Ridge trail, take the right fork from the parking on a forested stroll to Contour Road. For the first 1.5 miles after Contour Road, the trail twists and drops through rumpled topography, before coming upon the wide ridge. Open eucalyptus and koa forest allow occasional blue-water vistas, with glimpses of Ni'ihau and its lesser known satellite island, Lehua. About 3 miles in, stay left at a road fork (though the right fork loops back to join the left). A short trail leads from road's end on Kauhao Ridge to a lookout of the Napali. At this lookout you are about two miles up the coast from Polihale State Park. *Be Aware:* Don't get close to eroded cliffs.

For Ka'aweiki Ridge trail, walk left from the parking and cross Contour Road, about .5-mile later. This ridge lies between Kauhao and Polihale ridges. Ka'aweiki is narrower than its neighbors, with deeply cut Hikimoe Valley on its south side and Ka'aweiki Valley to the north. The trail is not inherently dangerous for the sure-footed, but watch your step during the last 1.5 miles. You reach a 1,300-foot cliff with a straight drop to the Pacific. *Be Aware:* Hunters may be out on weekends, so pick a weekday.

BIKE: Just as with their sister ridges in Pu'u Ka Pele Forest Reserve, **Ka'aweiki** and **Kauhao ridges** are a mountain biker's wonderland. *Be Aware:* Slick, packed dirt, road debris and ruts make these ridge roads a place where accidents do happen. Also make sure as you're breezing down that you have enough oomph to get back up.

63. HALEMANU VALLEY TRAILS   HIKE, BIKE

WHAT'S BEST: A tree-lover's hike-world with waterfall and canyon vistas, perfect for a day when fog is higher up the mountain.

Heading up Waimea Canyon on Hwy. 550, continue to mm14 and park off road at marked trailhead, at sign near Kokee State Park Boundary—as you leave Waimea Canyon State Park.

HIKE: Halemanu Trails: Cliff Lookout (2 mi., 525 ft.); Canyon Trail to Waipo'o Falls (4 mi., 1,150 ft.); Kumuwela Lookout (7.25 mi., 1,450 ft.); Black Pipe Trail loop (3.5 mi., 825 ft.)

Notes: Distances are for on-highway parking. A steep road from the highway leads .75-mi. to trailhead; if you choose to drive this road, subtract 1.5 mi. from hiking distances. If you plan to do a lot of hiking in the woodlands of Koke'e, stop by the park museum for expert advice and good gift ideas. Waipo'o Falls is a popular hike.

The **Halemanu Valley trails** skirt the edge of the forested birdlands where Koke'e Park gives way to the eroded red escarpments of Waimea and Po'omau canyons. **For all trails**, go down the steep, wide **Halemanu Road** from the highway, which takes a big bend at the bottom and comes to another trailhead sign after .75-mile. Go right a short distance to where the road ends, usually in a big mud-hole, and the trails begin.

After a short distance the trail forks: The **Canyon Trail (and other options)** are the left fork and the **Cliff Lookout Trail** is the right. The Cliff Lookout is a scamper up to an overlook with a pipe railing and picnic table. You'll get a big sense of place. From Cliff Lookout, you can see down the canyon to your left, including the eroded promontory that is part of the Canyon Trail.

Continuing left on the Canyon Trail to the falls and other destinations takes you down another 600 feet. You drop through dense forest and cross over part of the extensive irrigation ditch system. After the ditch, the Canyon Trail then climbs to where you get a view down the canyon, and where the **Black Pipe Trail** joins from

Halemanu Trail toward Waipo'o Falls

the left. The Black Pipe Trail—perhaps best done by making a semi-loop on the way back from the falls—curves through a plethora of trees back to the road you walked down. After about .5-mile on the Black Pipe Trail, make sure to switchback left up a hillside of koa trees, rather than continuing down to the stream. About .25-mile after this little climb, you go left again when you come to a road. Keep circling to your left on the Black Pipe Trail. You'll come to the trailhead sign that is just down the road from the highway.

For **Waipo'o Falls** and **Kumuwela Lookout**, you continue on Canyon Trail past the Black Pipe junction, dropping a few hundred feet onto a dramatic barren ridge with canyon views. Continue down the eroded ridge—watch your footing on log steps—and drop to **Koke'e Stream**. A very short spur trail goes left to a cascade and pool. The trail continues a few hundred feet to the top ledge of Waipo'o Falls, which falls 800 feet into the canyon. *Be Aware:* You don't get a good look at the falls. Check it out from across the canyon at Polihale viewpoint, TH61.

To Kumuwela Lookout, the trail crosses Koke'e Stream at the falls and then goes up gradually along a grassy slope. You contour to your left across the head of the canyon, dipping in and out. About 1.75 miles from the falls, you reach Kumuwela Lookout. You can see all the way down Waimea Canyon to the ocean, almost an entire cross section of the island. To your left is Po'omau Canyon, which wyes off Waimea Canyon to the northwest and abuts Alakai Swamp. *Be Aware:* Don't try to cross the top of the falls if the water is at all running swiftly. *More Stuff:* From Kumuwela Lookout you can continue about 2.5 miles back to the road near Koke'e Museum, a shorter route if you have someone to do the car shuttle.

BIKE: Mountain bikers can park at the trailhead and take off down **Halemanu Road**. By veering left at the first trailhead sign .75-mile in, and then veering left again after less than .5-mile, you can connect with **Faye Road**. Faye Road leads to Koke'e Park headquarters. Doing this involves escorting the wheels over a short trail that connects the Halemanu Road with Faye Road. You can also ride a spur off Halemanu Road by veering right after the trailhead sign. This spur takes you to the junction with the Black Pipe Trail, which can be ridden in most sections, but be sure to dismount for hikers. To explore this area, you may wish to buy a map at the park headquarters, if you care to know where you are. On the other hand, as long as you stay on rideable roads and avoid trails, the region is small enough that you will be able to ride yourself out.

64.   MAKAHA RIDGE ROAD   HIKE, BIKE

WHAT'S BEST: See a spectacular Napali ridge the easy way—by driving and taking short walks.

Canyon Trail

PARKING: Head up Waimea Canyon on Hwy. 550. Pass Pu'u Hinahina Lookout, and turn left on paved Makaha Rd., just before mm14. *For Makaha Arboretum:* Go about 3 mi. on Makaha Rd. and look for an unpaved road on left (which loops out to the main road about .5-mi. later). *For Miloli'i vista:* Go 4 mi. to the guard station and make a U-turn. Backtrack about .25-mi. to the top of the rise, with a red-dirt embankment and pine trees on the left—near where a utility line crosses over the road.

HIKE: Makaha Arboretum (3 mi., 350 ft.); Miloli'i vista (.25-mi.)

To **Makaha Arboretum**, which has sugi pine trees mixed among a number of native and introduced species, look for (unsigned) **Pine Forest Drive** on your left as you are making a long, straight descent to the Makaha Ridge. The trail to the arboretum spurs off this road about midway along its loop.

The pine forest here, not tropical at all in its appearance, underscores that climates exist for virtually every growing thing on the Garden Isle. After walking down for about .5-mile on Pine Forest Drive—and before crossing a drainage—take the road that drops away from the ridge and then contours seaward along the rim of **Kauhao Valley**. A mile after leaving Pine Forest Road, you come to a picnic area. Makaha Ridge isn't always a great lunch spot—during Hurricane Iniki in 1992, winds reached 227 mph, the most powerful ever recorded in Hawai'i.

The **Miloli'i vista** packs much of the scenic punch that you have to walk 10 miles and climb 2,000 feet to see on other ridge hikes. Make like a goat and wander down the crumbly red-dirt slopes that lead to near-vertical escarpments of the valley, about 1,500 feet high. There are many routes for curious and cautious hikers. *Be Aware:* Cliff

Nualolo Trail

edges are dangerous. Though not at this exact spot, fatalities have ocurred in Miloliʻi Valley, even among experienced hikers—including in 2007 to the island's beloved teacher and photographer, David Boynton.

BIKE: Beginning at the highway, the 4-mile **Makaha Ridge Road** is an easy roll in for cyclists, although you're looking at a 1,500-foot pump on the return leg. Cheaters can have someone drive down and pick them up. The paved road, which does have some dips along the way down, ends at a military guard gate. A side pedal to **Makaha Arboretum**, as per the hiking description above, is also a worthy excursion for mountain bikers.

65.   MILOLIʻI RIDGE   HIKE, BIKE

WHAT'S BEST: A long ride or hike to land's end on a little traveled Napali ridge.
PARKING: Take Hwy. 50 to Waimea and turn mauka toward Waimea Canyon on Hwy. 550. Go almost to mm14 and turn left on paved Makaha Ridge Rd. Go .3-mi. on Makaha Ridge Rd. and park off road on right at Miloliʻi Rd.

HIKE: Miloliʻi Ridge (11 mi., 1,800 ft.)

Miloliʻi Ridge road contours parallel to the highway for the first 1.25 miles, twisting through moist forest. It then drops and hooks seaward, beginning the first of its long descent over a 5.5-mile run. After 2.5 miles—amid a mature koa forest in the **Napali-Kona Forest Reserve**—you come to a picnic shelter. The shelter is set on a grassy flat with tree-filtered views of Makaha Ridge and Nualolo.

From the picnic area, the road becomes a wide trail. Most of the descent is over the last 3 miles. You drop on an eroded cut-bank, and then climb up and over two knobs that lie along the ridge. During the last 1.5 miles you descend more gradually, through a fresh-scented pine forest. Avoid spur trails and keep right as the trail keeps dropping. Finally, the road ends at a grass patch amid pine trees looking 1,600-plus feet down to **Miloli'i Beach**, where remnants of a heiau tell of the people who once lived there. Across the way is Nualolo Ridge. From the grass patch, you can walk up the eroded rise to your left, which leads out onto the ridge, with ultra views everywhere. Look for goats scampering about. *Be Aware:* Stay away from crumbling slopes.

BIKE: **Miloli'i Ridge** should be attempted by fit, experienced cyclists. Although not inherently dangerous—beyond the usual ruts, roots, slick mud and road debris—the road is a workout, with several steep segments. Less experienced mountain bikers might consider a "hike 'n' bike": Ride to the picnic area, about 2.5 miles in, and walk the rest of the distance.

66.   NUALOLO TRAIL   HIKE

WHAT'S BEST: Hike through the forests of Koke'e and break out to a narrow bench high above the Napali coast—one of the most exhilarating vistas in the world.
PARKING: Take Hwy. 50 to Waimea and turn mauka toward Waimea Canyon on Hwy. 550. Go .3-mi. past mm15 and look for trailhead sign on left, just before entering Koke'e State Park headquarters.

HIKE: Nualolo Trail to: Kuia Natural Area (.4-mi., 225 ft.), Napali Kona Forest Reserve (5.5 mi., 850 ft.), or Lolo Vista Point (7.75 mi., 1,600 ft.)

The steep and rutted **Nualolo Trail** descends through moist forest and then dry shrub lands to a precipitous terminus at **Lolo Vista Point**. Prepare for a challenging day hike. From the trailhead road, you jump up to the left and then climb for the first .25-mile, entering the **Kuia Natural Area Reserve**. From the area reserve you drop steeply, with difficult footing, through forest with the occasional clearing. Birds love it here. The descent continues, as forests give way to open areas, home to koa trees, ginger, and ferns. The trail swerves, making a left bend and then back to the right again as you descend a broad ridge top. About 2 miles in, you'll get the first blue-water views. At almost 3 miles from the trailhead, you enter the **Napali-Kona Forest Reserve**, as the trail drops steeply down a knob to drier, eroded relief.

Your route continues straight out the bench, descending steeply, and coming to the **Nualolo Cliff Trail** junction, which connects to the Awa'awapuhi Trail—although this trail *probably will be closed*. The last .5-mile of the Nualolo Trail is the big thrill. The trail drops down an eroded slope and onto the curving lip Nualolo Valley—a 2,000-foot free-fall to your right into a big bowl. Fortunately, the fall to the left into

Kawaiula Valley is not as sharp, and you can lean that way. The bench at Lolo Vista Point broadens out, with only dwarf flora in the vicinity, and it has a sturdy railing. Several Napali ridges provide views north and south. The rugged beach below where Nualolo Valley meets the Pacific is **Napali Coast State Park**. *Be Aware:* The earth is crumbly on the valley rim. There are places where people venture beyond the railing, but stay well back of edges.

More Stuff: The Nualolo Cliff Trail crosses around the rim of Nualolo Valley for 2 miles and connects with the Awa'awapuhi Trail, TH67. The Nualolo Cliff Trail can be in poor condition due to erosion—not recommended for those who fear heights. A car-shuttle hike between Nualolo and Awa'awapuhi trails is about 8.5 miles. If you plan this, inquire at the Koke'e Museum, since this trail *may be closed*.

67. KOKE'E STATE PARK — HIKE, BIKE

WHAT'S BEST: Discover the least-known face of Kaua'i, hidden in a birdland forest of countless varieties of trees, vines, and flowering shrubs. Repeat hikers and cyclists flock to these forests.

PARKING: Head toward Waimea Canyon on Hwy. 550. Go past mm15 and keep right at sign to Koke'e Museum and park headquarters. Continue on Hwy. 550 .1-mi. and turn right on Kumuwela Rd., which is marked with a sign to Camp Sloggett. Drive .4-mi. to first turnoff to the right and a sign for the camp and park. *Note:* The road beyond this junction is not always suitable for passenger cars.

Notes: If you plan on hiking this area extensively, stop by the museum and pick up an inexpensive park map. Plan on spending some time at the **Koke'e Museum** (Hui o Laka), which also serves as an interpretive center, gift shop, gallery and bookstore. In a beautiful setting, this is one of the best natural history museums in the state. The grand meadow in front is ideal for a picnic, and is also the site for the Queen Emma Polynesian Festival in October. Please donate.

HIKE: Halemanu-Koke'e Trail (2.5 mi., 375 ft.); Kumuwela-Waininiua loop (2.5 mi., 750 ft.); Ditch Trail loop (4.5 mi., 700 ft.); Berry Flat loop (2.75 mi., 250 ft.)

The **Halemanu-Koke'e Trail** is a good choice for birdwatchers and would-be botanists wishing a self-guided forest tour with easy hiking. Koa and ohia lehua trees dominate the forest, a drier forest that is still making a comeback from Hurricane Iniki in 1992. If you have a field guide, some plants to look for are mokihan, maile, pukiawe, hala-pepe, and ikiuki. Flitting among the branches, and providing the music, you may see i'iwi, apapane, elepio, and amakihi. In ancient times, exotic bird feathers were plucked here—the birds were captured and released.

To begin, walk toward **Camp Sloggett**—on the first road to the right off Halemanu Road—for .1-mile and look for the trailhead on your right. After 1.2 miles, the trail comes to **Halemanu Road**. You can turn around here; or make a longer loop hike by turning right on Halemanu Road. For a loop, follow Halemanu, keeping left, for about .2-mile to road's end, where you take an unnamed trail to the left. Stay on this trail for .2-mile to where you connect with **Faye Road**. Turn right on Faye, which joins Hwy. 550 in .5-mile, and from there it's another mile back to Koke'e and your car.

For the **Kumuwela-Waininiua loop**, walk to the next right turn from Kumuwela Rd, which is just past the Camp Sloggett Road. Go down the road, crossing **Koke'e Stream** near several cabins. About .25-mile after the stream crossing look for **Waininiua** trailhead on your left. The Waininiua Trail ascends gently but steadily for almost .5-mile, through koa trees and vines, before reaching a segment of **Kumuwela Road**. Turn right on Kumuwela. After a short distance a spur road leads to your left; this left turn goes to the **Ditch Trail** and you need to keep right. Continue on Kumuwela Road for 1.25 miles to where **Kumuwela Trail** comes in from the right, which is the route back to the car. You may wish to take a side-trip here: By continuing down Kumuwela Road for .5-mile to its end, you reach **Kumuwela Lookout**.

Turning right on **Kumuwela Trail**, you walk through dense woodlands, with a un-fathomable number of trees and shrubs. This woodland area, at the beginning of the 1900s was trampled and eroded by feral pigs and goats, with cows thrown in for good measure. In the 1930s, the animals were curtailed and a number of plants introduced. The trail continues for nearly 1 mile before reaching Kumuwela Road at its end. Walk Kumuwela Road, past the Waininiua trailhead and back to your car.

For the fairly strenuous **Ditch Trail loop** start out by following the above description for the Kumuwela-Waininiua loop. The Ditch Trail is perhaps the most scenic among

Kokee Museum

the interior Koke'e Trails. Inquire at the park museum or headquarters before taking this trail, however, as it sometimes deteriorates with bad weather. As you complete the Waininiua Trail section, and then turn right on Kumuwela Road, look for another road within .1-mile cutting back to your left. This is Waininiua Road, a .5-mile section that contours around and joins the Ditch Trail. Once at the Ditch Trail, turn left—the right-heading section is often not well-maintained. Turning left takes you both through woodlands and spots affording views of Po'omau Canyon. In about 1.5 miles of tough-walking terrain, the Ditch Trail joins with Mohihi Road. Go left on Mohihi Road, which becomes Kumuwela Road, and continue 1.75 miles back to your car.

The trailhead for **Berry Flat loop** is just under 1 mile in from Hwy. 550, at the first road that forks to your left. You can park at the Camp Sloggett Road, and walk to this trailhead, which adds .75-mile to the Berry Flat hike, making it about 3.5 miles roundtrip. Berry Flat, or Pu'u Kaohelo, is a forested nature trail, featuring koa, ohia, lehua, sugi pine and even a variety of redwood. Start up the road fork, which goes for .2-mile, and locate the trailhead on your left between two residences. The trail wiggles through a thicket of vines and ferns, under a shade canopy. At least two spur trails lead to nowhere; keep right as your contour in a circle for 2 miles, reaching Mohihi Road. Turn right on Mohihi and follow it back about .5-mile to your car.

More Stuff: For a loop of the Alakai Swamp-Pihea trail, you need to drive in 3.2 miles from Hwy. 550. Kumuwela Road becomes Mohihi Road. Although the road can be driven much of the way by passenger vehicles, it should be avoided in rainy conditions and is recommended for four-wheel drive. These trails provide other access to the swamp, which is described in TH68, Pu'uokila. *And More Stuff:* Mohihi Road continues for several more miles to Camp 10, with access to Po'omau Canyon Lookout Trail, Kohua Ridge Trail and Mohihi-Waialae Trail. Access to these trails should be in four-wheel drive vehicles. *Be Aware:* For all Koke'e trails bring rain gear and water. Keep your bearings and backtrack if you are unsure of your location.

BIKE: As you may gather from the hiking descriptions, the **Koke'e trails** lend themselves to mountain biking. **Kumuwela** and **Mohihi Camp roads** total 17 miles, and many visitors will consider this area more interesting riding than hiking. A mountain bike solves the dilemma of whether to take a rental car off-highway, which is a violation of most rental agreements. One hike-and-bike recommended for mountain bikers is to ride in about 4.5 miles on Mohihi Camp Road and take the walk to **Po'omau Canyon Lookout**, which is just after the road across Waiakoali Stream. The .5-mile walk takes you over a footbridge, passing Norfolk and sugi pines, to a viewpoint at the head of Po'omau Canyon. You look down to where this canyon joins Waimea Canyon. **Camp 10** is about 6 miles in on Mohihi Road, a slippery ride with stream crossings and a few roots to contend with.

WHAT'S BEST: This is one of Kaua'i's beauties. Hike through natural tropical gardens to an adrenaline-rush ridge, the jewel of the Napali. Or take a lesser-known adventure to the 'Valley of the Lost People.' Or, take a paved stroll from the car to a grand view. **PARKING:** Head up Waimea Canyon on Hwy. 550. Pass Koke'e Museum. *For Awa'awapuhi,* park at mm17 on left at signed trailhead. *For Valley of the Lost People,* continue to mm17.4 and park on the left at a dirt turnout, where the road makes a right, uphill bend with a concrete water ditch and berm on the right. *The Kalalau Valley Overlook* will be on the left, clearly signed near mm18.

HIKE: Awa'awapuhi (6.5 mi., 1,675 ft.); Valley of the Lost People (2.25 mi., 275ft.); Kalalau Lookout (.25-mi.)

The **Awa'awapuhi Trail** is to tropical ridges what the Golden Gate is to bridges and the Eiffel is to towers: powerfully beautiful and unique. For this reason it gets more hikers than many other trails, but not often overly crowded. The trail decends for most of its distance through abundant forest and then teeters across grassy spines to overlooks some 2,500 feet above the Napali Coast State Park. *Be Aware:* Prepare for rain and wind, and gear-up for a full-fledged day hike. Stay well back from cliff edges.

You begin walking through a good example of native dry forest, although dry for Kaua'i is different from dry in, for example, Nevada. The trail is in the **Napali-Kona Forest Reserve**, although the Awa'awapuhi Trail is managed as wilderness due to the rich number of native dryland plant species you see along the way. Just under 3 miles into the hike, the Nualolo Cliff Trail joins this trail from your left, which takes you 2

Awa'awapuhi

miles across the percipitous head of Nualolo Valley and joins the Nualolo Trail, TH66. As noted earlier, this connecting trail may be closed, so make inquiries.

The **Awaʻawapuhi overlooks** are less than .5-mile from the Nualolo junction, a breathtaking scamper to two different vantage points. You overlook the Nualolo and Awaʻawapuhi valleys, down vertical green escarpments. These valley floors, accessible only by boat, are part of the Napali Coast State Park. The right-side lookout gives up the point-blank view down to the valley. On the left, careful hikers can make their way down and across to a "goat perch," a platform of land that sticks out into the valley. Use utmost caution.

The **Valley of the Lost People** (formally called **Honopu Valley**) is where a band of the island's last Menehunes lived. The unoffical trail was closed due to deterioration, even before Hurricane Iniki in 1992, but local hikers manage to keep it passable—unless Mother Nature does a number. At the top of the bend in the highway, the trail starts as a level path through a thicket of vines and saplings. Stay left at a first junction after five minutes, and then go right at a second junction a few minutes later (plastic ribbons normally mark the spots). After nearly 20 minutes you'll reach another junction in a clearing—go *left* at this third junction, dropping through a fern hedge with overhanging trees. (Look down the valley to a knob on the ridge; the trail contours left around this knob.) After the descent, the trail traverses in the open, amid ferns and ohia. Honopu Valley is down to your left. Footing is tricky, but not dangerous. You contour around the front of the knob you viewed from above and find yourself in a healthy grove of koa trees, as well as red-flowering ohias. Pick your own turnaround.

New paths, tables, and a restroom make the **Kalalau Lookout** a sure thing for a family comfort stop. The view is a winner, though be sure to also continue to the Puʻuokila Overlook a mile ahead at the end of the road.

More Stuff: The **Kaluapuhi (Plumb) Trail** begins about .25-mile up Hwy. 550 from the Awaawapuhi trailhead; look for a red-dirt path heading up on a curve in the road. After 1.25-miles and 150 feet of climb, the trail pops back out to the highway .2-mile above the Kalalau Lookout—making for an easy car-shuttle option. Birds serenade the way through lush forest with wide-open spaces. Try Kaluapua on rainy or foggy days.

69.   PUʻUOKILA   HIKE

WHAT'S BEST: A tropicbird's view of Kalalau Valley, or a boardwalk into a primordial swamp to the edge of the world. (!!!) The lookout view graces book and magazine covers throughout the world—including *Kauaʻi Trailblazer*.

PARKING: Head up Waimea Canyon on Hwy. 550. Go past Kokeʻe State Park and the Kalalau Lookout at mm18. Continue 1 mi. to road's end at Puʻuokila Lookout.

Kalalau Valley from Pihea Trail

HIKE: Pihea Overlook (2 mi., 400 ft.); Alakai Swamp Trail to Queen Emma' Garden (3.75 mi., 300 ft.) or to Kilohana Overlook (7.5 mi., 950 ft.)

After taking in the view at the **Pu'uokila Lookout**, start down the trail along the rim of the valley, a rutted, often-slick slope that is indicative of the trail's worst parts for the first mile. *Be Aware:* Hiking poles will help. In some places, you'll need four limbs to negotiate the trail over sections of steps cut into hard-packed, greasy dirt—though the trail is not hazardous for the cautious hiker. The Pihea Overlook is on a hands-on spur trail beyond the junction with the Swamp Trail. At 4,280 feet, the **Pihea Overlook** is the highest point along the rim. You'll have to double back for the swamp trail.

To **Kilohana Overlook, Queen Emma's Gardens, and Alakai Swamp**, look for a signed junction a mile-plus from trailhead parking, just after completing a difficult hands-and-feet staircase. You drop down away from the rim, on a trail which at first is muddy and steep. But after a short distance you hit the boardwalk and series of stairs, rails, and ramps. But watch out for loose sections, although most the old two-plank walkway has been replaced by a new single-plank The rain forest is superlative. **Queen Emma's Gardens**, a particularly lush portion, is the flat section of the boardwalk about 1.5 miles into the hike. This trail approximates Queen Emma's route of personal healing, which she took often after the death of her husband King Kamehameha IV, and after the couple had lost their son, Albert, when he was a child. The queen's soirees were with hula dancers, who performed different rituals out of respect for each life-giving plant.

After about .75-mile on the boardwalk, you reach the **junction** with trails coming up from **Mohihi Road** (see TH67). To the Kilohana Overlook from the junction, go left toward Alakai Swamp. Don't forget to stop and admire the flora along the way. Not far after the junction, you descend on a long series of stairs and cross the stream. There's no boardwalk for a stretch as you climb up from the drainage through dwarf fauna on the other side. At the top, thankfully, the boardwalk begins again and continues through the 60-square-mile swamp—an open bog of ferns, grasses, shrubbery and dwarf trees spreading out at 4,000 feet above sea level. The caldera from Hawai'i's first eruption has evolved over millions of years to become the highest elevation swamp in the world. From edges of the swamp, including the ridge of **Mount Waialeale**, are the origins of all rivers and streams on the island.

Vegetation dwarfs and becomes more sparse over the last mile or so. Then the boardwalk ends at **Kilohana**, a small platform on the edge of the **Wainiha Pali**, 3,800-foot-high jungle cliffs rising above a river valley. If clouds are in your face, wait awhile since they are fickle and may well give you an opening, if you've been good. Wainiha Valley is a fissured green gorge similar in size to Waimea Canyon, but is rarely seen because it is privately held. See TH4. Hanalei Bay is in the center of a north shore view. *Be Aware:* Do not venture into the swamp. You'll be knee deep in mud and have a good chance of getting lost. When rain and fog come in, getting off the boardwalk can be a fatal mistake.

Alaka'i Swamp trail

A Brief History Of Kaua'i

Captain James Cook, an Englishman, made landfall in January of 1778 at Waimea Bay, thus "discovering" the "Sandwich Islands," though his real quest was for a fabled Northwest Passage to the Atlantic. But the Polynesians discovered Kaua'i about 16 centuries before the English, perhaps as early as 100 AD. The first Polynesians were from the Marquesas, an island group well below the equator, 2,400 miles to the southeast of Kaua'i and due south of California. What caused these Marquesans to take to the sea is not known, but their navigational skills remain a marvel of mythical proportions. The myth extends to the Americas, where some anthropologists suggest that early American peoples, those people known as the Anasazi, who pre-dated other tribal cultures in the Southwest, may have been of Polynesian descent.

The first Polynesians, perhaps coming in a series of migrations over the next several centuries, brought with them domestic animals, plants and seed stock to make a go of it in their new world. They became skilled stone workers, constructing many of the water ditches, agricultural terraces, fish ponds and heiaus—temples—that are in evidence today. Legend say these feats were accomplished by a mythical race of primitive engineers, tiny people, called the Menehunes.

The best guess now is that these Menehunes were actually the Marquesans, smaller in stature than the second wave of Polynesian settlers, who came from Tahiti as much as 1,000 years after the Marquesans. In the Tahitian language, the word for slave, or lower class worker is very close to today's "Menehune," giving credence to the theory that the Marquesans were subjugated and conquered by the Tahitians. The Marquesans who survived the Tahitian migration did so by retreating into river valleys, and, as recently as the late 1800s, the U.S. Census Bureau counted 65 "Menehunes" living in Wainiha Valley.

The Tahitian migrations are thought to have taken place in waves until the 1400s, including back-and-forth voyages on their double-hulled sailing canoes. Then, for reasons unclear, the migrations ceased and, like their predecessors, these Polynesian were on Kaua'i for good and without outside influence.

The second wave of Polynesians also brought with them domesticated animals, such as pigs, goats and dogs, as well as taro, breadfruit and other plants that were to sustain them over the next 400 years. Over the generations, the Hawaiians developed a way of life based on family communities sharing a self-sufficient plot of land, called an ahupua'a. The ahupua'a was usually a wedge-shaped plot, with an inland point encompassing a river or stream valley, and then fanning out over terraced agricultural lands to a seacoast.

From this ahupua'a, fruits, vegetables, livestock and sea foods—all that was needed to sustain the community—were cultivated by the members of the community, called the ohana. Today's aloha spirit has its roots in the ohana. Working together was a virtue among the Hawaiians, and all turned hands toward productivity. A person who was selfish and without friends did not survive in times of famine or natural calamity.

Hula Dancers

from a far away
friend here the mid-
Pacific
Angela H. Wright
Waimea Kauai

Aloha Nui

Early Kauaians lived in harmony with their surround for centuries, developing a philosophy that includes both their spiritual views and the accumulation of practical knowledge. Primary to this belief system is the 'ahupua'a (ah-hoo-poo-ah-ah), a division on land that includes a mountain stream valley and coast, providing all that is needed to sustain village life. The islanders' social fabric was held in check by a system of rules—the kapu—governing behaviors among individuals as well as their interactions with their natural world. Kapu violations of the severest nature were dealt with by swift capital punishment.

The Kauaian culture was transmitted over the generations by the hula—a dance performed by men and women, accompanied by chants and percussion—which kept alive both history and mythology. This ancient dance is alive today. The hula supplanted textbooks, for the Hawaiians had no written word. The Hawaiian alphabet of 12 letters and the spelling of all words were developed by academics.

To the Kauaians, place names, which sound similar and comically run-together to the Western ear, are very precise and descriptive. Each place on this complicated island was described in terms of its attributes and relation with all other places. Each place was part of an ahupua'a, which sustained the ohana (extended family), and all this fit together to make Kaua'i.

Hawaiian culture not only survived, it also thrived, and by the time of Captain Cook's arrival in 1778, the population of Hawai'i was about 600,000. Cook, an accomplished navigator and captain, had been leading an exploration of the South Pacific for a dozen years, searching for the theoretical Southern Continent. Ironically, he had been sailing right over it—Oceania, the Polynesian civilization of islands cast about the sea. Giving up on the Southern Continent, Cook set sail northward, this time in search of the illusive Northwest Passage.

Cook was on the furthest edge of the known world when his ships, the *Discovery* and *Resolution*, raised three islands, Oahu, Kaua'i and Ni'ihau. The ships dropped anchor in Waimea, staying not much longer than a vacation—about three weeks—making cursory notes and provisioning before resuming their quest. An officer with Cook was William Bligh, who was to lose the *Bounty* to mutiny ten years later.

A year later, Cook returned from North America, this time putting in at Kealakehua Bay on the Kona coast of the Big Island. He arrived during the Makahiki—a yearly time of celebration honoring the god of peace and fertility, Lono. His timely landing led local chiefs to proclaim that Cook himself was Lono. Cook's status as deity quickly wore thin, however, as his sea-weary men made increasingly greedy demands for women and food. After a few weeks, Cook and his men sailed from Kealakehua, but a storm damaged a ship's mast and they were forced to return.

Cook's return to Kona was as poorly timed as his arrival had been opportune. The Makahiki was over. While in harbor, local warriors stole one of Cook's cutters, a small boat. One thing led to another, a confrontation escalated. Cook was clubbed to death on the rocks of the bay, several Hawaiians were shot and Cook's ships skedaddled. Hawai'i was not visited by Western ships again for six years. Cook's arrival was coincident with the emergence of King Kamehameha the Great, nephew of an ali'i on the Big Island. Kamehameha was an intelligent, large man—over six-foot-six and north of three hundred pounds—whose political skills were matched by those as a warrior. By 1795 Kamehameha I, as he was later called, had unified all the islands under his rule, except for the island of Kaua'i.

Attempts to conquer Kaua'i were thwarted twice—once by the fierce waters on the Kaua'i Channel that separates it from Oahu, and a second time when the invading force was depleted by an illness that had been brought by Europeans. Kauaian warriors kept lookout for the invading ships for a dozen years, but the assault did not happen. Kaua'i did not come under Kamehameha's rule until Kaua'i's last ali'i, Kaumuali'i, voluntarily signed a treaty in 1810. The treaty was due in part to both kings' recognition that outside forces, represented by both American and Russian trading ships, were a part of the near future and it behooved the Hawaiians to be a unified people.

Kamehameha the Great ruled until 1819, during a time when whaling ships and other vessels traded with the Hawaiians to replenish their ships' stocks. The word was out on these abundant islands, and spreading fast. Sandalwood trade also flourished during the early 1800s, when forests of this fragrant wood on Kaua'i were denuded. Significantly, one year after Kamehameha's death, when his son, Liholiho or Kamehameha II, ascended the throne, the kapu system was abolished and the first New England Protestant missionaries arrived in Waimea. The onset of the missionaries left an American imprint on the islands, and dispelled any last hopes the Russians—who had built two forts on Kauaian soil—had of making Hawai'i a Russian territory.

Kamehameha's sons and grandsons, two of each, ruled the islands until 1872. During this time American influence came not just directly from the missionaries. The Gold Rush in California created a demand for Hawaiian sugar, meat and vegetables, and a decade later, the Civil War increased the demand for sugar, since the Union was cut off from Southern sugar supplies and had no other source to satisfy its sweet tooth. The development of the sugar industry—the first mill on Kaua'i was built in Koloa in 1835—also brought in workers from China, Japan and the Philippines to meet the labor demand. On Kaua'i since then no ethnic majority has existed, and therefore no minority. The blending of different races sharing an island is also part of the Aloha spirit, compatible with the concept of the ohana.

Another influence stemming from the mid-nineteenth century evident today is land ownership. About 41 percent of Kaua'i's land is owned by six private corporations and families who trace their purchases back to the 1800s. Owning land was not a concept in Polynesian culture.

The end of the Hawaiian monarchy came in 1893, the last year of the reign of its first woman leader—Queen Liliuokalani. Part of the monarchy's downfall was due to the excesses and economic foibles of the two kings after Kamehameha IV, Queen Liliuokalani's predecessors. A power struggle between the queen and her rivals—during which Queen Liliuokalani was betrayed—ended in a bloodless revolution. In 1898, about five hundred years after the Tahitians took over from the Marquesans, the U.S. Congress unlawfully annexed Hawai'i as a U.S. Territory. In 1900, Sanford B. Dole, a leader among plantation owners and one of Queen Liliuokalani's adversaries, became Hawai'i's first governor. In 1993, the U.S. formally apologized for the annexation.

Hawai'i's agriculture trade dominated development in the early 1900s, as more and more workers were brought in to meet demand. Most workers were from Japan, accounting for 40 percent of the island's population in 1930. U.S. Immigration put restrictions on Japanese immigration and workers from other Pacific locales were recruited. Tensions came to a head in 1941 when Pearl Harbor was attacked by Japanese planes. Midway Island, at the north of the Hawaiian Archipelago, became the strategic piece of real estate for American forces to defend.

In 1959, Hawai'i became America's fiftieth state, and thus the far north of Polynesia was linked with the way south of North America. Hawai'i is central to America's interests, both as a military force and an economic player with the Pacific Rim countries—the place where the Far East meets the West. In spite of this international context, visitors to Kaua'i will see that Hawaiian culture has endured. Hawai'i is the only state where the culture of its native peoples has retained such vitality, still the overriding influence on the island.

Driving Tours

Four drives feature the island's scenic, cultural, and historical points of interest, taking you on back roads as well as to major tourist attractions. The four tours together cover the whole island. Use the trailhead descriptions to explore more thoroughly the places mentioned in the tours.

Each tour can be driven in half-day to a day, but to see all the listed attractions takes well over a day—be selective. Some eateries and shops are mentioned in the text. Check *Resource Links* for other recommended places along the way.

McBryde Garden

top left going clockwise:
Haena
Hanalei taro
Waioli Mission House
Wailua Coast
Waimea Plantation Cottages
Poipu resort

DRIVING TOUR ONE

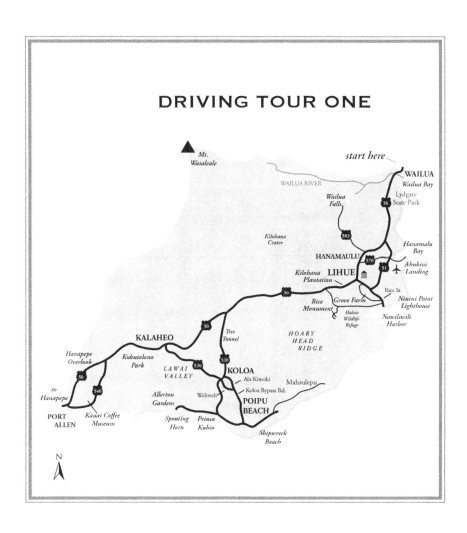

TOUR *one*

Waimea Falls, Hanamaulu Bay, Koloa Town, Poipu Beach, Allerton Garden, Spouting Horn, Kalaheo and Kauaʻi Coffee plantation. A good tour for a rainy day or for those wishing to see Kauaʻiʻs museums, historical buildings, and seaport.

START DRIVING TOWARD LIHUE ON HWY. 56. TURN RIGHT ON HWY. 583.

Wailua Falls is 4 miles up Hwy. 583, which is Maʻalo Road. Rainbows sometimes appear above the falls, especially in morning light when waters are brimming with storm runoff and mist roils from below. More often, twin cascades make the 80-foot plunge, which you may recognize as one of the shots for the opening of the television program, *Fantasy Island*. In ancient times, Kauaian chiefs would dive over the edge to prove their love and courage to chosen sweethearts.

BACKTRACK ON HWY. 583. TURN RIGHT ON HWY. 56.

Just after the turn, on the right you'll see **Kapaia Stitchery**, a must-stop for those interested in Hawaiian fabrics and quilts. Guys' bench is outside.

CONTINUE ON HWY. 56 AND TURN LEFT ON HWY. 570 WHICH IS AHUKINI ROAD. CONTINUE ON AHUKINI TOWARD AIRPORT, VEER LEFT AND TAKE AHUKINI ROAD 2 MILES TO END.

Ahukini Recreation Pier State Park, with its dilapidated labyrinth of a concrete pier, was the major port for the sugar industry until Nawiliwili Harbor was developed. Meaning "altar for many blessings," Ahukini today is where locals fish and talk story. The view inland is of **Hanamaulu Bay**, once the community of Portuguese cane workers. Above the bay, inland, is **Kalepa Ridge**, where Kauaian warriors kept a lookout for Kamehameha's invading army in the early 1800s, and U.S. servicemen kept a lookout for invading Japanese in the 1940s. Driving back out Ahukini Road you will notice the offices and take-off pads for many of the island's helicopter tour companies.

BACKTRACK ON AHUKINI ROAD AND TURN LEFT ON HWY. 51, KAPULE HWY. GO 1.25 MILE ON HWY. 51 AND TURN RIGHT ON RICE STREET. CONTINUE 1 MILE ON RICE STREET AND PARK NEAR UMI STREET.

Lihue was not much of a settlement until recent Kauaian history, in the late 1830s, when Kamehameha III's high chief was ordered to plant cane. The chief chose Lihue—meaning "gooseflesh" or "cold chill"—for its wetter clime.

Now the county seat, Lihue still has a number of buildings dating back to the 1800s—check out Kress Street which is two blocks down from Umi Street. If you're hungry, try the **Barbecue Inn** for local-style fare, or the **Hanamura Saimin Hut**. Don't wait for a rainy day to visit the **Kauaʻi Museum**, the lava rock building on Rice Street one block past Umi on Eiwa Street. The place is a visual treat. The main building colorfully depicts the nearly two centuries of Hawaii's history, tracing the aliʻi (royalty) from the first mariners to reach the Islands to the kings who traveled the world from here. An outrigger canoe, feather capes, and scads of tools, basketry, and

Kauai Museum, Lihue

other artifacts illustrated the tale. Included are recently salvaged items from the ship *Cleopatra*, which traveled the globe with Kamehameha II and later sank in Hanalei Bay. The annex building holds a potpourri of exhibits detailing Kauai's history after the landing by Captain James Cook in 1778. A large room holds the furnishings from sugar cane plantation homes. Movie posters tell of the island's post-WWII infulence on pop culture. Kauai's greatest surfers are honored, including the late Andy Irons from Hanalei, a three-time world champ. Check with the museum for special events featuring craftspeople and artisans.

CONTINUE UP RICE STREET PAST MUSEUM. TURN LEFT ON HALEKO ROAD. LOOK FOR LEFT-HAND TURN LANE, THE BLOCK BEFORE YOU GET TO THE STOP LIGHT.

Haleko Road takes you past what's left of the **Lihue Sugar Mill**, founded in 1849 and in operation until 2000. Most of Lihue's shopping areas, including **Kukui Grove Shopping Center** (local kine shops) were cane fields well into the 1900s.

CONTINUE ON HALEKO ROAD TO NAWILIWILI ROAD, WHICH IS HWY. 58. TURN LEFT ON NAWILIWILI ROAD, HEADING DOWNHILL TOWARD THE HARBOR.

Grove Farm Homestead

On the left, just past Aheahe Street, is **Grove Farm Homestead Museum**. Docents lead tours of the George Wilcox estate.

CONTINUE ON NAWILI-WILI ROAD FOR ABOUT .75-MILE AND VEER LEFT ON LALA ROAD.

Lala Road, which passes Kauaʻi High School, is the back road down to **Nawiliwili Harbor**. For a good view of Nawiliwili Harbor, veer right just past the school and drive up to **Kalapaki Memorial Park** at the top of the hill.

AT THE BOTTOM OF THE HILL, TURN LEFT, AND GO A SHORT DISTANCE AND PARK AT ANCHOR COVE SHOPPING CENTER OR NAWILIWILI BEACH PARK.

Nawiliwili Harbor is the main port for Kaua'i, both for glitzy cruise ships and get-down cargo freighters. A number of big gift shops cater to the wandering cruise ship passengers. Little do they know that during World War II, on New Year's Eve 1941, this harbor was shelled 15 times by a Japanese submarine but most of the shells were duds.

The **Kaua'i Marriott**, a world-class resort sitting above **Kalapaki Bay**, offers entertainment and Hawaiiana displays, including Prince Kuhio's vintage outrigger, *The Princess*. Both the lagoon at the resort's entrance and its poolside architecture are worth a visit. Then you can walk or drive out **Nawiliwili Jetty** for a view of the harbor, looking across the jetty to the **Kuki'i Point** light sitting at the edge of the golf course, and out to the mouth of the bay to **Ninini Point Lighthouse**.

CONTINUE, DRIVING AWAY FROM THE BAY ALONG THE HARBOR, ON WA'APA ROAD.

TURN LEFT ON WILCOX ROAD, PASS MATSON. TURN LEFT AT THE BOAT HARBOR.

Nawiliwili Small Boat Harbor, a nook in the bay sitting below majestic Hoary Head Ridge, is an anchorage for cruising sailboats You can take a short walk out the harbor's jetty to heighten the effect, and also check out the **Huleia Stream**, a kayaking spot.

BACKTRACK AND TURN LEFT AND THEN VEER LEFT ON HALEMALU ROAD.

In a short distance you'll come to the turnout on the left for the Alakoko, or **Menehune Fish Pond**, a pool alongside the stream built by the Menehunes more than 1,000 years ago. The Menehunes, several thousand workers, are said to

Kauai Marriott

have passed the stones from hand-to-hand from 25 miles away in Makaweli. The turnout also affords a view of the **Huleia National Wildlife Refuge**, which you can visit by kayak.

Menehune Fish Pond

CONTINUE ON HALEMALU ROAD FOR SEVERAL MILES, TURN LEFT ON KIPU ROAD AND FOLLOW TO END.

At the end of Kipu Road is the **Rice Memorial**, erected by Japanese workers after the plantation owner's death. The memorial is at the start of Rice's Norfolk pine-lined drive, heading on private property to Hoary Head Ridge.

BACKTRACK ON KIPU ROAD AND TURN LEFT AT JUNCTION WITH HALEMALU ROAD, DRIVING .5-MILE OUT TO HWY. 50. TURN LEFT ON HWY. 50, GO 3 MILES AND TURN LEFT TOWARD POIPU BEACH ON HWY. 520.

Highway 520 is known as the **Tree Tunnel**, named for the shaded corridor formed by the eucalyptus trees that border the road. The trees were damaged by direct blasts from hurricanes—Iwa in 1982, and Iniki in 1992.

CONTINUE TO KOLOA ON HWY. 520. TURN LEFT AT STOP SIGN AND THEN TURN RIGHT ON WELIWELI ROAD.

Koloa, which means "long cane," was the bustling center of Kaua'i

Koloa Town

from the building of the first sugar mill here in 1835 to the latter part of that century. An early mission was established here also, in 1835, by the Gulick family. Today, Koloa's town square and shops make it one of the better places on the island to walk around amid fragments of another time. Grab a cone and get lost in the small historical courtyard or stop at the **Snack Shop** outdoor counter for a local-style plate lunch of mahi-mahi, some Portugese

Koloa Snack Shop walk-up window

soup, or a hot-off-the-grill teriyaki burger. Poke around the back streets, since there's more than meets the eye here.

CONTINUE ON **WELIWELI** ROAD.

Note a right turn for **St. Raphael's Catholic Church**, a short distance off the road. St. Raphael's is the oldest Catholic Church on Kaua'i, built in 1854.

CONTINUE ON **WELIWELI**, FOLLOWING SIGNS FOR **POIPU**—**TURN RIGHT** ON **ALA KINAIKI**, THE BYPASS ROAD.

Grand Hyatt lagoon pool

Just as you near the bottom of the grade, look to your left for a glimpse of the crater, called **Pu'u Wanawana**, left by the island's last volcanic activity. Only a few lava spires stick up from cacti and brush. **TURN LEFT** AT STOP SIGN

On your right will be the **Grand Hyatt Kaua'i**, one of the world's best tropical resorts, and definitely worth a walk-through and perhaps a lunch or beverage at the Ilima Terrace restaurant. The resort is situated on **Shipwreck Beach**, even though the wrecks are now gone.

CONTINUE PAST **HYATT** ON **WELIWELI** ROAD. ROAD BECOMES **DIRT, BUT GRADED. PASS** ROAD TO STABLES, AND FOLLOW SIGNS TO **KAWAILOA**

Koloa Sugar Mill

BAY. IF YOU DON'T WANT TO DRIVE ON DIRT ROADS, OR WANT TO SPEND TIME ELSEWHERE, SKIP TO BACKTRACK BELOW.

Mahaulepu Beach at Kawailoa Bay was the site of a 13th century battle in which a Kauaian king outfoxed an invading armada of ships led by a king from the Big Island, who had already subjugated the rest of Hawai'i. This was 400 years before Kamehameha the Great failed twice to invade the island with consolidated forces. At Mahaulepu are rugged seascapes and a view of the other side of Hoary Head Ridge.

For a side-trip from the gated entrance to Kawailoa Bay, go straight on the cane road to the **Koloa Sugar Mill**, on the site of the original mill of 1835. Sugar production ceased in the late 1990s, and tropical foliage is creeping up the sprawling structure. (This road may be closed, so you will have to view from a distance.)

BACKTRACK TO THE HYATT. CONTINUE TO STOP SIGN ON WELIWELI ROAD AND TURN LEFT ON PE'E ROAD. PE'E ROAD CONNECTS WITH HO'ONE ROAD.

Pe'e Road takes you over a bluff, through beachside condos and homes and down to **Brennecke's Beach**, a popular surfing spot next **Poipu Beach County Park**. The park is the site for various weekend cultural events and fairs.

CONTINUE ON HO'ONE ROAD AND TURN RIGHT AT BEACH PARK ON HO'OWILI ROAD. THEN TURN LEFT AT STOP SIGN ON POIPU ROAD.

Mahaulepu

At the corner of Poipu Road is the restoration of the ancient village site of **Kahua o Kaneiolouma**. You'll see a lava wall at the corner, framing carved statues (called ki'i). Poipu Road bypasses the resorts, but is next to **Poipu Village**, a shopping mall with well known eateries (Roy's, Keoki's). To get a look at Poipu resorts, turn past the village toward the Sheraton on Kapili Road. Kapili Road quickly joins Hoʻonani Road, at the **Sheraton**. Also worth seeing are the **Moir Gardens** at the Outrigger Kiahuna Plantation across from the Sheraton. Going away from the Sheraton on Hoʻonani—or to your right as you come down—in about .5-mile you come to Koloa Landing at Whalers Cove, once the third most-used port in Hawaiʻi.

CONTINUE ON POIPU ROAD, TURN LEFT ON THE ROUNDABOUT TOWARD SPOUTING HORN ON LAWAI ROAD.

Poipu Beach

In less than a mile on Lawai Road, you come to **Prince Kuhio Park**, with its monument marking the 1871 birthplace of the prince who was the Territory of Hawaiʻi's congressional delegate until 1922. The park features remains of a homesite and heiau. Not far beyond Kuhio Park, on your right, is the visitors center for the **National Tropical Botanical Garden**. At the center are a gift shop and interpretive displays, and also a self-guided walk of the center's gardens. The center is also where you sign up for tours of **Allerton Garden** and **McBryde Garden**. The nearby gardens, once the favorite of Queen Emma, are now devoted to horticultural research and saving tropical plants.

Across the street from the visitors center is **Spouting Horn**, where wave-pressurized sea foam shoots geyser-like into the air from a hole in the lava reef. The gushing white water is a long-standing roadside attraction.

BACKTRACK ON LAWAI ROAD, TURN LEFT IN THE ROUNDABOUT ON ALA KA-LANIKAUMAKI RD. A SHORT DISTANCE.

The Shops at Kukuiula Village offers 50 cialty stores and many restaurants that feel like old sugar cane town. Touristy, yes, but they pulled it off. Dining ranges from Bubba's Burgers and **Kiawe Roots** to gourmet **Merriman's**, as well as island-organic **Living Foods**. A courtyard curves through palms and gardens of heliconia, ferns, and bananas. Tommy Bahama and Quiksilver add to a tropical shopping experience. For hair and body care, stop in at **Malie**. For Hawaiian

Merriman's

Allerton Gardens

handmade wares, the **Ohana Shop** is the place to stop in. For a rocking good time, come on a Wednesday at 3:30 for the **Kukui-ula Culinary Market**: music, tons of organic produce, and local artisan food.

CONTINUE UP ALA KALANIKAUMAKI RD. AND THEN TURN LEFT ON HWY 530, WHICH IS KOLOA ROAD.

Koloa Road takes you up through pastoral **Lawai Valley**. At the top of the grade past the old pineapple buildins is **Warehouse 3540**, epicenter for the growing art scene. Among the home grown artisans inside is **Ocean Paper**, creator of gift-quality cards and in-demand pigments for water colors. At the junction with Highway 50 on the right is **Hawaiian Trading Post**, known for its large collection of museum-quality Niʻihau shell necklaces. (Turn right at the highway to see Lawai town, and **Monkeypod Jam Company**—made onsite with local fruits. Try the tasting room. Yum!)

TURN LEFT ON HIGHWAY 50

Immediately on your left is small Wawae Road, entrance to the **88 Holy Places of Kobo Daishi**, a revered Buddhist-insprired shrine. The shrines are just beyond the gate for the **Lawai International Center**, to your right. It's open on the second and last Sundays of the month, or by appointment; 639-4300. Each miniature shrine is named for a Buddhist saint. The number 88 signifies the 88 sins committed by man, and it is believed that pilgrims worshiping here will be released from sins. Might as well give it a try. New on site is the **Hall of Compassion**, built using authentic 13th Japanese methods. Just past the shrines on Highway 50 is another spiritual place. Turn right near mm11 at Anuhea Place to see the factory that cooks **Kukui jams**. Inside is the sacred spot where Jimmy the Jar Man tightened lids for 25 years.

88 Holy Places of Kobo Daishi

CONTINUE ON HIGHWAY 50, 2 MILES TO KALAHEO. TURN LEFT AT LIGHT ON PAPALINA ROAD. CONTINUE 1 MILE AND TURN RIGHT ON

PU'U ROAD TO ENTER KUKUIOLONO PARK.

From the pavilion on the large knoll in **Kukuiolono Park** is a commanding view of the south and west coasts. On the grounds are small Japanese and Hawaiian gardens, as well as a collection of stones carved on by the Menehunes. Kukuiolono—which means "Lono's light," after the god of peace and fertility—was once the site of several heiaus and later the estate of sugar magnate Walter McBryde. McBryde, who is buried here, beautified the grounds in honor of his mother.

BACKTRACK TO HWY. 50. TURN LEFT ON HWY. 50. PASS THROUGH KALAHEO. CONTINUE ON HWY. 50, PASSING THE JUNCTION WITH HWY. 540, FOR 2 MILES. STOP AT HANAPEPE OVERLOOK.

Hanapepe Overlook is a preview for the beginning of Tour Four. From the rim of the canyon is a view of the lush river agricultural fieldss. The coffee orchard across the highway has a history of its own. In 1824, the last battle on Kaua'i took place here, a failed revolt led by Prince Humehume, the son of Kaua'i's last king. Prince Humehume would not accept his father's treaty with Kamehameha's forces.

CONTINUE DOWN HWY. 50. TURN LEFT BEFORE PORT ALLEN ON HWY. 540, WHICH IS HALEWILI ROAD. CONTINUE 1.5 MILES ON HWY. 540 TO KAUA'I COFFEE MUSEUM.

In addition to offering free samples of the local brew, **Kaua'i Coffee Visitors Center and Museum** exhibits planta-

Kukuilono Park, Kauai Coffee, Hanapepe Overlook

Kilohana Plantation

tion artifacts and shows a video detailing coffee production from the tree to the mug. Alexander & Baldwin sugar cane fields (now owned by an Italian corporation, Massimo Zanetti) were converted to the beans, and Kaua'i now surpasses Kona as the largest coffee grower in the islands. Work off the coffee high on a self-guided tour on a paved path, or on guided tours every two hours, starting at 10.

CONTINUE UP HWY. 540 BACK TOWARD HWY. 50 AT KALAHEO.

To your right as you head up Highway 540 is **Numila**, or "New Mill," with its row of classic sugar shacks. On the coast below Numila, which is private property, are two ancient fishing shrines and Nomilu Pond, a crater filled with seawater, where goddess Pele made her last attempt to make a home on Kaua'i.

TURN RIGHT AT HWY. 50, HEADING BACK TOWARD START OF TOUR.

Just after passing Kipu Road, look on the right for **Kaua'i Nursery & Landscaping**. Though set up to service landscapers, the nursery's many acres include a huge covered area (a rainy-day stop) with thousands of exotic and native plants and trees. Take your own free botanical tour. The nursery is certified to ship orchids.

A little farther on the highway is the **Kilohana Plantation Estate**, one of the top attractions in Kaua'i. Built in the 1930s, Kilohana is a 16,000-square-foot Tudor mansion, once home to the island's prominent Wilcox family. Wagon tours are available around the estate's 35 acres of manicured gardens and cane fields—wander around, but heed privae propery. Inside are top-rated Gaylord's Restaurant, fine art shops, locally crafted giftware, and history exhibits. A popular Sunday buffet features a history talk. Encircling the grounds is the **Kaua'i Plantation Railway**, a tour of agriculture fields aboard beautiful mahogany cars that are replicas of King David Kalakaua's Oahu Railroad. Kids will love the stop to feed wild pigs.

DRIVING TOUR TWO

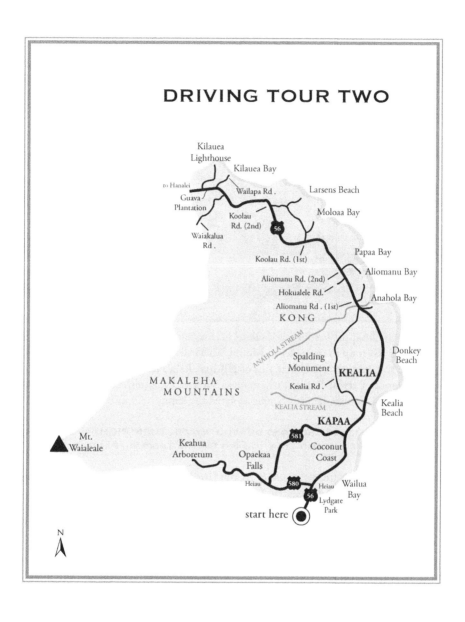

Kilauea
Lighthouse
Kilauea Bay
to Hanalei
Wailapa Rd .   Larsens Beach
Guava
Plantation
Koolau
Rd. (2nd)   Moloaa Bay
56
Waiakalua
Rd .
Koolau Rd. (1st)
Papaa Bay
Aliomanu Rd. (2nd)   Aliomanu Bay
Hokualele Rd.
Aliomanu Rd . (1st)   Anahola Bay
KONG
ANAHOLA STREAM
Spalding   Donkey
Monument   Beach
MAKALEHA   KEALIA
MOUNTAINS   Kealia Rd .
KEALIA STREAM   Kealia
Beach
KAPAA
Mt.   581
Waialeale   Keahua   Coconut
Arboretum   Opaekaa   Coast
Falls
Heiau   580   Heiau   Wailua
56   Bay
start here   Lydgate
Park

N

TOUR Two

Heiaus of Wailua Bay, Opaeka'a Falls, Kamokila Village, Keahua Arboretum, Kapa'a Town, Royal Coconut Coast, Sleeping Giant, Kong and Anahola Mountains, Larsens Beach, and Kilauea Lighthouse and Wildlife Refuge. A tour that blends scenery with shops, and beachcombing with resort beaches.

START DRIVING FROM LIHUE TOWARD WAILUA ON HWY. 56. TURN RIGHT ON LEHO DRIVE, BEFORE REACHING WAILUA RIVER. FOLLOW SIGNS TO LYDGATE PARK.

The mouth of the **Wailua River**, at today's **Lydgate Park**, is the cradle of Hawaiian civilization, where the royal ali'i built the first of seven sacred heiaus that led from here inland, following the Wailua River up to its source at Mount Waialeale. At a site on the grassy slope up from the river mouth are the remains of **Hikina'akala Heiau**. This area was also the site of **Hauola City of Refuge**, where miscreants and vanquished enemies could do time or escape punishment for having violated the kapu.

CONTINUE, TAKING LEHO ROAD OUT TO HWY. 56. TURN RIGHT ON HWY. 56, AND TURN LEFT IMMEDIATELY TOWARD SMITHS TROPICAL PARADISE.

Across Highway 56 from the resort is the largely intact, but hard-to-find, **Malae Heiau**. **Smiths Tropical Paradise** features luau hula shows and its own (excellent) tropical garden, and nearby are boat rides (do it!) to **Fern Grotto** up the **Wailua River**. The genuine, family-run gardens are one of Hawaii's top attractions and best tourist values. At Wailua State Park Marina is a postcard view of the river and Sleeping Giant.

BACKTRACK AND TURN LEFT ON HWY. 56, CROSS RIVER AND TURN LEFT ON HWY. 580, WHICH IS KUAMO'O ROAD. CONTINUE .25-MILE AND PARK ON LEFT AT WAILUA RIVER STATE PARK POLIAHU AREA.

Smiths Tropical Paradise

Located here are **Pohaku Hoʻoanau—Royal Birthstones**—on which the after-birth of royal babies were ceremoniously placed. The attributes of the animal which ate the afterbirth foretold the fortune of the child. This was also the site of the third heiau from the sea, Holoholoku Heiau, said to be used for human sacrifices. Across the street is another king's sacred site—the long-defunct **Coco Palms Resort**, where Elvis filmed *Blue Hawaii*. The Coco Palms will be remembered by longtime Kauaʻi visitors for its nightly torch-lighting ceremony, enacted to the sound of drum beats and an exotic narration. The lagoon

Coco Palms lagoon

predates the resort, built for Queen Emma in the 1800s. Behind the resort is the **Royal Coconut Grove**, for which this area is also well-known. The resort was closed by Hurricane Iniki in 1992, and plans to rebuild have floundered.

CONTINUE UP HWY. 580.

In less than 2 miles, look on the left for **Poliahu Heiau**, formerly the residence of kings—the aliʻi. The **Bell Stone**, a short walk down a nearby trail, was used to ring in a royal birth. Great views of the river are to be had from this five-star heiau.

CONTINUE UP HWY. 580.

Kamokila Village

On the right not far from the heiau is **Opaekaʻa Falls**, only 40 feet in height, but with a thunderous flow, especially during storms. Be sure to take the crosswalk to the other side of the highway to catch a panorama of the **Wailua River**. Just beyond the falls on the highway, a steep road veers to the left to **Kamokila Village**, a recreated folk village showing the ancient Hawaiian way of life. The riverside village, family-owned for generations and once a set for the movie *Outbreak*, is a quick-take on the ancient Hawaiian ways. Admission is cheap. Their tranquil docks are a good place to rent kayaks. For different cultural respite, drive farther up the road to the **Kauaʻi Hindu Monastery** (turn left near mm4.5 on Kaholalele Road).

Keahua Arboretum

CONTINUE up Hwy. 580 for 5 miles, passing the junction with Hwy. 581, to END OF ROAD at Keahua Arboretum. To bypass the arboretum, turn right on Hwy. 581, and skip paragraph below.

A spillway marks the end of the road for most rental car drivers, and to take a short walk around the **Keahua Forestry Arboretum** you may have to get your feet wet. If the water is low, drive across the spillway and park. The nearby University of Hawai'i station has set up an educational walk among native and exotic trees. The arboretum is also the taking-off point for a number of hikes, including one toward the Blue Hole at Mount Waialeale basin.

BACKTRACK on Hwy. 580. TURN LEFT on Hwy. 581, which is Kamalu Road.

This wide, green valley above the sea was where royal families made their homes and cultivated crops. You'll drive along the mountainside of the Sleeping Giant, so readily visible from Kapa'a and many places on the island. The **Sleeping Giant** is part of **Nounou Forest Reserve**, featuring a wide variety of species planted in the 1930s.

CONTINUE on Hwy. 581 and TURN RIGHT on Olohena Road, which is a continuation of Hwy. 581. CONTINUE on Olohena to Kapa'a. PARK before reaching stoplight.

Coconut Coasters

KIKO

Funky **Kapa'a Town** is the capital of island-style, a blend of Kaua'i's ethnic groups in a beachside community that is all local kine. Kapa'a was once the pineapple center of the island and fell on hard times when the industry cratered in the mid-1900s. Several beach parks border cottages along the coast, and the town's triangular "downtown" section. You'll discover a lot just poking around. Hemp kids hang around for the veggie stuff at **Mermaids Cafe**. Not far down the road are two places to feel like a local: **Kauai Juice Company**, and—next to Jim Saylor Jewelers on the main drag—**KIKO**, an arty-fun giftstore that holds the loving collection of three women with a lifetime of experience on the island. On the other end of town is low-key surf shop, **Tamba**, known-world wide by top surfers; buy a hat and you will be with-it on all Hawaiian beaches. The late Andy Irons, a world champ, started the trend. Low-key celebs hang at the **Art Cafe Hemingway**; try breakfast. **NoKa Fair** (North Kapa'a) is a community of colorful mini-cabins connected by a deck. Out front, look to **Chita's Fashion** for handmade aloha wear and accessories. But the big surprise is at the back, where a longtime New York fashion designer has opened **Ocean By the Sea Company**. For more locally produced art and keepsakes try the unassuming **Kaua'i Store**, just down the road; it's legit.

CONTINUE TO HWY. 56. TURN LEFT ON HWY. 56, AND CONTINUE TO KEALIA.

In 1877, the hills around **Kealia** were planted in sugar cane by Captain James Make'e. The former haul road along the coast from the beach also leads to a pier, used when Kapa'a's pineapple cannery was thriving. Just beyond the pier is **Donkey Beach**.

TURN LEFT ON KEALIA ROAD, ACROSS FROM MAIN GATE AT KEALIA BEACH.

Kong

Keep to your right on Kealia Road. On Mondays and Fridays, the open field becomes a farmers market. Next, the road climb heading toward the two rows of tall Norfolk pines at **Spalding Monument**. The stone edifice marks the former plantation of Colonel Zephaniah Spalding, son-in-law of Make'e.

TURN RIGHT AT SPALDING MONUMENT.

Anahola Beach Park

This portion takes you on an up-close look of **Kong**, a.k.a. Kalalea, the sharp peak in the Anahola Mountains. On top of Kong is a ruined heiau of three terraces. At the base of Kong was the **Hole in the Mountain**, which, legends told, was formed when a visiting king from the Big Island threw his spear clean through the ridge. The opening almost caved in during the late 1990s.

CONTINUE DOWN KEALIA ROAD TO HWY. 56. TURN LEFT ON HWY. 56 AND TURN RIGHT IMMEDIATELY ON ANAHOLA ROAD. CONTINUE .25-MILE ON ANAHOLA ROAD AND VEER LEFT AT BEACH PARK ON KAMANE ROAD.

The valley around **Anahola** was designated by the Land Act of 1895 as a settlement in which Hawaiians could acquire lands on 999-year leases. The Act was augmented in 1956 by the **Hawaiian Homelands** project, which allowed Hawaiians to finance homes on formerly government-leased sugar cane fields.

BACKTRACK TO HWY. 56 AND TURN RIGHT. CROSS OVER BRIDGE, PASSING THE STORE AND POST OFFICE AND TURN RIGHT ON ALIOMANU ROAD (FIRST). FOLLOW ALIOMANU DOWN TO THE RIVER MOUTH.

Anahola Bay, all of it a beach park, is split in two by the **Anahola Stream**—you can look across the bay to the other side of the park. **Aliomanu Bay** is to your left as you face the water. When you get back out to the highway, follow your nose across the street to the photogenic **Ahahola Baptist Church** (formerly Hongwanji Mission). The Anahola Mountains provide the scenic backdrop.

CONTINUE ON NORTH HWY. 56 TO JUST PAST MILE MARKER 14 AND TURN LEFT ON HOKUALELE ROAD.

This road, a dead end after less than one mile, gets you as close to **Kong** as you can get in a car. Along the way, you may see self-serve stands for gardenias and local produce.

BACKTRACK ON HOKUALELE ROAD TO HWY. 56 AND TURN LEFT. CONTINUE ON HWY. 56 AND TURN RIGHT ON

Moloa'a Bay

KO'OLAU ROAD (FIRST), WHICH IS PAST MILE MARKER 16. AFTER ABOUT 2 MILES ON KO'OLAU, TURN RIGHT ON MOLOA'A ROAD. FOLLOW MOLOA'A ABOUT 1 MILE DOWN TO BAY.

On the left before Ko'olau Road are roadside stands offering local produce, leis, and perhaps huli huli chicken fresh off the grill. At the highway turnoff to Ko'olau Road is **Moloa'a Sunrise Fruit Stand**. Along the road beyond the the fruit stand are dirt roads leading to small farms, including **Moloa'a Oranica'a**. Look for them at farmer's markets. It's okay to drive these backroad, but not into driveways. Next up is the paved road takes you down a lush tropical valley to scenic **Moloa'a Bay**. Fans of *Gilligan's Island* will like to know the television

Anahola

program was shot here. Moloa'a, meaning "tangled roots," was the island's main region for producing tapa, the paperlike cloth made from mulberry bushes.

BACKTRACK ON MOLOA'A ROAD AND TURN RIGHT ON KO'OLAU ROAD. CONTINUE ON KO'OLAU A LITTLE MORE THAN ONE MILE AND TURN SHARPLY RIGHT AT WHITE BEACH ACCESS POLE.

This road takes you one mile out to **Larsens Beach**, a pristine coral-reef beach perfect for strolling. You look down on the beach from the parking lot, an easy .25-mile walk. But don't forget to look seaward: whales and dolphins have been known to breach offshore, and seabirds, such as albatrosses and tropicbirds, might be winging about. *Be Aware:* Nudists.

Larsen's Beach

BACKTRACK TO KO'OLAU ROAD, TURN RIGHT, AND CONTINUE TO HWY. 56. TURN RIGHT AND CONTINUE TO MILE MARKER 21 AND TURN LEFT ON WAIAKALUA ROAD.

This one-mile, dead-end road is part of **Kilauea Farms**. Some of the island's organic fruit and vegetable growers reside up this pastoral drive. Waiakalua Road gives you a look at the open, grassy upslopes along this part of Kaua'i.

Na Aina Kai Botanical Gardens, Christ Memorial Episcopal Church

BACKTRACK TO HWY. 56 AND TURN LEFT. CONTINUE ON HWY. 56 AND TURN RIGHT ON WAILAPA ROAD, WHICH IS BEFORE YOU GET TO MILE MARKER 22. GO ALMOST .5-MILE AND VEER LEFT, DOWN A DIRT ROAD THAT ENDS AFTER .5-MILE.

Kilauea Bay has a large sandy beach and scenic stream, which borders the bluffs of the Kilauea Wildlife Refuge. At the end of Wailapa Road are the fanciful grounds of the **Na Aina Kai** botanical gardens—a must for green-thumbers and families with kids, who will like the village re-creation. Guided tours whiz through arboretum gardens, highlighted by a forest of bronze statues in lifelike settings.

BACKTRACK TO HWY. 56 AND TURN RIGHT. AT MM22.5 TURN LEFT ON KUAWA ROAD.

On the left, look for the store-on-wheels that is **Kaua'i Farmacy**, a tea-shop extraordinaire. Herbs are grown out back (turn left .4-mile from the highway), and the blends are complex and enticing. Owner Doug Wolkin's garden plot is a masterwork of biodiversity. At the end of Kuawa Road is **Common Ground** an organic garden

Anaina Hou community gardens

Anaina Hou Park, Silver Falls Ranch

and restaurant—though the grounds have new owners, and it's currently closed. Same goes for short trail (part of Wai Koa Trail) to an idyllic old stone dam; probably closed through 2019 due to flood damage.

CONINTUE ON HWY. 56 JUST PAST KILAUEA

Banana Joe's is a local institution, these days there's no Joe and seldom bananas; the main draw now is **Garden Island Chocolate**, offering farm tours. Behind Joe's is **Garden Ponds Nursery**, home to floating ecosystems in large pots. But the main event is next door at **Anaina Hou Community Park:** A unique mini-golf course through a botanical garden; cafe with wifi and locally made gifts; the 5-mile **Wai Koa Loop Trail** through ag lands; and farmers markets on Saturdays and Monday. Check it out. Then go back to the highway and turn left for a mile and then left again on **Kahiliholo Road**, which goes up several miles past opulant homes with sprawling gardens. On the left near the bottom is the **nonprofit dog park** (that connects to the Wai Koa Loop Trail). Near the top (go left on Kamo'okoa) is the main attraction in these uplands, trail rides at **Silver Falls Ranch** set in lush forests below Kalihiwai Ridge.

BACKTRACK TO HWY. 56 AND
TURN RIGHT TOWARD KILAUEA.

Kilauea was shaken by the 1971 closure of the Kilauea Sugar Mill, but has since reinvented itself as a tourist stopover and bedroom community for both the north shore and Kapa'a. Helping attract tourists is **Christ Memorial Episcopal Church**—located on Kolo Road—a small edifice built of lava rock and featuring detailed stained-glass

Kilauea farmers market

windows. Just down Kolo from this church is St. Sylvester's Church, an octagonal building of lava rock, featuring frescoes by Jean Charlot.

TURN LEFT ON KILAUEA ROAD AND CONTINUE TWO MILES TO END, AT LIGHT-HOUSE.

On the way to the lighthouse, browsers will want to stop at **Kong Lung**, a classy gift store and art store. In the courtyard **Coconut Style & Tugu** is a sartorial art world, with handcrafted aloha shirts and quilts. Outside the courtyard (next to the church), **Palate Wine Bar** offers bottles that make cheese a celebration. Across the street are stone-block storefronts; check the upscale **Kauai Juice** and **Kilauea Fish Market**. But to feed your mind, go to **Hunter Gatherer**: it's pleasing experience that is hard to pigeonhole as simply a gift store-gallery. The long-planned **Kilauea Lighthouse Village** shops are due to open in 2019.

Kilauea Natonal Wildlife Refuge and Lighthouse is the northern-most part of the populated Hawaiian Islands. From the tip of the bluff, you look down on tiny, wave-washed **Mokuaeae Island**. Among the birds soaring and flitting about are Laysan albatrosses, able to fly thousands of miles over oceans; great frigatebirds, ; tropicbirds; nene, or Hawaiian goose, the state bird; plovers; red-footed boobies; and wedge-tailed shearwaters, which nest around the visitors center near the lighthouse. The **Daniel K. Inouye Lighthouse** was built in 1913, featuring a French-made, 12-foot-high Fresnel lens, the tallest in the world. Free tours are available. *Note: Hwy. 56 at Kilauea is where Tour Two connects with Tour Three.*

Silver Falls Ranch, Laysan albatross

DRIVING TOUR THREE

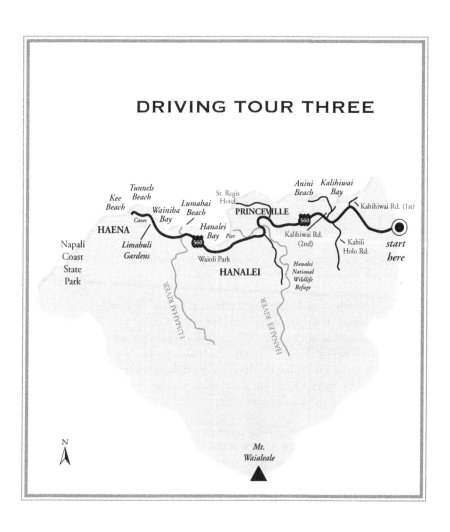

Tunnels Beach
Kee Beach
Anini Beach
Kalihiwai Bay
St. Regis Hotel
Lumahai Beach
Kahihiwai Rd. (1st)
Wainiha Bay
PRINCEVILLE
Caves
HAENA
Hanalei Bay Pier
560
Kalihiwai Rd. (2nd)
Kahili Holo Rd.
start here
Napali Coast State Park
Limahuli Gardens
560
Waioli Park
HANALEI
Hanalei National Wildlife Refuge
LUMAHAI RIVER
HANALEI RIVER
N
Mt. Waialeale

TOUR  Three

Anini Beach, Kalihiwai Bay, Princeville, Hanalei Town and Wildlife Refuge, caves, hula temple, and all the beaches along the tropical paradise of the north coast. Start early, especially on sunny days when road's end attracts many visitors.

START ON HWY. 56 IN KILAUEA AND PROCEED TOWARD HANALEI. CONTINUE ON HWY. 56, AND TURN RIGHT ON KALIHIWAI ROAD (FIRST), BEFORE MILE MARKER 24. FOLLOW ROAD ABOUT 1 MILE DOWN TO THE END.

Kalihiwai Bay is a locals' beach, for picnicking and surfing. Kalihiwai Bay was twice devastated by tidal waves, in 1946 and 1957. This bay historically was a favorite spot for a hukilau—when people of the ohana would gather and haul in a huge fishing net, reaping a bounty of fish, while shouting in unison, "Huki!" Surfers love the point break; a prime viewing spot is at the guardrail on the way down to the beach park.

BACKTRACK ON THE HIGHWAY, CROSS THE BRIDGE AND TURN RIGHT AFTER MILE MARKER 25 TOWARD ANINI BEACH PARK.

Along **Anini Beach** is the longest coral reef in Hawai'i. Windsurfers, kite-boarders, snorkelers, campers, and even polo players enjoy the pleasant park space that borders a two-mile beach. You can spot old-timers on Kaua'i if they call this place "Wanini Beach," its name before the "W" fell off a highway sign that no one bothered to fix. When leaving Anini for Princeville, look on the right at a large turnout for the **Coconut Experience**, an excellent fruit stand set in a trailer with an awning. It's full of organic goodies from the north shore.

CONTINUE ON HWY. 56 PAST MILE MARKER 27 AND TURN RIGHT ON KA HAKU ROAD, THE MAIN ENTRANCE TO PRINCEVILLE MARKED BY LARGE FOUNTAIN. CONTINUE ON MAIN ROAD FOR TWO MILES TO ST. REGIS PRINCEVILLE RESORT.

Kalihiwai Bay

Anini Beach

Both of Princeville's golf courses are championship quality, and the **Princeville Resort**, with its splashy **view of Hanalei Bay**, Wainiha Pali, and the tip of Bali Hai, is rated among the world's top tropical resorts. Hollywood types love it. Prior to becoming a manicured resort community, Princeville was a cattle ranch. Before that, in 1853, the lands were owned by British Resident Minister R.C. Wyllie. Wyllie, who made his fortune in Scotland in 1845, came here to find a new career as King Kamehameha IV's foreign minister, working for 20 years to get Hawai'i recognized as a sovereign nation. But Wyllie's personal dream was of a grand plantation on this bluff above Hanalei Bay to be named for Kamehameha's son, Albert—thus the name Princeville. Unfortunately, little Albert died at age four; Wyllie died three years later and the plantation was auctioned off in 1867.

Prior to being Wyllie's plantation, the Princeville bluff was the site of **Russian Fort Alexander**. An interpretive kiosk to the right of the hotel marks the spot, and provides an excellent viewpoint of Hanalei Bay and north coast. The Russians, under the leadership of Dr. Anton Schaffer, retreated here from Fort Elizabeth in Waimea after being banished by Kauaian chiefs. For several days they considered making a stand for the Russian Empire—Schaffer had proclaimed his country would claim Hawai'i at all cost—but they soon realized their predicament and left the islands for good.

BACKTRACK TO HWY. 56 AND TURN RIGHT. CONTINUE BEYOND THE PRINCEVILLE SHOPPING CENTER, TURN LEFT INTO THE HANALEI OVERLOOK.

St. Regis Princeville Hotel

Pu'u Poa Beach

The valley, like all such valleys with streams or rivers, was an ahupua'a—a division of land that provided the entire needs of a community. Taro is the prominent crop today, taking over from rice. Across the street, the **Princeville Shopping Center** is dedicated mainly to local and tourist commerce. A few of the shops are worthy of a walk through, notably the whimsical **Magic Dragon Toy & Art Supply**. On the way out of Princeville, go right at the police station and head to the end of the road to **Hanalei Organic Park**: a private and spectaular view of Hanalei Valley.

CONTINUE ON HWY. 56 AND CROSS ONE-LANE BRIDGE OVER HANALEI RIVER. TURN LEFT IMMEDIATELY AFTER BRIDGE AND CONTINUE TWO MILES ON OHIKI ROAD. *Note: Hwy. 56 becomes Hwy. 560 after Princeville.*

Waterfowl and shorebirds streak over the taro fields as you drive though **Hanalei National Wildlife Refuge**. About a mile in on your right is the restored (perhaps unsigned) Haraguchi Rice Mill, a remnant of large-scale rice production that took place alongside the taro from 1912 through the 1950s. During prohibition, bootleggers made a fiery spirit, called okolehao, from ti plants harvested in the hills above the mill.

BACKTRACK OUT TO HWY. 560 AND TURN LEFT. CONTINUE TO HANALEI TOWN.

You could easily spend the day, or years, wandering around **Hanalei Town**, with its long bay, beachside bungalows, historic buildings, and quirky shops. **Hanalei Pier**, at **Black Pot Beach** near the river mouth, was the link to civilization and commerce after it was built in 1912, and later became a set piece for a number of movies.

Hanalei Valley

Several churches draw visitors, including St. William's Church, a longhouse-style build-

Waioli Hui'i Church

ing with sliding doors as sides, and St. Thomas Episcopal Church, of Asian design. But the town's postcard is green-shingled **Waioli Hui'ia Church**. Near Waioli church is the **Waioli Mission House**, built in 1841, and refurbished in 2019. The mission was established by Bostonians Abner and Lucy Wilcox. The mission's 'back yard,' one of the fairest views in Hawaii.

Rising inland from the town are the ridges of **Waioli Valley**, called the "birthplace of rainbows." Numerous waterfalls appear in the dark green walls after rains. Much of Hanalei's walk-around shopping charm lies at the base of this valley, with the **Hanalei Center** set in the old elementary school. **Crystals & Gemstones**, on Aku Road, has a real-deal, world-class collection. At the Center, the **Hanalei Surf Company** buzzes with a wave of surf wear and gear. But don't spend all your clamshells before heading out back to **Yellowfish Trading Company** to see its esoteric collectibles; one of the better collections in Hawaii. Nearby **Havaiki** has trove of oceanic tribal art. Its courtyard features interpretive signs with colorful paintings depicting the Polynesian way of life. At **Ching Young Village** (across the street), you'll find shops tucked away. The **Ohana Shop** is worth a second and third look. **Hanalei Strings** is all things ukelele. If you're missing your pooch, pick up a doggie lei (money goes to local pet shelters) at **Spinner Dolphin**. They also print custom tees while you wait.

One of Hanalei's charms is **Ki Hoalu Slack Key Guitar**—in the **Hanalei Community Center**—where Doug and Sandy McMaster give low-key concerts.

CONTINUE ON HWY. 560.

Leaving Hanalei, you cross Waioli Stream and pass **Waikoko Beach**, which forms the far side of the bay. Across the street from the beach is on of Kaua'i's treasures, **Waipa Foundation**, a nonprofit set is a striking stream valley. Waipa is the site of a farmer's market on Tuesdays, and of workshops that include visitors who want to learn about the the Hawaiian methods

Surfer swap meet, Hanalei Center

of sustainable agriculture, around which the community thrives. Around the point From Waipa is **Lumahai Beach** and River, after mile marker 5. Lumahai is best known for its treacherous combers, able to snatch a stroller from the shore, and for being where Mitzi Gaynor wanted to "wash that man right out of her hair," in *South Pacific*.

CONTINUE ON HWY. 560. (THE HIGHWAY IS CLOSED HERE THROUGH 2019)

At mile marker 7 is **Wainiha**—the village, valley and river (spanned by one-lane bridges) are portrait quality. You can cover the vintage 'downtown' in a few paces. Before the devastating flood of April 2018, the attached storefronts included an old-school general store, a fresh sushi stand, and the Ohana Shop—one of the best giftstores on the island that has since re-opened in Hanalei and Poipu. Hard to say what businesses will come back once the highway is reopened, but you can be sure they will reflect the aloha of this most-Kauain of villages.

Much of the island's power is generated from the perpetual cascades deep up the Wainiha Valley. The **Wainiha Pali**—cliffs—rise nearly 4,000 feet from the river valley. They appear to be a ridge, but in actuality at the top of the pali is the Alakai Swamp, resting on a horizontal plane. The last of the Kaua'i's Menehune, 65 of them, lived in Wainiha, according to a late 19th century U.S. Census. The Hawaiians would try to lure them from the jungle with traps set with tasty foods, but the Menehunes were too swift, taking the food and fleeing in the night. Some Hawaiian families currently living in Wainiha trace their heritage back several hundred years.

CONTINUE ON HWY. 560.

Lumahai Valley

Rounding the turn from Wainiha, near mile marker 7, is a chance to buy fine art (and a latte fix) at the **Na Pali Art Gallery**. Among the offerings are keepsake necklaces made from local Ni'ihau-type shells. Then, after mile marker 8, you reach **Haena Beach Park** and **Tunnels Beach**, popular among campers and surfers, and also a premier snorkeling destination. From the beach are views of **Bali Hai Ridge**—correctly called **Makana** or "Fire Cliff." In pre-missionary times, specially trained men would hurl flaming logs from the summit to the sea, creating a shower of sparks that Kauaians would come to see, in canoes and on foot, from all parts of the island. The fire fall was not only for entertainment, but also to honor the sacred hula temple below.

On your left just past the spillway is **Maniniholo Dry Cave**, the end of a lava tube that extends several hundred yards under the cliff and finally, as a narrow opening, pokes out the top of the mountain. Legend tells that this cave was dug by Menehune, who used it to trap demigods who were stealing their fish.

Haena Beach

Beyond the dry cave, look to the mountains to spot Pohakuokane—the Rock of Kane—a large boulder sitting atop a rounded peak. It is said that when this rock falls, Kaua'i will sink beneath the sea. A sister rock, perched near the beach, was washed away in a tidal wave in 1946.

CONTINUE ON HWY. 560.

On your left past mm9 is **Limahuli Garden, a National Tropical Botanical Garden**, and one of the few spots on the north shore where you can get into one of the lush valleys. Most visitors miss this beauty, one of the top attractions in the state, on the way to the Kalalau Trail. Limahuli specializes in native plants, providing a historical as well as horticultural experience. The garden tour is self-guided along stream terraces,

Kalalau Trailhead

an authentic hale (hut), and hillside forests. Included is a plant booklet that alone is worth the price of admission.

On the left just beyond the garden entrance are **Waikapalae Wet Cave** and, a short hike up beyond the first cave, **Waikanaloa Wet Cave**. The volcano goddess Pele is said to have dug these caverns, in search of a fiery home for herself and her lover, Lohiau, but, alas, she came up wet, prompting her to flee Kaua'i and head south through the island chain. In the 19th century, Hawaiian boys would make sport of climbing the walls of the cave and diving 30 feet into its chilling waters.

Alula
Brighamia insignis
An endangered species native to Kaua'i and Ni'ihau presently being reintroduced into the protected wild habitat of Limahuli Garden

CONTINUE TO END OF HWY. 560 AT MILE MARKER 10.

The end of the road is better known as the beginning of the **Kalalau Trail**, a rugged path along 11 miles of the roadless Napali Coast. You can see down the coast from about .5-mile on the difficult trail—or by walking a short distance to your right down **Ke'e Beach**. In the winter, huge waves explode against the buttresses that stick out to the sea. During calm conditions, during the summer and also frequently in the winter, Ke'e is an excellent snorkeling pool.

Approach to Hankapiai Beach, Kalalau Trail

Napali Coast

A short trail from Keʻe Beach leads to the **Kauluolaka Heiau**, **Lohiau's hula temple**. The sacred heiau, the passionate meeting place for Pele and her lover, Lohiau, is the only dancing platform in Hawaiʻi dating back to mythological times.

Among Hawaiians studying the ancient dance, this site was the equivalent of the most prestigious university. The best young pupils from Hawaiʻi came, camping nearby, and were taught the traditions, chants and dances of their ancient heritage.

The graduation ceremony included a swim out the channel from Keʻe Beach, said to be guarded by a large shark.

The hula temple is in use today—treat it like a church. Just below the dance platform are the remaining ramparts of another heiau, Kaulu-paoa Heiau, dedicated to seafaring and navigation. This site is overgrown.

Kauluolaka Hula Heiau

DRIVING TOUR FOUR

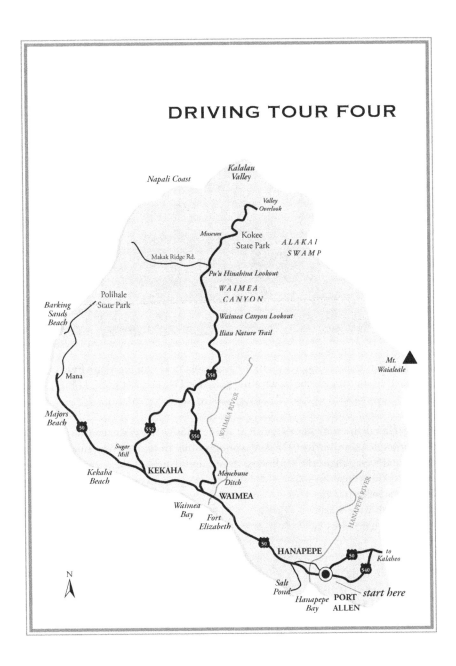

Kalalau Valley

Napali Coast

Valley Overlook

Museum

Kokee State Park

ALAKAI SWAMP

Makak Ridge Rd.

Pu'u Hinahina Lookout

WAIMEA CANYON

Polihale State Park

Waimea Canyon Lookout

Iliau Nature Trail

Barking Sands Beach

Mt. Waialeale

Mana

WAIMEA RIVER

550

Majors Beach

50

552

550

Sugar Mill

HANAPEPE RIVER

Kekaha Beach

KEKAHA

Menehune Ditch

WAIMEA

Waimea Bay

Fort Elizabeth

50

HANAPEPE

50

to Kalaheo

N

Salt Pond

540

start here

Hanapepe Bay

PORT ALLEN

TOUR *four*

Port Allen, Hanapepe and Waimea towns, Waimea Canyon, Koke'e State Park, Kalalau Valley overlook, Kekaha Beach and Barking Sands Beach. Take the Waimea Canyon portion on a clear day.

START AT SECOND JUNCTION OF HWYS. 50 AND 540. TURN LEFT TOWARD PORT ALLEN ON WAIALO ROAD. CONTINUE .5-MILE DOWN TO DOCK AREA.

Port Allen, on Hanapepe Bay, is Kaua'i's most active port for sportfishing, sightseeing and whale-watching excursions. Its breakwater and docks provide a glimpse of bustling harbor life, as does the small boat harbor down a road on the right from the larger dock. Some cruisers, like HoloHolo and Captain Andy's, take you offshore of **Ni'ihau**.

BACKTRACK OUT TO HWY. 50 AND TURN LEFT. AFTER A SHORT DISTANCE ON HWY. 50, VEER RIGHT TOWARD HANAPEPE ON HANAPEPE ROAD. PARK AFTER .5-MILE AT THE SWINGING BRIDGE.

Hanapepe, Kaua'i's "biggest little town," is known for its bougainvillea and an eclectic assemblage of old-style buildings, and wide-ranging galleries and shops, all set along the banks of the Hanapepe River. The town's historic markers tell the story. You'll want to take a walk across the **Swinging Bridge**. Hanapepe has a history that befits its Wild West look: In 1924, 20 people died here in a riot between police and striking sugar cane workers. And just up the road is where Prince Humehume, son of Kaua'i's last king, staged an unsuccessful revolt against the forces of Kamehameha the Great. If you want to get wild these days in Hanapepe, try Art Night (usually Fridays from sundown to maybe 9 p.m.) when the town is all prettied up. One of the town's better stops, the **Talk Story Bookstore**. Across the street is the **Storybook Theatre of Hawaii**, a creation of Mark Jeffers, a.k.a **Russell the Rooster**, whose TV shows both educate and amuse. Nearby **Kama'aina Cabinets** features keepsake koa tables and other furniture, made on-site. **JJ Ohana** you can get cheap-kitsch trinkets and also pricey (and worth it) Ni'ihau shell jewelry. *The* place for fine-art paintings is **Kalakoa Gallery**, offering the vibrant works of 14 artists. Cubbyhole **lu.la.** gallery has only made-in-Hawaii sarongs and bags, as well as tempting gift items. Across the street, **Blu Umi** curates art, jewelry, and fashion wear from around the world—and sends back some profits to the sources. On the highway is a local-

Hanapepe Town

kine shop with a national footprint: **Salty Wahine**. And you thought salt was just salt.

CONTINUE THROUGH HANAPEPE, CROSSING THE RIVER ON ONE-LANE BRIDGE AND REACHING HWY. 50. TURN RIGHT ON HWY. 50.

Salt Pond Beach Park

On the way to Waimea Town are three side trips. The first is immediately after Hanapepe on your left, the turnoff on Hwy. 543 to **Salt Pond Beach Park**. This is a good snorkeling and picnicking spot you might want to save for the return leg of the tour. The park includes salt ponds, dating back to the 1700s—they may look like puddles, but the salt was highly valued by seafaring vessels, and remains in use to this day.

Gay & Robinson Plantation

At mile marker 19, turn makai on Kaumakani Avenue and you'll be transported immediately to main street of a 19th century sugar mill town that leads to the former **Gay & Robinson Plantation.** The mill ran its last ceremonial harvest in 2009.

The third side trip, off Highway 50 after mile marker 22, is **Russian Fort Elizabeth Historical Park**. You'll have to use your imagination to see a fort amid the remnants, dating from 1817. The Russians, along with the Americans, established a trading presence on Kaua'i during the early 1800s. But, not long after the fort was built, Kauaian chiefs decided to boot the Russians and side with the Yankees.

CONTINUE ON HWY. 50 TO WAIMEA.

Along the weathered streets of **Waimea Town** are layers of the past that echo a diverse history. Captain James Cook made the first European landing here in 1778, and for nearly the next century, Waimea was the capital of Kaua'i—a favorite harbor and provisioning port for early whalers and traders. The red-dirt fields around town were well-suited for crops and livestock, in great demand by seafarers. The destructive sandalwood trade of the early 1800s, Hawaii's first commerce with the outside world, was also centered here.

In the 1820s, the first missionaries landed in Waimea, not branching out to other parts of the island until 1835, and Waimea then was the major settlement for whites. In 1850, the town was named the port of entry for all foreign ships, on par with Honolulu. Japanese, Chinese and Portuguese grew rice and taro in surrounding fields, their presence evidenced by the churches tucked away on back streets. Some of these historical strands, and other local lore, are on display at small **West Kaua'i Technology & Visitor Center** (at the Highway

Captain Cook Statue, Waimea

550 junction); they offer walking tours and talk story. On the way out of town are the **Waimea Plantation Cottages**, whose parklike grounds with huge banyans invite a stroll. Long before any of this, Waimea was a principal settlement for the Menehunes, who built heiaus and an ambitious water-conveyance ditch, extending 25 miles up the canyon. Drive one mile up **Menehune Road** to see a fragment of the ditch and walk a footbridge that spans the river.

Waimea Plantation Cottages

CONTINUE THROUGH WAIMEA TOWN ON HWY. 50 AND TURN RIGHT TO-WARD WAIMEA CANYON ON HWY. 550, AT THE EDGE OF TOWN.

Views of the canyon begin not long after starting up highway 550, and you could spend many days exploring the trails and viewpoints along the way to the top. On the other hand, for the first-time visitor to the "Grand Canyon of the Pacific," a drive to the top can deliver what seems like weeks' worth of experience in a few hours. **Waimea Canyon** is an eroded gorge of the **Alakai Swamp**—the swamp itself is the transition of a 60-square-

mile ancient caldera that was Hawai'i's origin and which lies at almost 4,000 feet in elevation on the side of the canyon opposite the road. The canyon is about one-mile wide, ten-miles long, and 3,700-feet deep, with other canyons branching off it. Several developed lookouts adorn the road, part of **Waimea Canyon State Park**. The first, after mile marker 7, is the **Kukui Lookout**, which features a nature walk. After mile marker 10 look for **Waimea Canyon Lookout** and after mile marker 13 look for **Pu'u Hinahina Lookout**, which includes another viewing area for **Ni'ihau island**. Note also, as you drive this stretch, on your left are a series of trails that head out onto ridges of the west Napali.

Kalalau Valley, Alakai Swamp

TURN LEFT ON MAKAHA RIDGE ROAD, JUST PAST PU'U HINAHINA LOOKOUT, BEFORE MILE MARKER 14.

This road takes you four miles out on **Makaha Ridge**, where Kaua'i's strongest winds were recorded during Hurricane Iniki—227 mph. Although a military installation prevents you from getting to the very end, you do get looks at steep valleys and ridges to either side on this lesser-known part of the Napali Coast.

BACKTRACK OUT TO HWY. 550 AND TURN LEFT. CONTINUE TO KOKE'E STATE PARK MUSEUM.

The boundary for **Koke'e State Park** is just after Makaha Ridge Road, and where Halemanu Valley Trailhead offers a series of trails to canyon viewpoints. **Koke'e Natural History Museum**, at the edge of the park's spacious lawn and towering trees, is a wealth of information about the natural and cultural history of the area. No trip to the canyon should exclude a stop here. Then wade your way through the wild chickens to the **Koke'e Lodge** next door, for a restful lunch and a browse of their gift store. Short and long trails network the park. Some trails, east of the park, are forested and others, the Nualolo and Awa'awapuhi west of the park, lead out

to spiny ridges far above the wild shores of Napali Coast State Park. Many Kauaians have cabins in the Koke'e area, and church and community organizations maintain camps along the many unpaved roads.

CONTINUE UP HWY. 550

Two miles beyond Koke'e's lawn area is **Kalalau Lookout**, a viewpoint of the fabled valley, 4,000 feet below steeply diving, rippling green walls. As recently as the early 1900s, 500 Hawaiians lived in the valley. Garden terraces rise above the beach. Now only adventuresome backpackers make the 11-mile hike down the Kalalau Trail, which begins at Ke'e Beach on the north shore. Kalalau means "the straying."

A mile beyond this first lookout is **Pu'uokila Lookout**, providing another don't-miss view of the valley. Listen and watch for goats on tangled perches of the valley's bowl. The **Pihea Trail** begins at this overlook, providing not only a walk along the valley rim, but also entrance to the **Alakai**

Kalalau Lookout, Napali Coast

Ni'ihau shoreline

Swamp and, at the edge of the swamp, a high-altitude look from the Wainiha Pali down to Hanalei Bay—a hike more than any other that underscores the island's peculiar and spectacular topography.

BACKTRACK DOWN HWY. 550. CONTINUE PAST MILE MARKER 7 AND VEER RIGHT ON HWY. 552, WHICH IS KOKEE ROAD, TOWARD KEKAHA.

From Highway 552 to Kekaha are dramatic views of **Ni'ihau**, lying less than 20 miles offshore the so-called Forbidden Island where only those of the purest Hawaiian blood are allowed to live. The 100-square-mile island remains in the hands of the Robinson family, whose ancestors bought it in 1864 for $10,000. A ferry each month brings Ni'ihau residents, who are known for intricate shell necklaces, to Waimea. Ni'ihau's two, tiny satellite islands, both uninhabited, also can be seen on the clearest of days—Lehua, a mile to the right, and Kaula, 19 miles to the left of Ni'ihau.

The only Japanese fatality on land during the Pearl Harbor attack took place on Ni'ihau, on December 8, 1941. After a Japanese pilot had crash-landed, he terrorized the locals with a pistol, searching for the persons who had taken his papers from the wreckage when he had been unconscious. The pilot threatened the wife of one Hawaiian, and the husband charged, taking three shots before he was able to get hold of the pilot and smash him, with one fatal toss, against the lava wall of his house. Since then, there has been a saying in the islands: "Don't shoot a Hawaiian more than twice. The third time he gets mad!"

AT THE BOTTOM ON THE GRADE IN KEKAHA, **TURN LEFT** ON KEKAHA ROAD.

You'll drive past the old **Kekaha sugar mill**, a red-dirt stained, gargantuan structure that washed and chewed tons of cane. The mill ceased operation in 2000.

TURN RIGHT ON PUEO ROAD, OR ANY ROAD THROUGH THE NEIGHBORHOOD. MAKE YOUR WAY SEVERAL BLOCKS BACK OUT TO HWY. 50. TURN RIGHT ON HWY. 50.

You drive along **Kekaha Beach**, playground for surfers, fishermen, strollers and horseback riders. Although it's hard to imagine, the area inland along this drive, surrounding the bygone village of **Mana**, used to be swamplands, created by water

Road to Polihale Beach

seepage from the ridges fanning down from the Alakai Plateau. A canal ran through the lower part of the bog, allowing the Hawaiians to canoe all the way to Kekaha. Water development for cane and seed crops have drastically altered the horticultural landscape. Also on these sloping lands was the Holua slide, a long chute paved with lava rock and padded with pili grass. In February, at the end of the Makahiki—a four-month festival during which work and war were prohibited—young Hawaiian athletes would fashion sleds from logs and ride the slide with abandon.

CONTINUE ON HWY. 50 TO ITS TERMINUS. FOLLOW SIGNS SEVERAL MILES TO POLIHALE. *Note: The road to Polihale is rough, often muddy, and subject to closures.*

The beach at **Polihale State Park**, including **Barking Sands**, is part of the longest sand beach in Hawai'i. A massive dune abuts the northwest section of the Napali Coast—the ridges loom over the beach—and fans all the way around Mana Point to Kekaha, although the Naval base makes some of the beach inaccessible. Surfers dare the waves at Polihale, but the only spot for swimmers, except during rare calms, is **Queens Pond**. Barking Sands, a fine mixture of coral and lava particles, gets its name from the "woofing" sound the sliding dunes make when settling or being trod upon. Legend says these are the barks of an ancient fisherman's beloved pets, directing him ashore after being lost at sea.

Polihale was the heiau on the island from which the etheral spirits of the deceased escaped their mortal coils and went to the next world. Two heiaus are in the area, Kapaula Heiau, inland from the camping area, and Polihale Heiau, also the site of Sacred Springs, located beyond where the beach meets the cliffs.

Polihale State Park

free advice & opinion

SAFETY TIPS THAT CAN SAVE YOUR LIFE
AND RECREATIONAL FACTOIDS OF MARGINAL USE.

HIKING

People have been walking here for centuries: If there is no trail already, you can't get there ... That nice green embankment may be tangled grass and air: stay back from drop-offs ... Carry an equipped day pack on hikes ... Drink plenty of water ... Don't trust rocks with footing: they break free ... If using your hands on the way up, the way down will be dangerous ... Use hiking poles ... Never walk downhill with your hands in your pockets ... Boink! Be aware of falling coconuts ... At hike-to beaches, make sure to memorize where you enter the sand: finding the trail on the return trip can be difficult ...

Use hunting trails on weekdays and wear bright colored clothes ... If you see hunters, don't hide behind bushes and snort or squeal ... Even bloodhounds get lost on Kaua'i: follow the trail, not your GPS ... Backtrack the moment you get lost or lose the trail ... Don't hike alone ... Give right-of-way to a wild pig ... If the sun rises on a clear Waialeale, head for Waimea Canyon ... Bring outerwear when hiking Koke'e ... Go south and west to look for sun in the winter ... You're in the tropics: protect your skin ... Drink more water ...

Loose rocks fall with waterfalls; don't dawdle beneath one ... On black rock beach trails: follow the mud and sand left by the flip-flops of your predecessors ... Flash floods happen on sunny days too, when it's raining inland: stay alert in stream beds ... A high stream will subside, so wait a couple hours rather than make a dangerous crossing ... Know the halfway point of your hike, and plan for enough time to get back ... Heed No Trespassing signs ... Public right of way on the coast is all land and rocks below the vegetation line, as a rule of thumb ... Let someone know if you're taking a long hike ... You need a permit to camp anywhere or to sleep on any beach ... Hikes on Kaua'i take longer than you expect, due to tough conditions and astounding scenery; add an hour for every four hours you think it will take.

WATER SAFETY

Good judgment beats the most dangerous conditions ... Throw a stick in the water before entering to see which way it floats ... Float face-down when you first get in to see which way the current takes you ... Observe the water for fifteen minutes before getting in ... Outgoing current is like a river, carrying out the surf surge: look for blue channels, riffles, and places in a wall of surf offshore where the waves aren't curling: that's where water is going out ... Wave for help if you're in trouble ... Be extra cautious at remote beaches ... High surf means stronger rip current ... Stay out of rocky areas with surge ... If possible, view swimming place from above to observe current ... Waves coming in means current is going out someplace ... Water isn't safe just because some tourist like you is in it ... Aloha Survival: Locals will be glad to tell you about water safety: ask a surfer or swimmer who knows ... Start your swim against a mild current, so you can swim with it when returning … Get out of a current too strong to swim against … Swim with fins … Waves are like thugs: don't turn your back on them … Every beach is both safe and unsafe, depending on the day … If you get swept out, go with it and then swim parallel to shore once the current has taken you out and released you … Don't panic and wear yourself out by swimming against a current you can't beat; it will release you … Surfers offshore are a safety net, but don't count on them … Locate the yellow life preservers, located at all beaches …

Shore break can break you … High surf rolls in on nice days from storms unseen far offshore … Local surfers will be safe in water that is dangerous for you … Tilted sand means deep water … But drop-offs can occur on flat beaches, too … Don't dive into unknown waters … Swim with a buddy, always … Go to the opposite side of the island from a high-surf beach: it should be calmer in the lee … Safest swimming is near a lifeguard … If you get stung by a jellyfish, put meat tenderizer on the wound … You don't need to fear the ocean; fear your bad judgment … When in doubt, stay out … All beaches are public places: keep your pants on … For health reasons, avoid swimming in murky waters at stream mouths.

BICYCLING

Bust a helmet, not your head … Lower your seat going downhill … Dismount for horses and speak so they know this helmeted thing is a person … Look: It's a vehicle! No, it's a pedestrian! Biking is the best of both worlds … Most of the backroads on Kaua'i are places rental cars can't go … Leaving bikes unlocked is a sign of a local … But why take the chance? … You can't take bikes on buses … A bike is the fastest wasy to get through Kapa'a …

You can continue past gates unless a sign tells you not to … Respect private property … Stay on trails to avoid erosion … Exception: Swerve onto grass on paved paths to avoid pedestrians … Dismount if you see hunters with dogs … Never ride down a road you can't get back up … Hard dirt becomes greasy slick after a few drops of rain … Add extra lube: rust grows here fast … Carry an extra tube … Don't assume cars see you: drivers are looking at scenery.

KAYAKING

It may be raining inland: watch for flash floods … Don't venture offshore without a local's advice … Paddling upstream, branches usually stop you before shallow water does … Remember your way back … Some of the island's best streams have no people on them … Ask a local if authorities ever found the anaconda in the Wailua River … … Don't paddle into mangroves … Keep open wounds out of stagnate fresh water: bacteria danger.

DRIVING AROUND

Driving is the most dangerous sport … Wear a seatbelt or get a ticket … Aloha driving: allow merges and turns … Speeding tickets are likely souvenirs … Park it or drive it: rubbernecking is dangerous … Hanging beads or a shell necklace from your rearview mirror will give your rental a local look … A box of baby wipes in the glove box provides an instant relief from red-dirt sweat … Signs that beckon: Dead End, No Outlet … On weekends, try to leave locals' beaches to the locals … Littering carries a stiff $1,000 fine.

GEAR

Hiking poles are a third leg and you'll need one … Bring a waterproof shell jacket … Spitting in your swim mask will clear fog … Muddy puddles make for great dye-your-own red dirt shirt dunking … It's cheaper to rent snorkeling gear for a few days, cheaper to buy for a week or more … It's cheaper to rent a bicycle for a couple days, cheaper to ship if biking for more than that … You can rent a bike rack for the rental car … Or hang the bikes out the trunk … It's cheaper to rent kayaks and surfboards … Call rental places first to make sure expert advice comes with the rental … See *Packlist* for what to bring … When mountain hiking, bring a plastic bag to put your shoes in after hike … Clothes are gear: No nudity on any Hawaiian beach … Attend to skin with antibacterial and fungicide: This is the Garden Island and everything grows here … Carry water, but if you do use a water pump, use iodine to go along with the filter … Most-common island footwear: bare feet … Bring lightweight hiking shoes that you can hose off.

DISCLAIMER

Think of this book as you would any other piece of outdoor gear: It will help you do what you want to do, but it depends solely upon you to supply responsible judgment and common sense. Weather and new rules may alter the condition of trails and beach access; please let us know. The publisher and authors are not responsible for injury, damage, trespassing, or legal violations that occur when someone is using our books. Furthermore, the publisher and authors hope that none of these bad things happen and that you have a great time.

ALOHA AUTHORS
Excerpts from some better known writers

"The far end of Kalalau Valley had been well chosen as a refuge. A sea of vegetation laved the landscape, pouring its green billows from wall to wall, dripping from the cliff lips in great vine masses, and flinging a spray of ferns and airy plants into its multitudinous crevices. Koolau had fought with this vegetable sea. The choking jungle, with its riot of blossoms, had been driven back from the bananas, oranges and mangoes that grew wild, and in every open space where the sunshine penetrated papaya trees were burdened with their golden fruit."

—Jack London,
Koolau The Leper

"The Pacific is inconstant and uncertain like the soul of a man. Sometimes it is grey like the English Channel, with a heavy swell, and sometimes it is rough, capped with white crests, and boisterous. When it is calm and blue, the blue is arrogant. The sun shines fiercely from an unclouded sky. The trade wind gets into your blood and you are filled with an impatience for the unknown, and you forget vanished youth with its memories, cruel and sweet, in a restless, intolerable desire for life."

—W. Somerset Maugham,
The Pacific

"No alien land in all the world has any deep strong charm for me but that one, no other land could so longingly and beseechingly haunt me, sleeping and waking, through half a lifetime, as that one has done. For me, its balmy airs are always blowing, its summer seas flashing in the sun; the pulsing of its surfbeat is in my ear, I can see its garlanded crags, its leaping cascades, its plumy palms drowsing by the shore. I can hear the splash of its brooks and in my nostrils still lives the breath of flowers that perished twenty years ago."

—Mark Twain,
Roughing It in the Sandwich Islands

"The sea was smooth under the lee of the island; it was warm besides, and Keola has his sailor's knife, so he had no fear of sharks. A little way before him the trees stopped; there was a break in the line of the land like the mouth of a harbor; and the tide, which was then flowing, took him up and carried him through. The next minute he was within, floated there in a wide shallow water, bright with ten thousand stars, and all about him was the ring of land, with its string of palm trees."

—Robert Louis Stevenson,
The Isle of Voices

"I wish I could tell you about the Pacific. The endless ocean. Reefs upon which waves broke into spray, and inner lagoons, lovely beyond description. I wish I could tell you about the sweating jungle, the full moon rising behind an ancient volcano."

—James A. Michner,
Tales of the South Pacific

HAWAIIWOOD

Take a self-guided tour to the locations of some of the more recent among 50-plus major motion pictures and television programs that have been filmed in Kaua'i. The first was *White Heat* in 1934. TH = Trailhead, DT = Driving Tour.

Ke'e Beach, TH1 — *Lord of the Flies, Throw Momma From the Train, Thorn Birds*
Haena Beach Park, TH2 — *North, Pirates of the Caribbean*
Kepuhi Point, TH3 — *Body Heat*
Wainiha Beach, TH4 — *Pagan Love Song*
Lumahai Beach, TH5 — *South Pacific, Pirates of the Caribbean*
Lumahai Valley, TH5 — *Uncommon Valor, Dragonfly*
Hanalei Bay, TH7 — *South Pacific, Soul Surfer, Wackiest Ship in the Army, The Descendants*
Hanalei Valley, TH8 — *Uncommon Valor, The Time Machine*
Anini Beach, TH13 — *Honeymoon in Vegas*
Kalihiwai Bay, TH14 — *Soul Surfer*
Pila'a Beach, TH16 — *None But the Brave*
Moloa'a Bay, TH21 — *Gilligan's Island, Castaway Cowboy*
Papa'a Bay, TH22 — *Six Days, Seven Nights*
Anahola Mountains/Kong, TH23 — *Raiders of the Lost Ark, Dragonfly, Avatar*
Kamokila Village, DT2 — *Outbreak, Tropic Thunder*
Kapa'a Town, TH28 — *Honeymoon in Vegas*
Coco Palms, TH33, DT2 — *Blue Hawaii, South Pacific*
Lydgate Park, TH34 — *Blue Hawaii*
Keahua Arboretum, TH32 — *Jurassic Park, Jurassic World, Avatar*
Wailua River, TH33 — *The Hawaiians, Islands in the Stream, Donovan's Reef, Outbreak*
Wailua Falls, TH36 — *Fantasy Island*
Ahukini Landing, TH39 — *Donovan's Reef, Pagan Love Song*
Nawiliwili, TH41 — *Diamond Head, The Lost World: Jurassic Park, Throw Momma from the Train*
Kalapaki Beach, TH41 — *Hawaiian Eye*
Huleia Stream, TH41 — *Raiders of the Lost Ark, Tropic Thunder*
Mahaulepu, TH42 — *Six Days, Seven Nights; Hook, Fast & Furious*
Kukuiula Harbor, TH45 — *The Thorn Birds, Islands in the Stream*
Allerton Garden, TH46 — *Jurassic Park, Acapulco Gold, Last Flight of Noah's Ark, Honeymoon in Vegas, Mighty Joe Young*
Hanapepe Town, TH51 — *The Thorn Birds, Jurassic Park, George of the Jungle*
Waimea Canyon, TH34 — *Wackiest Ship in the Army, Fantasy Island*
Barking Sands, TH57 — *South Pacific*
Kalalau Valley, DT4, TH1 — *King Kong*

KAUAIAN TIMELINE

5,000,000 BC Lava pokes above water; Kaua'i is born.

200 AD First Polynesians arrive from Marquesas; the Menehunes.

1100 Second Polynesian migration, from Tahiti.

1700 600,000 Hawaiians living on eight islands.

1778 British Captain James Cook arrives at Waimea; Hawai'i is discovered by the rest of the world.

1795 King Kamehameha unifies islands into one kingdom, except Kaua'i. Two attempts to conquer Kaua'i fail.

1810 Kauaian King Kaumuali'i signs peace treaty with Kamehameha.

1817 Russians driven from the island; their attempt at empire over.

1819 Kamehameha the Great dies.

1820 First New England missionaries arrive in Waimea. Kapu system of laws abolished by Kamehameha II.

1835 First sugar mill, Koloa; worker emigration from China, Japan, Portugal, Philippines and Korea. Kaua'i becomes major sugar supplier to U.S.

1842 United States recognizes Hawai'i as independent nation.

1864 Eliza Sinclair, ancestor of today's Gay & Robinson Corporation, buys island of Ni'ihau for $10,000.

1874 Rule of Kamehameha's two sons and two grandsons ends.

1893 Queen Liliuokalani overthrown. First hotel opened in Lihue.

1898 United States annexes Hawai'i as territory. Marines occupy Honolulu.

1912 Duke Kahanamoku wins Olympic gold medal. Goes on to win 5 more medals in swimming, ending with silver in 1932.

1930 U.S. restricts Japanese emigration to Hawai'i.

1941 Nawiliwili Harbor shelled during World War II.

1958 *South Pacific* movie released.

1959 Hawai'i becomes 50th state.

1967 One million people visit Hawaiian islands.

1982 Hurricane Iwa.

1992 Hurricane Iniki.

1993 United States formally apologizes for overthrow of Hawaiian kingdom.

2005 Kaua'i most popular island for outdoor recreation.

2006 40-day rains cause fatal floods in Kilauea.

2007 Flotilla of activists block inter-island Hawaii Superferry.

2009 Gay & Robinson harvests last sugar cane crop.

2011 Vog (volcanic fog) from the Big Island reaches the north shore.

2014 Waipa Foundation recreates ahupua'a.

2016 Kauai Conservation Alliance holds first-ever island-wide Expo.

2018 Epic rains and floodwaters wipe out much of the North Shore.

A GLOSSARY OF HAWAIIAN WORDS AND PHRASES

The Hawaiian alphabet consists of 12 letters: A, E, I, O, U, H, K, L, M, N, P, W.

The Polynesians transmitted their knowledge and culture through speaking, dance and chants; they had no written language. Missionary scholars in the 1800s derived word spellings from the Polynesian phonetics.

Kaua'i is pronounced: kow-WAH-ee

The apostrophe-like doohickey that goes between double vowels is called an okina. For instance, "a'a" is pronounced, "ah-ah."

Selected Hawaiian place name suffixes and prefixes, to give you an idea of how places were named and interconnected by their attributes:

A'a, rough lava
Ahi, land
Aina, land
Akau, north
Ala, road
Ana, cave
Anu, cool
Hana or *hono*, bay
Hema, south
Hikina, east
Haole, foreigner
Hau, spreading tree
Holo, run
Hono, bay
Hou, new
Hua, fruit, seed
Iki, small
Kaha, place
Kahawai, stream
Kai, sea
Kea or *keo*, white, clear
Koa, rocky, coral
Koko, blood
Komo, enter
Komohana, west
Kua, black
La, sun

Lani, heaven
Lau, leaf
Lena, yellow
Lolo, stupid
Lohi, slow
Lua, crater
Lulu, sheltered
Luna, high
Mala, garden
Malu, shelter
Maka, point
Makai, toward the sea
Mana, power or divide
Mano, shark or many
Manu, bird
Mau, moist
Mauka, toward the mountains
Mauna, mountain
Mele, merry or song
Mo'o, water spirit
Moi, king
Moku, island
Nalu, surf, wave
Nani, pretty
Niu, coconut
Nui, large
Ohu, fog

Olo, hill
Omao, green
Oluolu, please
One, sand
Papa, flat
Pau, finished
Pele, goddess of fire
Pono, harmony
Puna, water spring
Pu'u, hill
Tutu, aunt
Ua, rain
Uka, inland
Ula, red
Ulu, breadfruit
Uma, curve
Waa, canoe
Wai, water
Wailele, waterfall
Waimea, reddish waters
Walu, many
Wili, twist

SOME HAWAIIAN WORDS

Ahi, albacore or yellow tuna
Ahupua'a, land and coast segment that
    supported a community
'Aina, land, earth
Ali'i, king, royalty of highest nobility
Aloha, love, affection, welcome, hello,
    good-bye
Hale, house or building
Hana, work or activity
Haole, caucasian, originally any foreigner
He'enalu, surfing
Heiau, ancient temple or place of worship
Hoku, star
Huki, pull
Hukilau, hawaiian method of
    group net-fishing
Hula, the art of hawaiian dance
Ilio, dog
Kahuna, an expert, priest or
    religious leader
Kai, the ocean
Kama'aina, citizen of long standing,
Kanaka, human being, the Hawaiians
Kane, male
Kapu, prohibited, keep out
Keiki, child
Kona, leeward
La, sun
Lanai, porch or balcony
Lei, necklace made of flowers
Luau, Hawaiian feast
Mahalo, thank you
Mahina, moon
Makahiki, annual harvest and
    peace festival
Makai, toward the ocean
Mana, power
Mauka, toward the mountains
Mauna, mountain
Moana, ocean
Mu'umu'u, mother hubbard dress

Na Ala Hele, trails for walking
Ohana, the people of the community
Pali, cliff
Paniolo, hawaiian cowboy
Pele, goddess of volcanoes
Po, night
Poi, dish of mashed taro root
Popoki, cat
Pupu, hors d'oeurve
Spam, a traditional pork dish
Ua, rain
Wahine, female
Wikiwiki, fast, quickly

GREETINGS, TOASTS AND PHRASES

A Hui Hou, Until we meet again
Aloha Nui, A Big Aloha!
Hau'oli La Hanau, Happy Birthday
Hau'oli Makahiki Hou,
    Happy New Year
Hiki, Okay
Honi Kaua Wikiwiki, Kiss Me Quick
Kamau, Here's To Your Health
Kipa Mai, Welcome
Komo, Enter
Mahalo Nui, Many Thanks
Me Ke Aloha, With Love
Mele Kalikimaka, Merry Christmas
Okole Maluna, Bottom's Up

PIDGIN EXPRESSIONS

Pidgin is a form of English spoken by kama'aina. It is more a dialect and intonation of speech—flowing like a babbling brook—than a collection of phrases. Pidgin's origin is not Polynesian, but rather the rainbow of ethnicity that meld together as Hawaiian. Hang around places where locals shop or surf and you may hear snippets, though Pidgin-speak is waning.

'Ass awri, That's alright
'Ass why hard, That's why it's hard, life is tough
Auntie, Kids' word for all adult women in the calabash
Boddah you? You like to start something?
Brah, Brother
Bumbye, In the future; by and by, soon
Bummahs, Too bad
Bus laugh, Laugh out loud
Bus nose, Reaction to bad smell
Calabash, Friends and family, extended family
Calabash cousin, Not blood relation, but close friend
Chicken skin, Chills, goosebumps
Coast haole, Caucasian from the Mainland
Cockroach, To steal
Cool head main ting, Keep calm, don't panic
Da Kine, thingamajig, whatever speaker wants it to mean
Eh, Brah, Hey, you
Garans, Guaranteed
Grind, To eat
Grinds, Food
He been go, He went

Hey, Bruddah, Hey, Brother
Howzit?, How are you? Pidgin for Aloha
Huhu, to be upset
I shame, I'm embarrassed
J.O.J., Just off the Jet (tourist)
Junks, small personal things
Lesgo, let's do it
Local style, Hawaiian way of doing things
Lolo, Dumb-dumb
Moke, Local tough guy
Mo' bettah, Better
No boddah, Don't bother
No can, Cannot
No mention, Don't mention it, you're welcome
Not, No can be, You got to be kidding
Moah betta, More better
Plate lunch, Rice, meat or Spam and veggies, a fast counter lunch
Poi dog, Local mix of many breeds, small canine
Shaka, Right on, brah' (hand sign: fist with thumb and pinky out.)
Shave ice, Snow cones
Slack key, Hawaiian folk-blues played on loose-string guitar
Stick, Surfboard
Stink-eye, Dirty look
Stuffs, see Junks
Talk story, Tell stories, conversation
T'anks, Thank you, mahalo
Tita, Local tough girl
Uncle, Kids' word for all adult men in the calabash
Whack 'em, Eat up
Whatevahs, Whatever
Yeah?, Put anywhere in sentence

SURFER'S DICTIONARY

AIR: The invisible stuff that's on top of waves. Also, a gaseous substance necessary for a surfer to surf.

BAD: That which has nothing to do with surfing.

CAR: A disposable device sometimes used to transport a surfer and surf board to the surf.

CRUELTY: Taking a surfer's surfboard.

FEET: Things that allow a surfer to stand on a surfboard.

FOOD: A substance that surfers swallow in order to go surfing.

GOD: An entity that created waves and surfboards.

JOB: An activity by which a surfer acquires money in order to go surfing.

LIFE: Surfing.

KAUA'I PACKLIST

For two weeks, staying in hotel.

BASICS

Long pants/dress for airplane
Swimming suit (can buy here)
Rash guard (optional, for water sports)
Hat, sunglasses
Rain-proof shell (pants optional)
Aloha or polo shirt/dress for dress-up
2 pair hiking/riding shorts
1 pair dress shorts
4 T-shirts, one for every two days
1 or 2 lightweight long sleeve tops
(Dri-fit or polyester equivalent)
Waterproof watch

FOOTWEAR

1 pair flip-flops, a.k.a., zories, slippers
    (for driving, beach walking, shopping)
1 pair lightweight, washable
    hiking shoes; your mud shoe
2 pair lightweight hiking socks
1 pair hotel/airport/dress shoes
Optional boat shoes, sandals

KNAPSACK/DAYPACK:

Energy bar/emergency food
Flashlight
Swiss Army knife
First aid, sunscreen
Carry Water *(filter or treat only on long pack trips)*
Rain shell
Sunglasses/hat
Mosquito repellant
Camera/Cell phone

GEAR:

Hiking poles *(retractable, bring with you)*
Mask, snorkel, fins *(Bring or rent here. Cheaper to buy if you'll use for more than 5 or 6 days. Cost here about $35.)*
Surfboard *(Ship if you will use more than 5 days; otherwise rent. Contact airlines and outfitters to compare prices.)*
Bicycle helmet
Bicycle *(Contact airlines and outfitters to compare prices. Usually cheaper to rent here.)*
Kayak *(Rent, about $30 per day.)*

FACTSHEET

TEMPERATURES
Average, year around, day and night: 75 degrees

Extremes:	Record High	Record Low
Kilauea	87	50
Lihue	90	50
Poipu	92	40
Kokee	90	29

WIND
Summer: Trades and Kona winds from south

Winter: Trade winds generally from north

RAINFALL YEARLY AVERAGE IN INCHES

Waimea Town	28
Poipu	35
Koloa	65
Lihue	53
Kapaʻa	56
Princeville	98
Waialeale	460 (most in the world)

MAJOR HURRICANES

	average wind speed m.p.h.	maximum m.p.h.
1950 ʻHiki	68	93
1957 Nina	92	111
1959 Dot	81	103
1982 Iwa	65	117
1992 Iniki	145	227

HIGHEST PEAKS: Kawaikini, 5,243 ft.; Waialeale, 5,148 ft.

MILES OF COASTLINE: 110

SQUARE MILES: 550

AVERAGE DIAMETER, MI.: 28

LAND OWNERSHIP: (397,000 acres)
Six largest corporations: 41 percent
State of Hawaii: 39 percent
Small private landowners: 13 percent
Hawaiian Homelands: 6 percent
Federal government: 1 percent

POPULATION
Locals: 72,000
Visitors (average daily): 50,000
Total: 122,000

SUNSHINE MARKETS

all area codes are 808 unless otherwise noted

Outdoor markets offering home-grown produce. Times may vary, call 241-4946 for more information. Bring dollar bills, tote bags, and be on time!

Monday:	Koloa Ballpark, Maluhia Road, Koloa, 12 noon; Anaina Park, Kilauea, 4 p.m. Kealia (also Friday), 3 p.m.
Tuesday:	Kalaheo Neighborhood Center, 3:30 p.m. Hanalei-Waipa, (closed for 2019) 2 p.m.
Wednesday:	Kapa'a New Town Center, near Armory, 3 p.m. Kukuiula Culinary Market (Poipu), 3:30
Thursday:	Kilauea Ag Farms (past Kong Lung), 3:30 p.m. Hanapepe Park, behind fire station, 4:30 p.m.
Friday:	Lihue, Vidinha Stadium, Ho'olako St., 3 p.m.
Saturday:	Kekaha Neighborhood Center, 9 a.m. Hanalei Town Center, 9:30 a.m. Anaina Hou Park, Kilauea, 9 a.m.
Sunday:	**Kalalea** Anahola (Hokualele Rd), 10 a.m.

FREE HULA SHOWS
Call to verify times and inquire about other cultural events

South Shore Visitors Center (Allerton), Thursday, 2 p.m., 742-2623
Coconut Marketplace, Saturday 1 p.m., Wed. & Fri., 5 p.m., 651-0682
Kaua'i Beach Resort, nightly 7 p.m., 822-3455
Hyatt Regency Kaua'i Resort, nightly 6 to 8 p.m., also torch-lighting
ceremony daily at sunset, except Tuesday, 742-1234
Kaua'i Marriott Resort, Wednesday and Saturday at sunset;
also torch-lighting ceremony Monday and Thursday, 245-5050
Kukui Grove Shopping Center, Fridays, 6 p.m., 245-7784
Poipu Shopping Village, Tuesday and Thursday, 5 p.m., 742-2831
Queen Emma Polynesian Festival, October, Koke'e Park, 335-6466

THE MEANING OF *Aloha*

as adopted by a resolution of the State Legislature:

A is for Akahai. Kindness, to be expressed with tenderness.

L is for Lokahi. Unity, to be expressed with harmony.

O is for Oluolu. Agreeable, to be expressed with pleasantness.

H is for Ha'aha'a. Humility, to be expressed with modesty.

A is for Ahonui. Patience, to be expressed with perseverance.

The meaning of ALOHA not yet considered by the State Legislature:

A is for Attire. It's hard to be uptight or uppity in a place where nobody wears   pantyhose or neckties, and "dressing up" is colorful prints and flip-flops.

L is for Latitude. In the temperate tropics, with a lack of snow and boiling heat, everyone stays mellow.

O is for a Circle. On an island there's no point in rushing just to get where you've already been. Even the dogs don't chase their tails here.

H is for Healthy. With papayas, bananas, guava, mangos and spam, everyone enjoys the serenity of a healthy diet.

A is for Alone. The opposite of island fever is island euphoria; everyone is alone and isolated in the ocean, pitching in together to help out their neighbors. You don't outrun a bad reputation on a small island.

got aloha?

The Hawaiian word keiki (KAY-key) means both 'child' and also the green shoot of a new banana plant. Bananas are plants, not trees, and each year a new generation must be nurtured to maturity—just like children. By caring for each generation, the arts and skills of village life flourished for centuries on this beautiful, but isolated, island of Kaua'i. Your kids can see many of these arts practiced today. They can also do a lot of other fun stuff that will create life-long memories and bring the family together. The suggestions below will help you plan a day of family fun. Remember that trailhead numbers close together numerically will also be close geographically.

TH = trailhead. DT = driving tour. Activities are listed by ascending trailhead number. See *Resource Links* for telephone numbers.

KEIKI SWIMMING
Ke'e Beach, TH1, page 32
A reef-protected oval pool rests under the jagged Napali ridges. High surf, mainly in winter. Can be crowded.
Mola'a Baths, TH2, page 65
Drive down a lush valley and then walk the beach to a palm-shaded shore with natural pools in the coral reef.

FujiBeach, Kapa'a, TH28, page 78
This wading pool is popular among new moms. Beach cottage neighborhood setting.
Lydgate Park, TH34, page 99
Snorkeling is a sure thing year around at this big man-made lagoon.
Poipi Beach Park, TH44, page 120
A sand spit creates protected swim spots and Hawaiian sun graces this popular beach park, even when clouds frown elsewhere.

Waterhouse Beach, TH45, page 123
You'll have to look for this toddlers' beach, tucked away near Prince Kuhio Park. Bigger kids will like the snorkeling at Longhouse Beach.

Salt Pond Beach, TH52, page 140
West Kaua'i's best swimming beach. To the far right of the beach is a smaller splash area. Good facilities.

Queens Pond, TH57, page 150
Families with a sense of adventure will like this calm spot along the long Polihale Beach. High surf often makes conditions very unsafe. Bring your own shade and water to these open sand dunes.

FAMILY NATURE WALKS

Limahuli National Tropical Botanical Garden, TH1, page 31
You might expect dinosaurs to stride down the green ridges and onto the garden terraces. Native and endangered plants abound, many unique to Kaua'i.

Wai Koa Loop, TH16, page 51
Do the whole five miles through scenic tropical farms, or opt for a shorter trip to a very pretty stone dam with waterfall.

Sleeping Giant, TH30, page 81
You get a fantastic view of interior mountains and the Coconut Coast from the top of the Giant (Nounou Mountain.) The Norfolk Pine forest on the way up will have everyone's interest. Kids will get a sense of accomplishment.

Keahua Arboretum, TH32, page 84
You've got many options at the arboretum, all beginning where the Wailua River crosses a spillway in the jungle. The Kuilau Ridge is green fantasy land—but make sure to stay on the trail on the steep parts.

Smiths Tropical Paradise, TH33, page 95
The little ones may shriek like the peacocks that float down from the treetops. Bridges span the lagoons of Kauai's best-value gardens and arboretum.

Kukui Trails-Iliau Loop, TH58, page 152
Make this commanding overlook your first stop on the way up Waimea Canyon. Bigger kids in active families can make the trek to the bottom of the canyon.

Koke'e State Park, TH66, page 163
With all the trails and overlooks around Waimea Canyon, many families might miss these woodland, bird-lover's strolls.

BEACH PICNICS

Haena Beach Park, TH2, page 33
Stop by on the way back from Ke'e Beach. Surfers and a play stream add interest to this developed park. The cool caves are across the road.

Pine Trees Beach, TH7, page 37
Large ironwood trees cast shade on a few tables, about midway around Hanalei Bay.

Surfers and joggers pass by. (Access via
Ama'ama Road, down from the City
Pavilion on Weke Road.)

Anini Beach, TH13, page 49
Drop down to this long coral-reef park.
Large trees shade camping and picnic
areas. A polo field and windsurfers add to
the charm.

**Kilauea Bay-Kahili Beach, TH18,
page 54**
No facilities here, but you can take sand
seats where Kilauea Stream emerges from
a tropical valley at a big sand beach. The
drive down is a mini-adventure.

Anahola Bay, TH23, page 66
The road to the beach curves down
through a leafy canopy. This side of the
bay is rustic, but you can get comfy along
the sandy river bank.

Poipu Beach Park, TH44, page 121
You may have company at the pavilions,
since sun and safe swimming make this
Kaua'i's most-popular beach park.

Prince Kuhio Park, TH45, page 122
The scant-sand beaches nearby are great
for snorkeling, but this is the place for a
quiet family repast.

Salt Pond Beach Park, TH52, page 140
Palms shade the grassy shores, and swimming is normally safe. Pull off here if
cruising West Kaua'i—the locals do.

**Kikiaola State Boat Harbor, TH54,
page 144**
Watch adventure cruises set sail for Napali. Palm trees provide shade and scenery
at this off-the-beaten track respite on the
sunny west side. The little harbor will
have a calming effect on the whole family.

**SHORT WALKS
TO BIG PLACES**
**Hula Platform, Ke'e Beach, TH1,
page 30**
The Kalalau Trail is well-known, but the
short walk to the scenic terraces above
crashing waves packs a punch. Tread
lightly at this sacred Hawaiian site.

Hanalei Pier, TH7, page 37
Watch fishermen haul 'em in and surfers whiz by. The covered pier at Black Pot Beach is a short walk down past the surfer cars to where the Hanalei River enters the bay.

Aliomanu Beach, Anahola, TH22, page 66
Easily reached, this hike-to beach holds the promise of treasure found—shells, coral bits, or maybe a message in a bottle.
Kukui Point Light, TH41, page 107
A path curves from the posh grounds of the Marriott to the entrance to Nawiliwili Harbor. Pick a sunset when a cruise ship is leaving the harbor.

Mahaulepu, Poipu, TH42, page 115
A bumpy ride out sets the tone for a walk along sculpted bluffs and wild waves. A a short-crawl hole enters the Makauwahi Cave Reserve. Out side are tortoises in huge enclosures.
Kukuiolono Park, Kalaheo, TH48, page 127
Wild chickens flit about formal gardens and a path skirts the golf course to a pavilion with a big view.
Pu'uokila Overlook, Waimea Canyon, TH69, page 168
Thrilling overlooks of the Kalalau Valley from the get-go. A trail skirts the rim. Trekking families can pile on the adventure by taking the boardwalk trail across the Alakai Swamp.

EASY & ENTERTAINING & EDUCATIONAL
Waipa Founation, Hanalei, TH6, page 35
Volunteer and you'll see a magical valley and perhaps plant taro and other crops in the traditonal Hawaiian way.
Anaina Hou Mini-Golf, Kilauea, TH16, page 51
Free Play 18 holes through a botanical garden that displays Hawaiian plants from native species to today's exotics.
Kilauea Lighthouse, Kilauea, TH17, page 53
Free binoculars aid in the bird-and-whale watching at this dramatic northerly spot.

Lydgate Play Bridge, TH34, page 99
The ocean snorkeling pool here is the big draw, but you've also got Kamalani Playground andthe awesome Play Bridge.
National Tropical Gardens-Spouting Horn, Koloa, TH46, page 124
Kaua'i's sea geyser gets the oohs and ahhs, but the garden visitors center across the street is an escape into remarkable flora.
Storybook Theater, Hanapepe, TH5, page 144
Meet TV's Russell the Rooster in real life, and take a tour of the town.
Koke'e Natural History Museum, Koke'e, TH67, page 164
Caps off a visit to the to Waimea Canyon. Hurricane and natural history exhibits are eye-openers.
Kauai Museum, page 180
The story of the island unfolds through photos and displays. Giftshop gets an A+.

GUIDED ADVENTURES
—see resource links for phone numbers
Princeville Ranch Zipline
The ranch has added a kids-only adventure camp to its menu of outings.
Smith's Fern Grotto Boat Ride
Kaua'i's classic since the 1950s. Hula and ukulele performers enliven the ride.

Pedal the Coconut Coast
A beach path winds along the coast from Kealia to the Wailua River.
Float through the Hanalei Wildlife Refuge
The Hanalei River leads through taro fields, and into Hanalei Valley.
 Learn to Surf
Beginners may like Poipu, but many think Hanalei Bay is the best for beginners..
Wailua River Paddle
The first Hawaiian kings chose to make their home along these banks. Wailua River Kayaks leads a tour to Secret Falls.
Na Aina Kai Botanical Gardens
Separate children's garden.
Kilohana Plantation
All aboard! Ride the vintage railway or hop on a horse-drawn carriage.
Kauai Coffee's Safari
Ride an open-air vehicle from the ocean up to the moutains,—and then plant one yourself! (Kids must be eight or older.)
Hi ho Silver Falls.
Pick a sunny day and ride through wideopen fantastic scenery—on happy horses handpicked for all-levels of riders. Silver Falls Ranch is one of a kind.

FUN PLACES TO EAT

Duke's Canoe Club, Kalapaki
*Surfboards and other memorabilia
adorn this special occasion resort restau-
rant right on Kalapaki Beach. Duke
Kahanamoku was a surfing legend and
Olympic medalist.*

Keoki's Paradise, Poipu
*Gardens, water features, and teak-
beamed breezeways create an open-air
atmosphere that feels like a vacation.
The kid's menu is a plus, not an after-
thought.*

Hamura Saimin Stand, Lihue
*Enough noodles to reach the moon and
back have been served up at the counter
in Lihue's old-town. Spills okay, the
counter is Formica. Chopsticks optional.*

Koke'e Lodge
*Stop in at the old building after a
visit to Waimea Canyon and watch the
chickens and roosters flit about outside
plate glass windows that frame a green
expanse of the park.*

Lava Lava Beach Club, Kapa'a
*Open air and on the beach at old-timey
resorts on the Coconut Coast. It's behind
the Coconut Marketplace.*

JoJo's Shave Ice, Waimea
*One of these sweet coolers (a traditional
Hawaiian treat) might save the day if the
family got ornery after a little too much
sun at Polihale. The funky joint is part of
the fun.*

Hanalei Dolphin, Hanalei
*Tables are set along the river for lunch,
making birds and kayakers part of the
show. Their kids' menu is tops.*

HULA SHOWS

With chants, dancing, and percussion,
the hula tells the story of Polynesian
culture. Performances vary from keiki
dance clubs and resort performers to
Hawaiian cultural groups from Ni'ihau
and Kaua'i. A listing for free performances is on page 229. Smith's Tropical
Garden also holds a Polynesian dance
extravaganza, and traditional luaus also
come with entertainment. (St. Regis
Hotel Princeville and the Sheraton
in Kapa'a are two popular feast sites.)
Many performances include impromp-
tu lessons for kids. If you're here in
October, don't miss the **Queen Emma
Festival** in Koke'e State Park.

Princeville Ranch Adventure zipline

CAMPING PERMITS AND INFORMATION

Try to call for permits a month ahead of your trip. Camping is by permit only in established campsites. Backpacking in the tropics is challenging, even for experienced hikers; be prepared. Car camping in Koke'e and forest reserves is often at unimproved sites; get specifics from agencies listed below. Beach park camping is on small sites on lawn areas near parking, pavilions and restrooms. Plan for rain: Consider bringing a car-camping tent rather than a backpack tent.

Kaua'i State Parks, 274-3444
Kalalau Trail, Napali Coast, http://www.hawaiistateparks.org/parks/kauai/napali.
cfm *Backpacking. State Parks*
Koke'e Forest Reserves, including Waimea Canyon, 274-3344
> *Department of Land and Natural Resources, Forestry & Wildlife*
County Beach Park Camping, 241-4460
www.kauai.gov/government/departments/parksrecreation/tabid/515/default.aspx
> *County of Kaua'i. Including these beach parks: Haena, Anini, Hanamaulu, Salt Pond, Lydgate, Kekaha, and Lucy Wright; see Trailhead Maps.*

OUTFITTERS/RENTAL GEAR

Each outfitter is listed once, under primary activity; ancillary services also noted for each outfitter.

HIKING

Most of the trails in Kaua'i, both coastal paths and mountain routes, were laid down centuries ago by native Hawaiians. In addition to these historic paths are forest reserve trails and four-wheel drive roads.

Native Hawaiian Hiking Expeditions, 652-0478, *Charlie Cobb-Adams will take you to the wild places out of Waimea Canyon and the Napali. True adventure.*
Pedal 'n Paddle, Hanalei, *camping gear, clothes, maps*, 826-9069
Princeville Ranch Adventures, 826-7669, *guided tours, equipment included. 2,500-acre ranch, also has cross-valley zipline rides and kayak tours.*
Storybook Theatre Walking Tour, 335-0712; *Mark "Russell the Rooster" Jeffers leads tours of Hanapepe, starting from the family-oriented nonprofit center.*
West Kaua'i Visitors Center, 338-1332, *call Friday to reserve a spot on a history tour of Waimea—a look at Old Hawaii.*

SNORKELING, SCUBA & CRUISES

Kaua'i has 110 miles of coastline, with waters supporting 650 different kinds of fish. Generally speaking, calmer waters and better snorkeling will be found during the winter months on south and east side beaches. During the summer months, calmer waters will generally be on north and west shore. East and west shore beaches are the least predictable.

all area codes are 808 unless otherwise noted

BEACHES WITH FULL OR PART-TIME LIFEGUARDS:
Wailua Bay, Lydgate Park, Anahola Beach Park, Anini Beach (coming) Poipu Beach, Hanalei, Kealia, Haena Keʻe, Kekaha, and Salt Pond Beach Park.

Captain Andy's, Port Allen, 800-335-6833, *south coast specialists, ranging from Kipu Kai Beach to the Napali. Large to smaller vessels, great crews.*
Blue Dolphin Charters, Port Allen, 335-5553
HoloHolo Charters, Port Allen, 800-848-6130, 335-0815, *daily excursions, boat tours to Niʻihau, Napali.*
Kalapaki Beach Boys (True Blue), Kalapaki Beach, 246-6333, *rentals, tours, lessons, also surfing, windsurfing, kayak, hiking.*
Kayak Kauaʻi, Hanalei, 800-437-3507, 826-9844
Liko Kauaʻi Cruises, Waimea, 338-0333
Napali Explorer, Waimea, 877-335-9909, 338-9999
Smiths Fern Grotto Cruise, Wailua, 821-6892

BICYCLING

With miles of forest reserve roads and trails, resort bike paths, disused cane roads and quiet rural roads, Kauaʻi is made for biking. The paved Kapaʻa Coastal Path is a great family ride of one of Hawaii's top outdoor attractions. On the down side, highway bike lanes could be better, and it's too bad buses aren't equipped to take cyclists over one or two highway stretches that are unsafe. Rentals are from $5 to $25 a day. You may want to inquire with your air carrier about shipping your own bike.

Bicycle John, Lihue, 245-7579, *sales, service--been here forever*
Bike Doktor, Hanalei, 826-7799, *rentals, sales, service, for years*
Coconut Coasters, Kapaʻa, 822-7368, *Sparky & Melissa Costales can set you up with first-class cruiser; centrally located on the Kapaa Coastal Path. Top gear.*
Kauaʻi Cycle and Tour, Kapaʻa, 821-2115, *rentals, tours, sales, service*
Kauaʻi Courtyard by Marriott, Kapaʻa, 822-3455, *your basic wheels, $5 in the lobby*
Outfitters Kauai, Poipu, 742-966, *down Waimea Canyon is their specialty*
Pedal ʻn Paddle, Hanalei, 826-9069, *rentals; also kayaks, snorkeling, boogie boards, camping*

KAYAKING

Kauaʻi has the only navigable waters in Hawaii, including six rivers and as many streams that are wide enough to be called rivers in most states. Rivers and streams can rise fast after storms, but more often river kayaking on the island is on quiet lagoons that curve inland. Coral reefs and bays also provide dozens of places for sea kayaking, under calm conditions.

Aloha Canoes and Kayaks, Nawiliwili, 246-6804, *tours, rentals*
Kamokila Village, Wailua, 823-0559, *their docks are upriver and out of the wind*
Kayak Hanalei, 826-1881
Kayak Kaua'i, Wailua Marina, 826-9844
      tours, rentals; also bikes, snorkeling, surfboards, camping
Napali Kayak Tours, Hanalei, 826-6900, *specialize in coast camping*
Outfitters Kaua'i, Nawiliwili and Poipu, 742-9667, *tours; also bicycles, hikes*
Pedal 'n Paddle, Hanalai, *north shore's best adventure store*, 826-9069
Princeville Ranch Adventures, also hikes and zipline, 826-7669
Kauai Beach Boys, Kalapaki, 246-6333, *kayak Huleia Wildlife Refuge, surf lessons*
Kayak Wailua, 822-5795, 639-6332
      rentals and paddle-hike tours to Secret Falls on Wailua River;
      smaller groups and special requests

SURFING AND WINDSURFING

Surfing originated here, and is called the sport of kings, since Hawaiian royalty began riding the waves centuries ago. Winter months usually bring the biggest surf to north shore and west side beaches. During the summer, look for the biggest surf on the south and east sides of the island.

Garden Island Surf School, Poipu, 652-4841
Hanalei Surf Company, 826-9000, *rentals, lesson referrals, and the island's*
      best surf shop; also snorkeling
Kaua'i Beach Boys, Kalapaki-Nawiliwili, 246-6333
Learn To Surf, 826-7612, *lessons, rentals, island-wide*
Nukomoi Surf Company, Poipu, 742-8019, *rentals, surf shop*
Tamba Surf Company, Kapa'a, 823-6942, *rentals, surf shop— known world-wide*
Titus Kinimaka, Hawaiian School of Surfing, 652-1116 *one of Hawaii's greatest*
      surfers; Titus or staff will teach from novice on up
Dr. Ding's Westside Surf Shop, Hanapepe, 335-3805, *custom boards*

HELICOPTERS

Beautiful Kaua'i has been 5 million years in the making, nuanced by numerous river valleys, seacliffs, and ragged ridges, all of it adorned with a tangle of life that would put Darwin in a tizzy. The sure way to see how it all folds together is by helicopter. Recent economic hard times have brought the demise of several companies, including Air Kauai, but several good choices remain.

Blue Hawaiian, 245-5800, *has respected operations on all the islands; This is your best*
      bet; features quiet Eco-star choppers
Safari Helicopters, 326-3356
Sunshine (Will Squyres) Helicopters, 240-2577

all area codes are 808 unless otherwise noted

HORSEBACK RIDING
CJM Country Stables,
Poipu, 742-6096
Esprit De Corps Riding Academy,
Kapaʻa, 822-4688
Princeville Ranch Stables, 826-6777
Silver Falls Ranch, Kilauea, 828-6718, *Rides on a private ranch take in a huge palm aboretum, the falls, and an ancient caldera which is now a lush bog.*

GOLF
Kauaʻi Lagoons Golf Club, Kalapaki Bay, 800-634-6400
Grove Farm Golf Course at Puakea, 245-8756
Kiahuna Golf Club, Poipu, 742-9595
Kukuiolono Golf Course, Kalaheo, 332-9151
Poipu Bay Resort Golf Course, 800-858-6300
Princeville Golf Club, 800-826-1105
Wailua Golf Club, 241-6666

MAPS
Kauaʻi Trailblazer's maps and descriptions are all you need for recreating on the island. However, you may want a supplemental map. Generally speaking, the trick to hiking in Kauaʻi—whether coastal or inland—is knowing where to go and finding the trailhead; and then following the trail, not a map.

Full Color Topographic Map of Kauaʻi, The Garden Isle.
Best overall for use with this book; indexed place names, widely available, inexpensive. By University of Hawaii Press.
Northwestern Kauaʻi Recreation Map, 800-828-MAPS
Best for Kalalau Trail, very good for Kokeʻe area. By Earthwalk Press.
Basically Books, 800-903-6277. *Bookstore on Big Island that does credit card phone orders; handles USGS and other maps.*
The Ready Mapbook of Kauaʻi, Odyssey Publishing, 935-0092.
Handy companion street atlas.
Kauaʻi Island Atlas and Map, http://www.envdhawaii.com
Loaded with recreational sites, plus lots of natural history. Also a good choice to work in tandem with Trailblazer.
Kokeʻe Trails, 335-9975. *Inexpensive map for hiking woodland trails of Kokeʻe State Park. Available at museum at the park.*

MUSEUMS, HISTORICAL ATTRACTIONS, CHURCHES

Grove Farm Homestead, Lihue, 245-3202
Kaua'i Coffee Company Visitors Center, Port Allen, 800-545-8605, 335-0813
Kaua'i Hindu Monastery, Kapa'a, 822-3012, 822-3152
Kaua'i Museum, Lihue, 245-6931
Kilohana Plantation, Lihue, 245-5608, Plantaton Railway 245-7245
Kukui Jam Factory, Kalaheo, 332-9333
Koke'e Natural History Museum, Kokee, 335-9975
Lawai International Center-88 Holy Places of Kobo Diashi, 639-4300, 212-1349
Po'oku Heiau Preserve, Princeville, 692-8015
Waioli Mission House, Hanalei, 245-3202
Waioli Hui'ia Church, 826-6253
West Kaua'i Technology & Visitor Center, Waimea, 338-1332

GARDENS AND OUTDOOR ATTRACTIONS

Allerton/McBryde National Tropical Botanical Gardens, 742-2623, 742-2433
Anaina Hou Community Park (and mini golf), Kilauea, 828-2118
Kamokila Hawaiian Village, Wailua, 823-0559
Kaua'i Coffee, Kalaheo, 335-0813, *tasting, self-guided walk, orchard tours*
Kaua'i Farmacy, Kilauea, 828-6526, *call for special event tour*
Kaua'i Fresh (sustainable) Farms Tour, Wai Koa Plantation, Kilauea, 826-0077
Kaua'i Nursery & Landscaping, Lihue, 888-345-7747, 245-7747
Kaua'i Products Fair (NoKa), Kapa'a, 246-0988
Kilauea Point National Wildlife Refuge, 828-1413, 828-0383, 246-2860
Kukuiolono Park, Kalaheo, 332-9151
Limahuli National Tropical Botanical Garden, Haena, 826-1053
Makauwahi Cave Reserve, Poipu, 631-3409
Moir Gardens, Kiahuna Plantation, Poipu, 742-6411
Na Aina Kai Botanical Gardens, Kilauea, 828-0525
North Shore Dog Park, Kilauea, 240-2670
Peace Garden and Storybook Theatre, Hanapepe, 335-0712
Smith's Tropical Paradise, Wailua, 821-6895
Smith's Fern Grotto Cruise, Wailua, 821-6892, *a Hawaiian tradition.*
Taro Patch (John & Suzanne Pia), Anahola, 822-9563, 245-8101
Waipa Foundation, Waikoko (Hanalei), 826-9969

CULTURAL CONTACTS

Anahola Ancient Cultural Exchange, 822-9563, 245-8101
Kamanawa Foundation (Hula), 335-6466
Kaua'i Heritage Center of Hawaiian Culture & Arts, 821-2070
Kikiaola Foundation (plantation heritage), Waimea, 337-1005
Poipu Beach Foundation (Heritage Trail), 742-7444
West Kaua'i Main Street, Waimea, 338-9957

all area codes are 808 unless otherwise noted

HAWAIIANA SHOPS & GALLERIES

Bambulei, Wailua, chic antiques, 823-8641
Blu Umi, Hanapepe, 634-0101
By the Sea Company, Kapa'a (NoKa Fair), 639-0002
   A New York designer has opened shop in Kaua'i
Chita's Fashion, Kapa'a (NoKa Fair), 652-2369 *Handmade on Kaua'i*
Coconut Style-Tugu, Kilauea, 828-6899
Crystals & Gemstones Gallery, Hanalei, 826-9304
Dawn M. Traina Gallery, Hanapepe, 335-3993
Hawaiian Trading Post, Lawai, 332-7404
Haviki Oceanic Tribal Art, Hanalei, 826-7606, 635-7404
Hunter Gatherer, Kilauea, 828-1388
   It's a cool experience, along with being a gift store-gallery
Island Soap & Candle, Princeville, Kilauea 827-8111, Koloa, 742-1945
JJ Ohana, Hanapepe, 335-0366
Jungle Girl, Koloa, 742-9649
Kalakoa Kauai, Hanapepe, 335-6468
Kapaia Stitchery, Hanamaulu, 245-2281
Kaua'i Fine Arts, Hanapepe, 335-3778
Kaua'i Museum Gift Shop, Lihue, 246-2470
Kaua'i Store, The, Kapa'a, 631-6706 *All quality and created on island*
KIKO, Kapa'a, 822-5096 *'Simple goods,' workshops, and a fun place to be*
Kilohana Galleries, Lihue 245-2452
Kong Lung, Kilauea, 828-1822
lu.la., Hanapepe, 855-0215
Lemurian Light Alchemy, Kapa'a, 639-8133
   Real-deal healing bodywork by Wai-Sum.
Maile, Kukuiula (Poipu), 339-3055 *Hawaiian body and skin care*
Magic Dragon Toy & Art, Princeville, 826-9144
   Fun gift ideas for all ages. Next to Foodland.
Margaret Joy Jewelry, Hanalei, 639-2298 *by appointment*
Ocean Paper, Lawai, www.theoceanpaper.com
Ohana Shop, Hanalei, 826-7888, Poipu (Kikuiula), 212-1208
Spinner Dophin Designs, Hanalei, 826-7461
Carmen's Wai'iti Botanicals, Kilauea, 639-6956
Warehouse 3540, Lawai, 635-6576
   Happening place for a burgeoning art scene
Yellowfish Trading Company, Hanalei, 826-1227
   An artfully curated gift shop, among Hawaii's best

LOCAL INFORMATION

County of Kaua'i Transportation (public buses), 241-6410
Kaua'i Visitors Bureau, 245-3971, 800-262-1400

Where to eat

A calabash of island-style eats, ranging from take-out plates to Pacific Rim gourmet. Lunch carts are springing up everywhere. For cheap local-style plates, try the small places in forlorn shopping centers.All listed below are recommended; special selections are boldfaced. Area codes are 808.

(C)   **Cheap or take-out (under $12)**
(M)   **Moderate, family ($12-$22)**
(P)   **Pricey, special occasion (over $22)**

KILAUEA
PRINCEVILLE
HANALEI

Bar Acuda, Hanalei	(P) 826-7081
The Bistro, Kilauea	(M-P) 828-040
Hanalei Dolphin	(M-P) 826-6113
Hanalei Gourmet	(C-M) 826-2524
Healthy Hut Natural Foods	(M) 828-6626
Kilauea Bakery-Pau Pizza	(M) 828-2020
L&L Barbecue, Hanalei	(C) 826-7388
Moloa'a Sunrise	(C) 822-1441
Nourish Hanalei, Princeville (C-M)	
	760-420-7096
Namahana Cafe, Kilauea (C-M)	828-2118
Tahiti Nui, Hanalei	(M) 826-6277

Note: Multiple new food trucks in Hanalei

KAPA'A
COCONUT COAST

Cafe Hemingway	(M) 822-2250
Bubba's, Kapa'a	(C) 823-0069
Caffe Coco, Wailua	(M) 822-7999
East Side Grill & Bar	(M)823-9500
Huli Chicken	(C) 639-2163
Kauai Pasta	(M) 822-7447
Lemongrass Grill	(M) 821-2888
Lava Lava	(M) 769-5282
Mermaids Café	(C) 821-2026
Nana's Snack Shop	(C) 639-3849
No. 1 Chinese BBQ	(C) 821-8800
Olympic Cafe,	(M)822-5825
Papaya's	(C) 823-0190
Pono Market	(C) 822-4581

LIHUE
NAWILIWILI

Barbecue Inn   (C-M) 245-2921

Dani's Restaurant   (C-M) 245-4991

Duke's Canoe Club,

    Kalapaki   (M-P) 246-9599

Garden Island Barbecue   (C) 245-8868

    Local style plates are tops (C) 245-3271

The Greenery Cafe   (C) 635-2752

Hamura Saimin Stand   (C) 245-3271

Mark's Place, Lihue   (C) 245-2522

Kauai Pasta   (M) 245-2227

Kiibo Restaurant, Lihe   (M) 245-2650

Rob's Good Times Grill (C-M) 246-0311

Tip Top Motel Cafe   (C) 245-2333

KOLOA
POIPU

Beach House, Prince Kuhio   (P) 742-1424

Kiawe Roots, Kukuiula   (M) 631-3622

Koloa Deli   (C) 742-9998

Gaylord's, Kilohana Plantation (P) 245-9593

Ilima Terrace and Tidepools

    Grand Hyatt Poipu   (M-P) 240-6566

Eating House 1849 (Roy's)   (P) 742-5000

Living Foods, Kukuiula (M-P) 742-2323

Makai Sushi, Koloa   (M) 639-7219

Merriman's, Kukuiula Village (P) 742-8385

Sueoka's Snack Shop, Koloa (C) 742-1112

Keoki's Paradise, Poipu   (M-P) 742-7534

Plantation Garden, Poipu   (P) 742-2121

HANAPEPE
WAIMEA

Bobbie's, Hanapepe   (C-M) 335-5152

Japanese Grandma's Cafe (M-P)

    Hanapepe, 855-5016

Jo Jo's Shave Ice, Waimea

           (C) 378-4712

Koke'e Lodge   (C-M) 335-6061

Little Fish Coffee, Hanapepe

           (C) 335-5000

Monkeypod Jam Cafe, Lawai (M)

      378-4208

Yumi's, Waimea   (C-M) 338-1731

Island Taco, Waimea (C-M) 338-9895

Where To Stay

Hyatt Regency

Give these places a call to inquire about amenities and location. Be sure to ask if you're getting the lowest rate, including weekly offerings. Calling is also a good way to find out which places have Aloha. Also contact Kaua'i Visitors Bureau, 800-464-2924. For island-wide referrals, try **Hawaii's Best Bed & Breakfast** at 800-262-9912 or Hawaiian Beach Rentals, 808-262-6968.

Area code is 808 unless otherwise provided. All listings are recommended; special selections are boldfaced.

TYPE
(**Rustic**) Cabins, hostels
(**B&B**) Bed & Breakfasts, cottages, homes
(**Condos**) Condominium complex
(**Hotel**) Mid-range, mid-size hotels and motels
(**Resort**) High-end, larger, luxury
(**Agent**) Real estate broker for private residences

(C) Cheap ($60 to $100)   (M) Moderate (low-$100 to $200)   (P) Pricey ($200 & up)

NORTH SHORE — KILAUEA, PRINCEVILLE, HANALEI

Jagged green ridges, secret beaches, and waving palms on the North Shore will fulfill everyone's fantasy about what a tropical vacation should be. Hanalei is hip, funky, and beautiful, with walk-around sightseeing. Princeville is manicured condos and two hotels, set on a bluff and buffeted by golf courses and hike-to beaches. Anini Beach is a quieter, more remote beach community, and Kilauea has more of a pastoral feel. During the winter months, storms hit this shore, along with larger surf. During the summer, blue lagoons await. The North Shore is also a long haul to visit other parts of the island.

Aloha Sunrise Inn, Kilauea (cottages)	(**M**) 888-828-1008, 828-1100
Hanalei Bay Resort, Princeville (Resort)	(**M-P**) **826-6522**
Hale Hoo Maha, Hanalei (B&B)	(**M**) 826-7083
Hanalei Colony Resort, Haena (Condos)	(**P**) 826-6235, 800-628-3004
Hawaii Life	(**M-P**) 652-9777
Hanalei Dolphin Cottages	(**P**) 826-1675
Ocean Properties of the Pacific (Agent)	(**M-P**) 826-4280
Princeville Vacations (Agent)	(**M-P**) 800-800-3637, 828-6530
Princeville Resort	(**P**) 800-826-4400, 826-9644
Westin Princeville Resort Villas	(**P**) 827-8700

COCONUT COAST — KAPA'A, WAILUA

With palm groves and coral reef at the shore and mountainous forest reserves inland, the Coconut Coast is a place to visit, no matter where your room is on the island. Weather is decent year around, and the central location makes the rest of Kauai easily accessible.

Garden Island Properties (Agent)   (C-P) 822-4871

Aston Islander on the Beach (Hotel)   (M-P) 822-7417

Courtyard Marriott Kaua'i (Resort)   (M-P) 877-622-2975, 822-3455
> *The place has aloha, and is the site of various community events.*

Hilton Garden Inn (Resort), Wailua   (C-M) 823-6000

Kauai Beach House Hostel, Kapa'a (Rustic)   (C) 652-8164

Kaua'i International Hostel, Kapa'a (Rustic)   (C) 823-6142

Kaua'i Shores (Hotel)   (M) 822-4951

Kumu Camp, Anahola (Rustic)   (C) 631-9082

Plantation Hale, Best Western (Condos)   (M) 800-775-4253

Pono Kai (Condos)   (M-P) 800-535-0085

Sleeping Giant Realty (Agent)   (C-M) 800-247-8831

LIHUE AND NAWILIWILI

Lihue is the county seat and business district, meaning fewer tourists stay here, except on cruise ships in the harbor. Central location is good for outings.

Garden Island Inn (Hotel)
     (C-M) 745-7227

Kauai'i Marriott Resort
     (P) 888-236-2427, 245-5050
     Grounds and pool are fabulous.
     On Kalapaki Beach. Rooms
     fairly small. (Nearby, Marriott's
     Kalanipu'u has big rooms, but
     no grounds or beach.)

Kaua'i Beach Resort (Resort)
     (M-P) 866-536-7976,
     954-7419
     On miles of open beach. Well-
     run with nicely appointed
     (small) rooms. Nice pools.

Kauai Inn Resort   (C) 245-9000

Waimea Plantation Cottages

POIPU and KOLOA

Beach potatoes will like sunny Poipu, particularly in the winter when surf is lowest and the weather is approaching from the other side of the island. (Surf's up in the summer here.) The environs are arid, with low scrub on the coast, giving way to indigenous forests inland. Good snorkeling and coast walking, along with ready access to Waimea Canyon. Hanalei is a long haul, but reachable on a day trip. Rates vary from mid-range condos—which tend to be spaced fairly close—to the luxury rooms at the fabulous Hyatt Regency. In Koloa and inland communities, you can find low- to mid-priced cottages in garden settings. Suite Paradise rents spacious condos at affordable prices.

Hale O Kapeka, Poipu B&B)	(M) 742-6806
Grand Hyatt Kaua'i (Resort)	**(P)** 800-233-1234, 742-1234
Kiahuna Plantation (Condos)	**(M-P)** 800-367-8020

Large greenspace opens up to the middle of Poipu Beach. Close to great dining.

Koloa Landing Cottages (B&B)	**(C-M)** 800-779-8773
Kuhio Shores (Condos)	**(C-M)** 800-367-8022
Lawai Beach House (Guest Home)	**(M-P)** 800-325-5701
Nihi Kai Villas (Condos)	**(M)** 800-367-8020
Poipu Crater Resort (Condos)	**(C)** 800-367-8020
Poipu Kai Resort (Condos)	**(C-P)** 800-367-8020

Ocean views with easy walks to Poipu Beach and coastal trails.

Poipu Shores (Condos)	**(M-P)** 800-367-8020
Sheraton Kauai (Resort)	**(P)** 888-847-0208
Suite Paradise (Agent)	**(C-P)** 800-367-8020

Selection, guest services, and extra amenities make them the first choice. A wide selection of reasonably priced, top-end condos, many located on a quiet walking path that connects Poipu with the Grand Hyatt and Shipwreck Beach. Beach gear available to guests and the staff are always ready to help.

WEST SIDE — WAIMEA, KOKE'E, KALAHEO

The West Side is basically non-tourist, although during the day rental cars parade to Waimea Canyon and Barking Sands Beach. This is the arid side of Kauai, which means sun most often graces its long beaches. Hanapepe and Waimea draw visitors looking for old-style rural settings. Poipu is close by, but the North Shore is a long day trip. Koke'e State Park is a few thousand feet up, so prepare for cool weather if that's your choice.

Camp Sloggett, Koke'e (Rustic, also campsites)	**(C)** 245-5959
Kauai Tree Houses, Kalaheo (B&B)	**(C-M)** 635-3945, 332-9045
Koke'e Lodge Cabins (Rustic)	**(C)** 335-6061
Waimea Plantation Cottages (Resort)	**(M-P)** 800-922-7860, 338-1625

Spruced-up authentic cottages set on huge, parklike grounds. Oceanfront, but the water is often murky due to Waimea River runoff.

INFORMATIONAL/CULTURAL
www.trailblazertravelbooks.com
www.ancientkauai.com
www.gohawaii.com
www.gohawaii.about.com
www.hawaii.com
www.hawaii.gov/dlnr/dsp/kauai.com
www.hawaii-nation.org
www.hawaiitrails.org
www.hawaiiweathertoday.com
www.hotspots.hawaii.com
www.kauaiexplorer.com
www.kauai-hawaii.com
www.kauaipolynesianfestival.org
www.kauaigov.org
www.kauai-hawaii.com/parks
www.hawaii-stuff.com
www.kauaimonkseal.com
www.kauainews.com
www.kauaivisitorsbureau.org
www.kauaiworld.com (weather)
www.mele.com
www.nativebooks.com
www.ntbg.com
www.oleo.hawaii.edu
www.planet-hawaii.com
www.thegardenisland.com
www.tripadvisor.com
www.thisweek.com
www.trailblazerhawaii.com
www.islandergroup.com
http://en.wikipedia.org/wiki/Kauai

ACTIVITIES & SERVICES:
www.trailblazerhawaii.com
www.adventureskauai.com
www.bikehawaii.com
www.campingkauai.com
www.cjmstables.com
www.scuba.about.com
www.kauaiseatours.com
www.hawaiianair.com
www.hawaiioutside.com
www.hulasource.com
www.kauaiexplorer.com
www.kauaiwedding.com
www.kayakkauai.com
www.outfitterskauai.com
www.trailblazerhawaii.com
www.napali.com
www.uhpress.hawaii.edu
https://www.bluehawaiian.com/en/kauai/tours

ACCOMMODATIONS:
www.wheretostay.com
www.bestplaces.com
www.bnb-kauai.com
www.hanaleisurf.com
www.kauai-bedandbreakfast.com
www.kauaivacationrentals.com
www.poipubeach.org
www.princeville-vacations.com
www.staykauai.com
www.suiteparadise.com
www.travel-kauai.com
www.tripadvisor.com
www.hawaiianbeachrentals.com
www.vrbo.com

index

Notes

For publisher-direct savings to individuals and groups, and for book-trade orders, please contact:

DIAMOND VALLEY COMPANY

89 Lower Manzanita Drive, Markleeville, CA 96120

Phone 530-694-2740
www.trailblazertravelbooks.com
www.trailblazerhawaii.com (blog)
e-mail: trailblazertravelbooks@gmail.com

Check for paperback and eBook versions on Amazon.com.
Please contact us with comments, corrections, and suggestions.

DIAMOND VALLEY COMPANY'S
TRAILBLAZER TRAVEL BOOK SERIES

ALPINE SIERRA TRAILBLAZER
Where to Hike, Ski, Bike, Fish, Drive
From Markleeville to Tahoe and Yosemite
"A must-have guide. The best and most attractive guidebook for the Sierra. With you every step of the way."—Tahoe Action

GOLDEN GATE TRAILBLAZER
Where to Hike, Walk, Bike
In San Francisco and Marin
"Makes you want to strap on your boots and go!"—Sunset Magazine

KAUAI TRAILBLAZER
Where to Hike, Snorkel, Bike, Paddle, Surf
"An amazing book for all types of people, no matter what you like to do."—Aloha Update

MAUI TRAILBLAZER
Where to Hike, Snorkel, Surf, Drive
"The best of them all."—Maui Weekly

HAWAII THE BIG ISLAND TRAILBLAZER
Where to Hike, Snorkel, Surf, Bike, Drive
"For seekers of the adventure of Old Hawaii, this is the guide."—Tropical Travels

OAHU TRAILBLAZER
Where to Hike, Snorkel, Surf
From Honolulu to the North Shore
"Marvelously flexible. A well-marked trail of tropical adventures."
—San Francisco Chronicle

NO WORRIES HAWAII
A Vacation Planning Guide for
Kauai, Oahu, Maui, and the Big Island
"Really a travel planning guide without peer. If only other travel destinations had someting this good."
—Guide to Travel Guides

NO WORRIES PARIS
A Photographic Walking Guide
"A wonderfull, worry-free journey."
—Chicago Tribune

RANGE of LIGHT TRAILBLAZER
Where to Hike, Camp, Drive from
Mono Lake south to Mount Whitney,
and the Pacific Crest Trail east to Death Valley
—*Coming in 2020*

"Trailblazers are deserving of ongoing praise. You are guaranteed a unique experience that is high quality and perfect for independent travelers."—Midwest Book Review

"Trailblazers are the essential books to pack when planning a trip to Hawaii."—About.com

The one you'll want to have along. Kauai's most respected and best loved book.—TripAdvisor.com

Poipu Beach, Menehune Bridge, Waimea Canyon

Kalalau Trail, Limahuli National Tropical Botanical Garden, Tunnels Beach

Hula at Waimea Canyon rim, Awaawapuhi, Wailua Falls

Kilauea Point National Wildlife Refuge, Wailua River paddlers, Donkey Beach, Salt Pond Beach Park

Made in the USA
Las Vegas, NV
21 September 2023

77887983R00144